REASON
and
IMAGINATION
in
C. S. LEWIS

A Study of
Till We Have Faces

Peter J. Schakel

WILLIAM B. EERDMANS PUBLISHING COMPANY
GRAND RAPIDS, MICHIGAN

The United Library
Garrett-Evangelical/Seabury-Western Seminaries
Evanston, IL 60201

To my Mother and Father,
with deep affection and appreciation

Copyright © 1984 by William B. Eerdmans Publishing Company
255 Jefferson Ave. S.E., Grand Rapids, Mich. 49503
All rights reserved
Printed in the United States of America

Library of Congress Cataloging in Publication Data

Schakel, Peter J.
Reason and imagination in C.S. Lewis.

Includes bibliographical references.
1. Lewis, C. S. (Clive Staples), 1898-1963. Till we
have faces. 2. Cupid and Psyche (Tale)—History and
criticism. 3. Reason in literature. 4. Imagination in
literature. I. Title.
PR6023.E926T5437 1984   823'.912   84-1482
ISBN 0-8028-1998-2

PR6023
.E92T54
GESW

Contents

Contents

Acknowledgments

RESEARCH for and the writing of this book were made possible by a National Endowment for the Humanities Summer Seminar—I am particularly grateful to its director, Alasdair MacIntyre, for his encouragement and support—and a Faculty Development Grant and sabbatical leave from Hope College.

I was given permission by C. S. Lewis PTE Limited to quote from two unpublished letters by Lewis and from his unpublished diary. Owen Barfield kindly allowed me to quote from an unpublished lecture. Portions of the book were published previously in *Mythlore* and *VII: An Anglo-American Literary Review;* my thanks to the editors for allowing me to reprint them here. I have, in the book, modified considerably the positions taken in the article in *VII*.

I am indebted to a number of people who read parts of or the entire manuscript and made valuable suggestions for its improvement: Tom Andrews, John Cox, Paul Ford, Douglas Mantz, and Merold Westphal; from Peter Macky I learned a great deal about Lewis's use of imagination and from Peter Kreeft a great deal about Lewis's use of reason. I owe an especially large debt to my colleague Charles Huttar, who read the manuscript at various stages and was a continual source of encouragement, information, suggestions, and corrections.

As a hunt-and-peck typist, I am very thankful to my wife Karen, to Dee Bakker, and to Bev Kindig, who typed parts or all of the manuscript at different stages. And I am grateful to my students at Hope College and at the Center for Christian Study in Charlottesville, Virginia, for their patience, enthusiasm, answers, and questions.

Grateful acknowledgment is given to the following publishers for permission to quote from their publications.

CURTIS BROWN, LTD.

Letters to Malcolm: Chiefly on Prayer by C. S. Lewis. Copyright © 1963, 1964 by the Estate of C. S. Lewis and/or C. S. Lewis.

Spirits in Bondage by Clive Hamilton (pseud.). Copyright © 1919 by Clive Hamilton.

Surprised by Joy by C. S. Lewis. Copyright © 1955 by C. S. Lewis.

Till We Have Faces: A Myth Retold by C. S. Lewis. Copyright © 1956 by C. S. Lewis.

JAMES BROWN ASSOCIATES, INC.

They Stand Together: The Letters of C. S. Lewis to Arthur Greeves, 1914–1963, ed. Walter Hooper. Copyright © 1979 by the Estate of C. S. Lewis.

WILLIAM COLLINS SONS & CO. LTD.

The Great Divorce by C. S. Lewis. Copyright © 1946 by William Collins Sons & Co. Ltd.

The Problem of Pain by C. S. Lewis. Copyright © 1947 by William Collins Sons & Co. Ltd.

HARCOURT BRACE JOVANOVICH, INC.

Letters to Malcolm: Chiefly on Prayer by C. S. Lewis. Copyright © 1963, 1964 by the Estate of C. S. Lewis and/or C. S. Lewis.

Spirits in Bondage by Clive Hamilton (pseud.). Copyright © 1919 by Clive Hamilton.

Surprised by Joy by C. S. Lewis. Copyright © 1955 by C. S. Lewis.

Till We Haves Faces: A Myth Retold by C. S. Lewis. Copyright © 1956 by C. S. Lewis.

MACMILLAN PUBLISHING COMPANY, INC.

The Great Divorce by C. S. Lewis. Copyright © 1946 by Macmillan Publishing Co., Inc.

The Problem of Pain by C. S. Lewis. Copyright © 1947 by Macmillan Publishing Co., Inc.; copyright renewed 1975.

They Stand Together: The Letters of C. S. Lewis to Arthur Greeves (1914–1963), ed. Walter Hooper. Copyright © 1979 by the Estate of C. S. Lewis.

SEABURY PRESS, INC.

A Grief Observed by C. S. Lewis. Copyright © 1961 by N. W. Clerk.

Preface

PERHAPS the most haunting of C. S. Lewis's poems is a sixteen-line sonnet entitled "Reason." In it Lewis contrasts the cool clarity and strength of reason (symbolized by Athena, the "maid" of the poem) with the warm darkness and creativity of the imagination (Demeter, the earth-mother, in the poem). The poem concludes,

> Oh who will reconcile in me both maid and mother,
> Who make in me a concord of the depth and height?
> Who make imagination's dim exploring touch
> Ever report the same as intellectual sight?
> Then could I truly say, and not deceive,
> Then wholly say, that I BELIEVE.[1]

The poem is haunting in part because it does not reveal if Lewis ever found the concord of depth and height he so earnestly sought. If the poem was written before his conversion to Christianity in 1931, one could assume that a reconciliation was effected by that experience and that through it he was made able to "believe." The date and occasion of the poem, however, are not known, so one cannot assume that it was an early poem or that reason and imagination were reconciled through Christianity. Indeed, reason and imagination appear in works throughout Lewis's career, in varied relationships, but not unquestionably unified and harmonized until near its end. The questions about reason and imagination raised by the poem clearly suggest that this is a very significant theme in Lewis, but equally clearly these questions can be answered only by a careful examination of Lewis's works as a whole.

This book examines the place of reason and imagination

in the thought of C. S. Lewis and shows that a shift, not in basic positions or theory but certainly in emphasis and practice, occurs, not at the time of his conversion but in the late 1940s or early 1950s. Prior to that—in *Mere Christianity* and the Ransom trilogy, for example—Lewis relied heavily upon, or put his ultimate trust in, reason (the capacity for analysis, abstraction, logical deductions), with imagination (the image-making, fictionalizing, integrative power) playing a valued but limited supporting role.[2] After that, Lewis's confidence in imaginative methods increases, and imagination becomes the more striking feature of his work from 1950 on—in the Chronicles of Narnia, for example. My purpose is to chart the changes briefly, account for them as fully as possible, and show that in some of his later works, such as *Till We Have Faces* and *Letters to Malcolm,* reason and imagination are, at last, reconciled and unified.

Till We Have Faces has a crucial place in this study. Not only is it Lewis's finest imaginative work, but it also explores the tension between reason and the imagination as a central theme. Furthermore, *Till We Have Faces* is the culmination of efforts Lewis made in a number of works throughout his life to use similar images and imaginative structures to resolve that tension. One cannot fully understand or appreciate Lewis's thought and work as a whole without a sound understanding of *Till We Have Faces.* But *Till We Have Faces* is also the most difficult of Lewis's works, one which constantly gives the sense that "something more is going on here than I am comprehending fully." Many readers who enjoy Lewis's other apologetic and fictional works are perplexed and discouraged by *Till We Have Faces.* Because of these difficulties, many readers are denied access to the motif which is the most helpful in pulling together the diverse threads of Lewis's thought and work.

I have, therefore, adopted a rather unusual structure for this book. Chapters I–IX explore reason and imagination in *Till We Have Faces,* while walking through the story with the reader, providing aids for those who have difficulty with it: making sure the plot line is clear, pointing out structures and figures which bring out meaning, and reflecting upon the issues and ideas which underlie each section. This book is not designed to take the place of reading the work itself; rather, the two might well be read together—Chapter I of this book, then Chapters 1–2 of *Till We Have Faces,* then Chapter II of this book, and so on. Upon completing the process—and I think this is important—one should reread *Till We Have Faces* consecutively, without the pauses and breaks the previous process entails, to get a sense of the continuity and flow of the story. Chapters X–XIV revert to conventional essays. With *Till We Have Faces* now as common background, they examine the use of reason and imagination in works that precede and follow it—particularly *Dymer, The Pilgrim's Regress, The Great Divorce, Surprised by Joy,* and *Letters to Malcolm*—tracing in them myths and images which find their mature expression in *Till We Have Faces.*

In doing so, I want to assert the importance of considering Lewis's works in historical and chronological context. Robert H. Smith, in a recent study of Lewis, posited that "Lewis's thought appeared almost full-blown in the earliest Christian writings that came from his pen. With only a few exceptions one may refer to his early or late works alike for the explication of any given subject without risking significant wrenching of his meaning."[3] Smith here assumes what ought instead to be proved; and if one starts with this as an assumption, the evidence will of course seem to confirm it. Combining early and late statements may not "wrench" Lewis's meaning, but on a number of topics it can blur valuable distinctions and obscure changes in emphasis; and it fosters the tendency, in Lewis studies, to treat Lewis as an authority figure and concentrate on summarizing his positions on various topics. If Lewis studies are to progress beyond this and to become increasingly precise and illuminating, it will be necessary to attend to chronology and to the specific context which generated particular works, as well as the general historical milieu in which Lewis's thought developed.

I have sought to describe and examine Lewis's works objectively, pointing out strengths and weaknesses as needed.

But criticism can never be wholly objective—the very act of reading inevitably involves the reader's assumptions and experiences, and this book surely reflects mine, often no doubt in ways and to extents I am unaware of. My goal, therefore, is not to convince readers of a particular hypothesis about change or growth in Lewis, but to offer an approach to Lewis which will encourage and enable others to reread his works more closely and attentively. My approach will modify earlier readings and later readings will modify mine; our combined efforts should result in a fuller and more accurate understanding of Lewis and the value of his work.

Quotations from *Till We Have Faces* are from the 1980 reprinting of the American paperback edition (New York: Harcourt Brace Jovanovich); page numbers are cited parenthetically in the text. The pagination of that edition is the same as that of the original American clothbound edition (New York: Harcourt, Brace, and World, 1957) and an earlier paperback edition (Grand Rapids, Mich.: Eerdmans Publishing Company, 1966). On page 203 I have appended a table by which those using other editions can identify the chapter in which a cited passage appears and thus locate it quite easily. Quotations from other works by Lewis are from the earliest published form, unless stated otherwise. I have not included a bibliography; all published studies of *Till We Have Faces* known to me are mentioned in the notes.

SECTION **I**

TILL WE HAVE FACES:
THE WORK ITSELF

I

Introduction:
The Background

*T*HOSE who come to *Till We Have Faces* after reading
the Chronicles of Narnia or *Out of the Silent Planet* and
wanting more of the same are always surprised and often
disappointed. The story lacks, or seems to lack, the simplic-
ity of plot and style and clear embodiment of Christian
themes they expect of Lewis. There is no doubt that this
story is different. It offers more to readers than his earlier
stories, because of its greater maturity and sophistication
in technique and style, but it also demands more of readers,
who may therefore require some guidance and helps in dealing with it. A relatively small amount of background information will do a great deal toward removing apparent
difficulties and permitting full enjoyment and appreciation
of the work.

1

Lewis first expects his readers to know the story of Cupid
and Psyche. From its earliest known version, by the Latin
author Apuleius two centuries after Christ, the tale has
often delighted readers and has been retold again and again
throughout the centuries. Lewis's book is another retelling
of the story, one which brings out far more of its significance
and power than any of the earlier versions. Lewis takes for
granted that his readers will know the basic plot of his story
and will notice and appreciate the points at which he makes
changes in the original. A summary of "Cupid and Psyche"

may be useful as an introduction to or reminder of the myth his story is retelling:

ONCE upon a time there lived a king and queen who had three daughters, two of them beautiful, but the third, the youngest, so beautiful that people worshipped her as a goddess and neglected the worship of Venus for her sake. Therefore, although her sisters were married to kings, Psyche (the youngest) had no suitors; because of her beauty and supposed divinity, no man dared aspire to her hand. Her father consulted the oracle of Apollo about her marriage and was told that she was not to marry a human: rather, she was to be exposed on a mountain where a dire serpent would take her as his bride. With great sorrow and funeral rites, Psyche was abandoned on the mountain.

Venus, jealous of Psyche's beauty and of the honor given to her, had a different fate in mind for her; she ordered her son Cupid to use his magic arrows to cause the girl to fall in love with the most deformed and ignoble man he could find. Cupid set off to do so, but, upon seeing Psyche, fell in love with her himself. When she was left on the mountain, therefore, he had the West-wind carry her to his palace. Invisible servants welcomed her, bathed her, sang to her, and brought her a sumptuous banquet. That night Cupid came to her and made her his wife, but left before daybreak, having forbidden her to see his face.

After some days, Psyche longed to see her sisters and begged that they might visit her. The god consented reluctantly, warning her of possible consequences, and had the West-wind waft them to the palace. Psyche entertained them with baths, music, and divine delicacies; when they inquired about her husband, Psyche said he was a handsome young man who spent most of his time in the hills, hunting. She loaded their arms with jewels and treasures as they left, and urged them to return.

Although to Psyche they expressed delight at her good fortune, inwardly they were consumed with envy, for Psyche's palace, wealth, and spouse were superior to their own. They conspired to destroy her happiness, and found the means upon their next visit, for the simple Psyche (now pregnant, and forewarned that her sisters intended her harm) forgot her earlier story and said that her husband was a middle-aged merchant with grey hair. Realizing that Psyche had not seen her husband and suspecting that she was married to a god, the sisters returned the next day and persuaded Psyche that her mysterious husband must actually be a monstrous serpent

3

who devoured pregnant women. They instructed her to hide a lamp and a sharp knife in the room and, when her husband was sleeping, to take out the lamp and by its light to cut off his head.

All this the gullible Psyche, terribly frightened by their words, promised to do. That night she brought out the lamp and saw not a monster but Cupid, sweetest and most beautiful of gods. She gazed on him with insatiable love, until a drop of hot oil from her lamp fell on his shoulder and woke him. He, injured by the burning oil and wounded by her lack of faith, rebuked her and vanished from her sight.

Psyche, wretched and desolate, first attempted to drown herself; but the river would not let her drown and the god Pan warned her never to try again. Psyche wandered on and came to the city where one of her sisters lived. She told her sister that her husband was Cupid, that he had turned her out for her disobedience, and that he had said he would marry the sister instead. At this the sister hastened to the mountain and flung herself over the cliff from which she had been wafted down before; but the West-wind did not aid her this time, and she was dashed to pieces on the rocks. After doing the same to her other sister, Psyche traveled about the country seeking her husband. She was refused shelter by the goddesses Ceres and Juno, because of Venus's anger toward her.

In despair, Psyche finally decided to seek out Venus, hoping to be reconciled to her. Venus, however, beat her, had Sorrow and Sadness torment her, and set her a series of seemingly impossible tasks. The first, of separating a great heap of wheat, barley, millet, poppy-seed, peas, lentils, and beans into separate piles, was carried out for her by a host of sympathetic ants. Next, she had to get a handful of golden wool from some man-killing sheep; a reed by the river whispered to her that this could be achieved by plucking the wool off the briars amongst which the sheep had been grazing. Then she had to fetch a cupful of water from a fountain fed by the river Styx, at the top of a sheer and slippery rock face guarded by dragons who never slept; but an eagle came to her, took the cup from her, filled it with the water, and returned it to her.

Finally, Psyche was sent to the world of the dead and told to bring back to Venus a box containing beauty from Persephone, Queen of the Underworld. A mysterious voice told her how to enter the Underworld, make her way through it, and return; it warned her in particular that three times she would be asked for help by people who would seem to deserve her pity, but she must refuse them all. And when Persephone gave her the box, she must above all things not open it to look

4

inside. Psyche obeyed all this and returned to the upper world with the box; but curiosity overcame her and she looked into it. It contained only an infernal and death-like sleep, which overcame her at once.

Cupid, his injury now healed, and searching for Psyche, found her, put the sleep back into the box, woke her, and sent her on to Venus. He then interceded with Jupiter, who agreed to permit him to marry Psyche and made her a goddess. Venus, no longer having reason to be jealous of Psyche, was reconciled to her, "and thus Psyche was married to Cupid, and after in due time she was delivered of a child, whom we call Pleasure."[1]

Readers have always sensed that deeper meaning lay under the simple story. The names invite such a response, of course. *Psyche* is the Greek word for "soul"; the story from the first has been allegorized as the human soul's quest for love. It readily lent itself to Christian meanings. The Italian writer Boccaccio, in the fourteenth century, saw Psyche as the rational function of the soul needing to reject the sisters (the lower, physical functions) and be joined to noble love or God himself. William Warburton, in the eighteenth century, interpreted the story as tracing "the progress of the soul to perfection, in the possession of divine love, and the reward of immortality." And Robert Graves, in the twentieth century, calls it "a neat philosophical allegory of the progress of the rational soul towards intellectual love."[2]

This tale frustrated Lewis, partly because he saw that such interpretations miss the real point and vastly oversimplify the story, and partly because he saw that Apuleius missed the whole point himself. The story was the sort out of which the great myths are made: and myth for Lewis, of course, meant not "a fictitious story or unscientific account," but a use of narrative structure and archetypal elements to convey through the imagination universal or divine truths not accessible to the intellect alone.[3] Apuleius had failed to develop the story's mythical potential. In particular he had failed to give the tale the sense of divine mystery or awe— Lewis, using Rudolf Otto's term, called it "numinousness"[4]— which is characteristic of myth: for Lewis this failure was epitomized by the fact that the sisters could *see* the palace of the god. From his first reading of the story he thought that could not have been the way it was.

So he tried to retell the story the way it should have been told. In his youth he tried to write "a poem on my own version of the Cupid and Psyche story in which Psyche's sister would not be jealous, but unable to see anything but moors when Psyche showed her the Palace."[5] Fragments of two such attempts in couplets remain.[6] In 1922, according to his diary, he was considering how to make a masque or a play of the story.[7] Not until three decades later, however, was he able to rewrite the story, and then not as a poem but as *A Myth Retold,* as his subtitle puts it. In a paragraph prefaced to the first British edition, Lewis accounted for it this way: "This re-interpretation of an old story has lived in the author's mind, thickening and hardening with the years, ever since he was an undergraduate. That way, he could be said to have worked at it most of his life. Recently, what seemed to be the right form presented itself and themes suddenly interlocked."[8]

What interlocked for Lewis was a profound picture of the central elements of Christianity, presented not in the apologist's form of his early works, enabling readers to "see," or understand, truths through the reason, but in mythical form, giving a "taste" of Reality through the imagination. This represents a significant change in Lewis's attitude toward and ideas about myth, which will be discussed in the final five chapters of this book: Lewis, who in his thirties put his fullest trust in reason, came in his fifties to regard myth as one of the best means available for embodying and conveying the Truth.

2

Other difficulties which readers encounter in *Till We Have Faces* involve the style. A few readers are put off by the sentence structures and word choice. These are, indeed, less simple and direct than those of the Narnian Chronicles or even the Ransom trilogy. The extent to which they are, however, is largely part of the total fiction Lewis is creating. We are to imagine not Lewis writing this in the twentieth century, but the character Orual writing it more than 2,200 years ago. And we are to imagine she is writing it in Greek, which is a second language for her, and a language for conducting business and legal matters, thus more formal and less flowing for her than if she were writing in her native language. To give some sense that one is reading an ancient document, in Greek, Lewis slips into a slightly stiff, artificial tone. It may at first require a bit of extra attentiveness in reading, but it is clear and direct and soon should give no difficulty.

Potentially a larger barrier, initially, is the use of an "unreliable narrator." The story is told, or narrated, in the first person by the person to whom it happened. This is a major change from the ancient myth Lewis is retelling. In Apuleius's version the story was told by a third-person storyteller, an objective reporter who simply described things the way they occurred. In a brilliant move, Lewis has one of the participants relate the story, which gives a more intimate view of the events. Orual aims to be wholly truthful in her account, but it is very important to realize that she fails to understand a good many things about herself and those around her. She will report honestly, reliably, what happens to her; but her interpretation of the meaning of what happens, and her knowledge and understanding of what is happening to other characters, cannot fully be relied on. We are, therefore, required to read critically, to observe to ourselves "She's rationalizing" or "That may be the way it seems to her, but . . ."—as we do when listening to an acquaintance complain of how badly he or she has been treated. Of course, all the mistakes and self-deceptions are made clear in the end—that in one sense and at one level is the purpose of the book, and part of its greatness: it is the story of a character coming to know herself, to understand how she has treated those around her, and to take the steps needed to put herself right with her god. For the alert and careful reader, however, the revelations at the end are no surprise: he or she has already seen in Orual what she will come to see for herself.

A final difficulty involves the book's references to names and ideas which may be unfamiliar—Iphigenia, Antigone, or Stoicism, for example. Their unfamiliarity is to a great extent the result of narrowness, or perhaps shallowness, in modern education; in using such references, Lewis was not attempting to make the book difficult or obscure. For a person with even a much less rigorous education than Lewis had in the classics, literature, and philosophy, the references are generally familiar. Often the meaning of such allusions will be clarified in the text of this study, as part of the explanation of the background or meaning of the section at hand. Other times I will identify them in the notes to avoid interrupting the flow of the text or turning the study into a handbook of entries pertaining to the story.

In sum, one must expect that *Till We Have Faces* will make slightly heavier demands than Lewis's earlier stories. It requires more alertness, more involvement in the narrative process, more willingness to become informed so that material will be meaningful. It requires, then, an adult level of reading (which, it must be added, some people reach at a very early age, and others never reach), but it will yield, therefore, adult-level understandings of Lewis, of life, and of oneself.

II

Part I, Chapters 1–2:
Methods, Motives, Materialism

THE death of Orual's mother is followed by the arrival of the Fox, a Greek slave whom the King, Orual's father, purchased to teach the sons he expects to have and meanwhile to teach his daughters, Orual and Redival. Preparations begin for the marriage of the King to a Princess from Caphad, which the King hopes will yield him a son. The young queen dies in childbirth, after giving birth to a daughter, a beautiful child whom the King names Istra, or Psyche. Orual loves her devotedly and tends to her upbringing; she becomes a close companion to Orual and the Fox.

THE key function of Chapters 1 and 2 is to establish the perspectives from which the story is told and to introduce the central characters. With that in mind, the opening paragraphs repay attentive reading and close examination:

> I am old now and have not much to fear from the anger of gods. I have no husband nor child, nor hardly a friend, through whom they can hurt me. My body, this lean carrion that still has to be washed and fed and have clothes hung about it daily with so many changes, they may kill as soon as they please. The succession is provided for. My crown passes to my nephew. (p. 3)

I explained in Chapter I the extra task of understanding imposed on the reader by the first-person narration, to which the first word in the book, "I," alerts us. The word "now" is equally important. The narrator is old "now," a signal that the story operates at different levels, or different stages in time. "Now," in the first sentence, is contemporary with the

9

events at the end of Part I; Part I looks back over the events of a lifetime, perhaps six decades. Part II follows Part I by a few weeks at most. The narrator is always looking back at things after they happen, not simply reporting them as they occur, although she generally tries to tell things as they were and to avoid commenting on them. The important thing is that the narrator understands a great deal more at the end of Part II than at the end of Part I, because she learned much in the writing itself. And that has important implications for the reader: one can understand Part I fully only after finishing Part II. *Till We Have Faces* is, therefore, a book to be read twice, or three times, or more, for one begins then to appreciate levels of meaning and insinuations and ironies that could not be noticed on a first reading.

From the rest of the opening paragraph, and the one following, we learn a great deal about the narrator: that she is female ("I have no husband"), lonely ("hardly a friend"), of royal standing ("the succession," "my crown"), and well educated (as the sophisticated style and structure of the third sentence indicate). We learn that she is unhappy, and blames her unhappiness on the gods, and that her purpose in writing Part I is to present a case against the gods demonstrating the injustice of their dealings with her: "I will accuse the gods, especially the god who lives on the Grey Mountain. That is, I will tell all he has done to me from the very beginning, as if I were making my complaint of him before a judge" (p. 3). Part I, therefore, will be a mixture of diary and court case (along with romance and myth), and we must remember as we read that although this is at one level an autobiography, an account of the narrator's life, it is always told with a purpose—that of building a case against the gods. Thus it is written, we are to suppose, in Greek in the hope that the book will sometime be carried to Greece, where wise men will read it and "know whether my complaint is right" (p. 4). This dates the story some centuries before the birth of Christ—200–300 B.C., perhaps—and establishes a criterion—Greek thought, rational, objective—by which the narrator intends us to judge what will be said.

The third paragraph introduces another major change

from the ancient myth, in addition to the use of a first-person narrator. In Apuleius's version the setting is vague, unspecified, and undetailed. Lewis adds greatly to the interest and impact of the story by constructing an imaginary place and time for the story, and filling out its scene in detail. As he put it in a letter to Clyde S. Kilby, shortly after the book was published, it is "a work of (supposed) historical imagination. A guess of what it might have been like in a little barbarous state on the borders of the Hellenistic world of Greek culture, just beginning to affect it."[1] Lewis draws on his imagination and his knowledge of ancient times for specific details which bring out, for example, the crudity and cruelty of that world—in the references to the girls sliding on ice formed from "the stale of beasts" in the palace yard, to the sores on the legs of a slave where the irons had been, to the pouring of human blood over the stone statue of the goddess Ungit. James Como has described Lewis's method as not demythologizing but remythologizing: the events and characters do not exist in another world and another dimension, but in a real and believable setting in this world.[2] And that has an important effect: it takes the story out of the realm of allegory, in which people and things "stand for" abstract qualities or meanings, and places it firmly in a mode of realism, in which things simply are themselves. Thus, in the letter cited above, Lewis gently corrected Clyde Kilby on this matter: "The children made mud pies not for symbolic purposes but because children do. The Pillar Room is simply a room. The Fox is such an educated Greek slave as you might find at a barbarous court—and so on." Lewis had a fine ability to bring a setting to life and enable his readers to enter imaginatively the feelings and experiences of people very different from themselves. That is his initial and basic purpose here.

The most important character, naturally, is Orual. Since the entire book is a development of her character, only the initial elements can be laid out here. The main impression created in the early chapters is of a person very honest and fair. That impression starts at the end of paragraph two, as Orual hopes her case will be read and discussed by Greek readers, who will assess its strength: "Perhaps their wise men will know whether my complaint is right or whether the god could have defended himself if he had made an answer" (p. 4). It is reinforced by her forthrightness about herself, especially her refusal to hide or mitigate the fact of her ugliness. Some readers suggest that she wasn't as ugly as she had been made to feel she was, but her ugliness, I believe, must be accepted as literally true: first, because so many parts of the story hinge on it or point toward it, particularly as other characters, characters sympathetic to Orual, say or imply it is so; and second, because her physical appearance later becomes a symbol of her inner, spiritual condition, she must be literally ugly. From the beginning, then, Orual seeks to be open and honest as a person, accurate and trustworthy as a reporter.

Given those aims, the fourth paragraph is striking and significant. "I will begin my writing with the day my mother died and they cut off my hair, as the custom is" (p. 4). Why should she begin here? Why not earlier, so that we might know something of the formative influence of her mother, or later, with the coming of the Fox? One could attempt to justify this starting point as being where the story really begins, for the King's first wife must die in order that he can take a second, who will be Psyche's mother. But the real reason for Orual's choice of a starting point lies not in what is to come in the story but in her character and attitude. The reason she remembers that episode comes out in two key sentences: "As the shears snipped and Redival's curls fell off, the slaves said, 'Oh, what a pity! All the gold gone!' They had not said anything like that while I was being shorn" (p. 5). Here is an early expression—perhaps even the beginning—of the rivalry between the two sisters and of Orual's attitude toward herself. It may mark the first time Orual is made aware of a significant difference in appearance between her and Redival—thus it is that she remembers this particular day and event. Beginning here shows something more, although she herself may not be aware of it. She is writing a case against the gods because, she believes, they have been unjust in taking Psyche from her and not revealing themselves to her. What we realize—though she may not—is that her lasting feelings of injustice and jealousy go as far back as this: her later attitudes grow out of a sense of unfairness that Redival should be golden and beautiful, while she is drab and ugly.

Till We Have Faces is a story of the resolution of Orual's charges of injustice, but it is also an account of Orual's movement between the experience and attitudes of the other two main characters, the Fox and Psyche. The Fox's thought draws mainly upon the philosophy of the Stoics. When the Fox calls the old Greek myths "only lies of poets, lies of poets, child. Not in accordance with nature" (p. 8), or says conception of male children comes not from magic bedsteads but "by natural causes" (p. 10), or asserts that wind and weather "are all part of the same web, which is called Nature, or the Whole" (p. 85), his ideas can be traced back to Zeno, Cleanthes, and Chrysippus, Greek philosophers of the third and fourth centuries before Christ. His scoffing at death, because "at death we are resolved into our elements" (p. 17), and his idea that "all men [are] of one blood" (p. 9), have the same origin. Diogenes Laertius, author of a third-century history of Greek philosophy, summarizes the key aspects of early Stoic thought as follows: "The end [of life] may be defined as life in accordance with nature, . . . a life in which we refrain from every action forbidden by the law common to all things, that is to say, the right reason which pervades all things."[3] To the Stoics, the world is endowed with soul and reason, and nature is either that which holds the world together or that which causes things to come to life: "They hold that there are two principles in the Universe, the active principle [God] and the passive [matter]. . . . God is one and the same with Reason, Fate, and Zeus. . . . The substance of God is declared by Zeno to be the whole world and the heaven."[4] On this belief in nature as "the Whole" rest the basic Stoic beliefs in an "endless chain of causation" (that is, Fate or Destiny),[5] in acceptance of natural processes like death, and in the common rational system inclusive of all human beings.[6]

More important than identifying sources for specific remarks by the Fox, however, is to notice that Stoic philosophy is characterized by rationalism and materialism. The Fox's thinking, therefore, is similar to that of Lewis's tutor, W. T. Kirkpatrick, a rationalistic naturalism grounded in the scientific writings of Darwin and Huxley. Lewis described Kirkpatrick as "a purely logical entity . . . a 'Rationalist' of the old, high and dry nineteenth-century type."[7] He insisted on precise observation and careful inference therefrom, and dismissed entirely matters of "belief" and "opinion." That there is much of Kirkpatrick in the Fox has frequently been noted, and is pretty much beyond doubt.[8] But there is also much of Kirkpatrick in Lewis. Lewis was highly impressionable, and there is no doubt that Kirkpatrick's system of thought and modes of argument left a deep and lasting imprint on him. He ceased to be a rationalist even before he became a Christian, but the love of dialectic and "talking for victory" lasted long thereafter and helped shape his methods in his apologetic works.[9] To some extent, then, the Fox is Lewis, who for much of his life was drawn toward rationalistic thinking despite his love of the imagination.

There is much of Lewis in Psyche as well. The non-rationalistic way in which she approached others and the gods also appealed to Lewis, and pulled against the rationalist tendencies in him. In Psyche there is a natural, almost intuitive response to God, an inner loveliness and lovingness which is reflected in her physical beauty. The Fox on several occasions compares her to Helen, in Greek legend the most beautiful woman in the world. Orual says of her, "She made beauty all round her. When she trod on mud, the mud was beautiful; when she ran in the rain, the rain was silver. When she picked up a toad—she had the strangest and, I thought, unchanciest love for all manner of brutes—the toad became beautiful" (p. 22). In fairy tales, when a princess kisses a frog, it turns into a beautiful prince; in this tale, Psyche's touch will, eventually, give beauty to an ugly queen, for among the strangest and unchanciest of Psyche's loves is her love for a brute, Orual.

In his letter to Kilby, Lewis describes Psyche as having a "naturally Christian spirit." Her life, characterized by love

14

and by a series of sacrifices, has led some to call her a symbol, or a type, of Christ.[10] Such a reading is suggested, for example, by the fact that she heals the sick, calls herself a "ransom for all Glome" (p. 72), and dies at "a single leafless tree" on a hilltop (p. 98). It is supported also by such lines, referring to the sacrificing of Psyche, as "the victim must be perfect" (p. 49) and "it's only sense that one should die for many" (p. 61). Lewis himself, however, preferred that she not be interpreted as a symbol of Christ; the resemblances to Christ are important for a different reason, as he said in his letter to Kilby: "She is in some ways like Christ because every good man or woman is like Christ. What else could they be like?"[11] In the story Orual says Psyche was "what every woman, or even every thing, ought to have been and meant to be, but had missed by some trip of chance" (p. 22). We are not to assume, therefore, that Psyche's loving attitude, self-giving concern for others, responsiveness to spiritual urgings, and understanding of divine matters reflect something unique and unattainable; rather, they exemplify what all of us could be and indeed should be.

The initial indications of character are enriched by ironies, allusions, and anticipations, literary devices Lewis introduced in these chapters and used throughout the book. Irony enables a writer to be indirect, to convey shades of meaning, to bring out aspects of character subtly and naturally; it demands more alertness and flexibility in a reader than nonironic prose. The ironic tone employed in much of *Till We Have Faces* is established in the description of Orual's hair being cut by the slaves after her mother's death: "While Batta was using the shears many other of the slave women were standing round, from time to time wailing for the Queen's death and beating their breasts; but in between they were eating nuts and joking" (p. 5). The ironic contrast, or discrepancy, between their apparent and actual feelings prepares the way for several types of irony later in the book. There is the irony created by the use of a first-person narrator, who often is less fully aware of the implications of what she says than the reader should be. There is also simple verbal irony, where one thing is said but the opposite is

15

meant. When the King arranges to marry the third daughter of the King of Caphad, he believes he has "made a great match" (p. 9); but as the now much older Orual writes these words, she means just the opposite, as she points out a few sentences later. There is a sort of situational irony when the King says to the Fox, "It can't often have fallen to the lot of a mere Greekling to rule the grandson of so great a king as my father-in-law that is to be. . . . You're all pedlars and hucksters down in the Greeklands, eh?" (p. 9)—irony in the striking discrepancy between the King's estimate of a situation and that of the reader and the rest of the world. And there is irony when the King, having purchased at great expense a bed "made of an eastern wood which was said to have such virtue that four of every five children begotten in such a bed would be male" (p. 10), has another daughter. The ironies in the book, often humorous, enhance the character of Orual as an incisive, wry, but understanding person.

Equally important in adding depth to the characterizations are allusions, such as the references to Aphrodite and Anchises (p. 8), and the lines *"Virtue, sought by man with travail and toil"* and *"The Moon's gone down, but / Alone I lie,"* quoted from Greek lyric poems by Simonides and Sappho, respectively.[12] An author expects a reader to recognize such explicit allusions and to draw relevant parts of their original contexts into the story: thus the comparisons of Psyche to Helen (p. 23) are disturbing because Helen was not only beautiful but also a source of discord, the cause of the famous Trojan War (which is alluded to on page 33). But allusions are often less explicit; there may be no more than a key phrase to indicate that the author is pointing toward an external reference and invoking its associations. One such allusion appears in the second paragraph of *Till We Have Faces*. Orual writes,

> I will accuse the gods, especially the god who lives on the Grey Mountain. That is, I will tell all he has done to me from the very beginning, as if I were making my complaint of him before a judge. But there is no judge between gods and men, and the god of the mountain will not answer me. (p. 3)

The phrase "there is no judge between gods and men" closely resembles a phrase from the Old Testament book of Job: "There is no umpire between us, who might lay his hand upon us both" (9:33 RSV). The similarity in the wording and situation suggests strongly that, although for Orual this is simply the most effective way to state her point, for Lewis it is an allusion to Job and thus an initial signal that *Till We Have Faces,* like the book of Job, is a reply to a charge of alleged injustice on the part of God or the gods. And it suggests that the answer to that charge in *Till We Have Faces* should be considered in relation to that in Job, either as similar to and thus reinforced by it, or as a contrast, probably a dramatic and striking contrast, to it.

Also important to the characterizations are foreshadowings or "anticipations" of later actions or events. Thus the use of veils as the twelve girls sing a Greek bridal hymn on the King's wedding day prepares for the importance of veils later in the story. Similarly, the first mention of Psyche's love for the Grey Mountain and the stories she made up about being a queen and living in "a castle of gold and amber . . . on the very top" (p. 23) should lead one to expect something of the sort to occur to Psyche, literally or symbolically, in the future. In Chapter 1 a more subtle foreshadowing occurs when the Fox tells Orual a tale of how Venus (Aphrodite) fell in love with Prince Anchises, who was to be the father of Aeneas, the mythical founder of Rome:

> She dimmed her glory and made herself like a mortal woman and came to Anchises and beguiled him and they went up together into his bed. . . . Anchises woke from sleep and saw Aphrodite standing in the door of the hut, not now like a mortal but with the glory. So he knew he had lain with a goddess, and he covered his eyes and shrieked, "Kill me at once." (p. 8)[13]

This anticipates the story, later in the book, of Psyche's marriage to the God of the Mountain: the sexes are reversed, but the same theme of a divine-mortal union, the same emphasis on not looking at a god, are there. Lewis has placed it here partly as a preparation: the strange story to come will seem slightly less strange because it was preceded by this one. But it is here also as an initial undermining of the Fox. The Fox, upon finishing the story, hastens to add, "Not that this ever really happened. . . . It's only lies of poets, lies of poets, child" (p. 8). The Fox, as a Stoic and rationalist, will admit into his world only that which is open to scientific explanation. We are introduced here to the first of many mysterious but meaningful occurrences which lie outside the domain of the Fox's understanding. As the motif of human-divine union recurs, we should recall this episode and the Fox's inadequate response to it.

III

Chapters 3–5:
Of Divine Mysteries and Sacrifice

REDIVAL, neglected by the threesome of Orual, Psyche, and the Fox, turns for companionship to Tarin, a young soldier. Discovered together at night, Tarin is castrated and Redival put under the eyes of the Fox and Orual. The golden days of Orual's life are spoiled by Redival's presence and by Orual's fear that the gods will become jealous over people's attention to Psyche's beauty. The Tarin incident is followed by bad harvests, a rebellion, and the plague—even the Fox takes ill, but Psyche nurses him back to health and gains the reputation of a miracle worker. The people force Psyche to come out to touch those who have the fever, though it nearly costs her her life. The fever is followed by drought and famine, and public opinion shifts from praising Psyche as goddess to calling her "the Accursed." The Priest comes to the palace to tell the King that Ungit must be appeased through the Great Offering, in which a perfect victim is sacrificed to the gods and becomes the husband of Ungit or the bride of Ungit's son. Told that the lot fell on the royal family, the King grows angry and threatens the Priest—who doesn't so much as flinch—until he learns that subsequent lots fell, not on him, but Psyche. When Orual protests and begs the King to save Psyche, the King gives vent to his fear and relief by beating her savagely and accepts the Priest's words as what must be.

IN these chapters Lewis takes us back to the rites and thought forms of an ancient and pagan society, asking us thus to broaden our range of human experience and begin, at least, to question naturalistic assumptions taken for granted in the twentieth century.

The first such question, carried over from the end of the previous chapter, involves the existence and nature of the gods: is it characteristic of the gods to be jealous? At the end of Chapter 2, Orual is filled with fear when the Fox calls Psyche prettier than Andromeda, Helen, and Venus Aphrodite: he reassures her that "the divine nature is not like that. It has no envy" (p. 24). In Chapter 3, Orual is similarly frightened when she hears that many times Psyche has been worshipped as if she were a goddess. "Oh, it's dangerous, dangerous," Orual responds; "The gods are jealous. They can't bear—" (p. 28).

Lewis introduces here a central issue of the story, the problem of how Ungit on the one hand and her son on the other can be expressions of the same divine nature. Until that can be understood, Orual will remain, necessarily, an enemy of the gods. To the Fox, divine nature could not be jealous, because, as Stoic "Reason" or "Fate," it is not personal. But both of the main traditions which bear upon this work suggest the contrary. In the Apuleian myth, Venus's jealousy of Psyche's beauty supplies the central conflict of the plot, and this suggests one level of thematic interpretation of the myth for Lewis: Ungit is the Glomian equivalent of Venus, the Greek goddess of love.[1] Thus Orual's words, "The gods are jealous," characterize not just the goddess but also *eros*, or natural love: such love itself is, or tends to be, jealous and dangerous.

Her words also introduce a parallel to the Old Testament injunction against worshipping other gods: "You shall not bow down to them or serve them; for I the Lord your God am a jealous God" (Exodus 20:5). Jahweh is jealous in that he claims for himself the total allegiance and devotion of his people and warns them of consequences if they do not follow his injunction. For a proper understanding of the Old Testament it is crucial to recognize that the jealousy of God is inseparable from the love of God. As Gerhard von Rad puts it, "In this commandment declaring the zeal of Jahweh Israel was told two things: Jahweh's turning towards her—of this Hosea speaks in terms of the passion of a lover—but at the same time his threat, in case she should only yield to him with a divided heart."[2] The revelation of God's love without the revelation of his jealousy would not make clear the proper and necessary relation of his people to him. That in God which inspires fear and trembling, Rudolf Otto writes, "sets free as its accompaniment ... the feeling of personal nothingness and abasement before the awe-inspiring object directly experienced."[3]

Till We Have Faces is purportedly written for Greeks, that is, for rationalists, for people who, like the Fox, think of the gods—if at all—in terms of reason and benevolence rather than of sacrifice and fear. Lewis had made the point previously in *The Problem of Pain*:

> By the goodness of God we mean nowadays almost exclusively His lovingness; and in this we may be right. And by Love, in this context, most of us mean kindness. . . . [But] love is something more stern and splendid than mere kindness: . . . even the love between the sexes is, as in Dante, "a lord of terrible aspect." . . . If God is Love, He is, by definition, something more than mere kindness.[4]

A major purpose of *Till We Have Faces* is to convey a fuller, more adequate awareness of the divine nature than that of the rationalists, which "will not produce that fear of the Lord in which wisdom begins, and, therefore, will not produce that love in which it is consummated."[5]

Ungit, too, is a "numinous" god, not a god of the rationalists. There is about her a sense of "the holy" which creates fear in the young Orual (p. 11) and later gives rise to "the horror of holiness" (p. 54). And Ungit, like Jahweh, is jealous: as Lewis makes clear in *That Hideous Strength,* the ancient conception of Venus was not as a warm, sentimental, indulgent goddess, but as a powerful and dangerous force to those who crossed her. The tension between mother and son is similar to the dynamic in Christianity between a God of wrath and a God of love, a dynamic Lewis elsewhere dramatizes in Aslan, who is "good and terrible at the same time."[6] One key theme of the story, then, is the need for Orual to find beauty in both Ungit and her son—to move from fear to awe to appreciation to love—and it is vital to realize that for much of her life she finds beauty in neither.

Important as divine jealousy is in *Till We Have Faces,* Orual's very raising of the issue is of nearly equal interest at this point in the story. The Fox asserts that the divine nature has no jealousy—whether it has or not, human nature certainly does. We are invited, I think, to ask if Orual's fears are in part a projection (perhaps unconscious) of her own feelings. Orual has shown several evidences of a protective and possessive attitude toward Psyche. As others notice Psyche, praise her, do obeisance to her, Orual may even at this point be protesting against sharing Psyche with others, against Psyche's obtaining from others the assistance Orual wants to come only from herself.

In Apuleius's myth Psyche's exposure on the mountain is not a direct result of Venus's jealousy. Venus is indeed jealous of Psyche's beauty; but the exposure comes as a result of the oracle's directive, either to assist the working out of fate which has determined that Cupid and Psyche will meet, or at Cupid's instigation. Lewis accepts Venus's jealousy as a given part of the myth and incorporates it into his plot by making it a basic and adequate motivation for Psyche's being sacrificed on the mountain: she was the Accursed because her beauty made her, unintentionally, a rival to Venus. But Lewis also draws on ideas of the pagan worldview he was depicting to add a secondary motivation by raising questions about the relationship between the spiritual world and the material world as reflected in events which follow the castration of Tarin. Later that year is "the first of the bad harvests" (p. 26). In a pagan world one might ask if this is only coincidence, or if there is a connection between the two. Might the land be responding to the physical desexing inflicted, perhaps unjustly, on the young man? In the next case there clearly is a connection: "The year after that we had rebellion. It came of my father's gelding Tarin" (p. 29). The King must wage a war against Tarin's father and his allies, a war which the King wins, but at the cost of weakening the monarchy. To the modern mind, the connection is political, not spiritual, but the ancient mind would not make such arbitrary divisions: in the King, after all, runs the blood of the gods. "That year was the second bad harvest and the beginning of the fever" (p. 29), followed by a drought and famine: "The Shennit was now no more

22

than a trickle between one puddle and another amid dry mud-flats; it was the corpse of a river and stank. Her fish were dead, her birds dead or gone away. The cattle had all died or been killed or were not worth the killing" (p. 40). The question raised by all this, then, is whether there is in nature a responsiveness which extends beyond the Fox's notion of a web of wholly naturalistic causes. Lewis, I think, does not desire to affirm the existence of such a natural sympathy—but I suspect he is very willing to shake our confidence that it could not exist.

These mysteries take on a further dimension as well, a religious one. For the Priest assumes that there is a specifically sympathetic relation between occurrences: "All the woes that have come upon us," he says, are because "the land is impure." Ungit's anger, he continues, "never comes upon us without cause, and it never ceases without expiation." There will be "no mending of all our ills till the land is purged" (pp. 45–46). Thus one explanation for the natural disasters is Ungit's jealousy: "I hear of terrible doings in this land, mortals aping the gods and stealing the worship due to the gods" (p. 47). On this view, the guilty party must be found and must pay the penalty. This, in a strict view, is not sacrifice: it is justice.

But as the Priest goes on, he moves easily, if inconsistently, from purgation to appeasement, from "expiation" by the ferreting out and elimination of the "Accursed" to the "offering" of something set apart for the gods to win their favor. As he describes the nature of the Great Offering, he is clearly discussing not justice but sacrifice: "In the Great Offering, the victim must be perfect. For, in holy language, a man so offered is said to be Ungit's husband, and a woman is said to be the bride of Ungit's son. . . . That is why you are so wide of the mark, King, when you think a thief, or an old worn-out slave, or a coward taken in battle, would do for the Great Offering. The best in the land is not too good for this office" (p. 49). The Latin roots of *sacrifice* convey the meaning "make sacred": one offers a thing to the gods, sets it apart or consecrates it to them, in order to win or regain their favor or good will. To peoples who regard property as an extension of their persons (and we have barely emerged from that stage ourselves: witness the use of capital punishment for theft, on that grounds, as late as the nineteenth century in Europe), to offer an animal to a god was literally to offer a part of themselves: our donation, even "sacrificially," of money, a thing clearly external to, separate from, ourselves, is not even a pale shadow of what sacrifice was to an ancient people. This is precisely the way the King interprets the act in *Till We Have Faces*: "It's I who should be pitied," he protests. "It's I who am asked to give up part of myself" (p. 61). For, of course, in an ancient society, children—and women generally—were regarded as possessions of their fathers or husbands: "No one seems to remember whose girl she is. She's mine; fruit of my own body. My loss" (p. 60). In that sense the Great Offering could be seen as required by the King's gelding of Tarin, which caused the drought and famine. Ungit, a fertility goddess, was offended by an act which prevents conception of life, and the King must make reparation to her to regain her favor.

To the extent that impurity in the land has been caused by the King's actions, his death could achieve purgation, but his death could not be a sacrifice. For, as the Priest insists, in the Great Offering, the victim, who becomes the husband or bride of the god (p. 49), "must be perfect," and the King is not perfect, not suitable as reparation. Expiation and offering could be achieved simultaneously, however, if a perfect part of the guilty party were to be offered on the guilty party's behalf. And this, of course, is the essence of sacrifice: the setting apart, consecrating to the gods, of something perfect, in the place of the imperfect thing which deserves to die, as the reparation which can restore the favor of and proper relationship with the gods.

There is nothing reasonable about all this—why should a part, logically, be accepted for the whole? Thus the Fox finds it incomprehensible and repulsive (pp. 7–8), even apart from the emotional outburst prompted by his fears for Psyche: "A moment ago the victim of this abominable sacrifice was to be the Accursed, the wickedest person in the whole land, offered as a punishment. And now it is to be the best

24

person in the whole land—the perfect victim—married to the god as a reward. . . . It can't be both" (pp. 49–50). The Priest's answer sets up a central theme of the rest of the book: "We are hearing much Greek wisdom this morning. . . . It is very subtle. But it brings no rain and grows no corn; sacrifice does both . . ." (p. 50).

The mystery implicit in this part of the Priest's reply reaches deep: at every level of being—the natural, the human, and the spiritual—life arises from death, and without death—sacrificial death—there can be no life. The Priest continues,

> "Much less does [Greek wisdom] give [people] understanding of holy things. They demand to see such things clearly, as if the gods were no more than letters written in a book. . . . Holy places are dark places. . . . Holy wisdom is not clear and thin like water, but thick and dark like blood. Why should the Accursed not be both the best and the worst?" (p. 50)

The answer lies in the nature of sacrifice: the victim of the Great Offering will be both the worst and the best—the best, because of Psyche's goodness and beauty, and the worst, since Psyche not only represents the King but also has provoked the jealousy of Ungit.

That the victim can be both, that such substitution can be effected, that life and strength can come from such a death, are mysteries, divine paradoxes, contrary to Stoic (and modern) reason. That the Fox cannot accept such paradoxes is part of the book's central, crucial contrast between him and the Priest:

> The Fox had taught me to think—at any rate to speak—of the Priest as of a mere schemer and a politic man who put into the mouth of Ungit whatever might most increase his own power and lands or most harm his enemies. I saw it was not so. He was sure of Ungit. Looking at him as he sat with the dagger pricking him and his blind eyes unwinking, fixed on the King, and his face like an eagle's face, I was sure, too. (p. 54)

Later in the book (pp. 144 and 147), the Fox is compared to Oedipus, who used his intelligence to solve the riddle of the Sphinx and thus saved the city of Thebes. If the Fox is like

Oedipus, able to answer riddles (p. 144), the blind Priest must be like the blind prophet Tiresias, and his confrontation with the Fox closely parallels the key juxtaposition in Sophocles' play. When Tiresias tells Oedipus that he, Oedipus, is the cause of the plague which is now afflicting the city, Oedipus rejects the idea and ridicules the prophet because he cannot see. Tiresias responds: "And I tell thee— since thou hast taunted me even with blindness—that thou hast sight, yet seest not in what misery thou art, nor where thou dwellest, nor with whom."[7] Tiresias is blind physically, but he has spiritual sight: he sees the truth, knows divine wisdom. Oedipus, for all his human knowledge and physical sight, is blind to wisdom and the truth. So it is, Lewis is suggesting, with the Priest and the Fox. The divine paradox of sacrifice is repugnant to the human understanding. But a central theme of the book is that such understanding must "die," must be "sacrificed," must be transformed, so that it can see past the clearness of knowledge into the dark recesses where wisdom lies, and thus truly see and truly understand.

IV

Chapters 6–7:
Love and Longing

THE Fox and Orual try to convince the King to take measures, any measures, for saving Psyche, but he refuses. Orual's offer to take Psyche's place is refused, because she lacks beauty, and Psyche is imprisoned in an inner room of the palace. When Bardia, who is guarding the door, refuses to allow Orual to enter, she takes a sword and tries to fight him. He disarms her easily, but allows her to enter. The interview with Psyche seems the reverse of what it should be: Psyche, strong and controlled, comforts Orual, who is bitter and resentful, partly at Psyche because the latter seems so little moved over their parting. When Psyche begins to talk of her old longing for the gods and for death, Orual accuses her of cruelty and lack of love, and their interview ends on a very unpleasant note.

*L*EWIS once commented, in response to the difficulty people had with *Till We Have Faces,* "I'm surprised that people don't see that it is about jealousy and possessive love."[1] The difficulty may be less a failure to see that it is about possessive love than a failure to understand the way possessive love and love-longing oppose each other in Orual and the way Platonic and Christian ideas about love and longing give shape to a conflict which threatens to tear her life apart.

It would not be unfair or misleading to call *Till We Have Faces* a development in fiction of the central themes Lewis would spell out a few years later in *The Four Loves.* Each of the four loves—*storge* (to use its Greek name), or affection; *philia,* or friendship; *eros,* or love between the sexes; and *agape,* or unselfish love, godly love—has an im-

27

portant place in *Till We Have Faces,* though only the first appears in Chapter 7. Lewis calls *storge, philia,* and *eros* the "natural loves," and *agape* "divine love." His thesis about the loves is that the natural loves can remain themselves, can remain loves, only if they are infused with, or transformed by, divine love, or *agape;* left to themselves, cut off from *agape,* the natural loves will become corrupted, will gradually cease to be loving and will in fact, eventually, turn into forms of hatred.

Lewis had illustrated all this much earlier in *The Great Divorce,* in which he describes two women, now in hell, who have characteristics resembling Orual's. One is a mother who loved her son, Michael—gave up her whole life to him, she says, did her best to make him happy, and, after his death, lived only for his memory: "Keeping his room exactly as he'd left it: keeping anniversaries: refusing to leave that house though Dick and Muriel [her husband and daughter] were both wretched there."[2] All this points toward the fact that her love went bad, became "uncontrolled and fierce and monomaniac" (p. 84; *92*). She admits finally that she would rather have her son with her in hell than free to be happy in heaven. The other is a wife who devoted her life to her husband, Robert. "It was I who made a man of him! Sacrificed my whole life to him!" (p. 77; *85*). It was she who forced him to work thirteen hours a day, to strive for promotions, to buy a more expensive home, and to give up his old friends and begin to entertain "properly." She still thinks that she could make something of him: "I'll take charge of him again. I will take up my burden once more" (p. 81; *89*). The real concern of both women is themselves, not Michael or Robert: "I want my boy, and I mean to have him. He is mine, do you understand? Mine, mine, mine, for ever and ever" (p. 86; *95*); "Please, please! I'm so miserable. I must have someone to—to do things to" (p. 81; *89*). Such, Lewis affirms, is the inevitable fate of all natural loves left to themselves: "They all go bad when they set up on their own and make themselves into false gods" (p. 84; *93*). The natural loves need to be converted, infused with divine love, if they are to remain loves. They must be recognized as second things, not mistaken for first things: this is the principle underlying all love, that "you cannot love a fellow-creature fully till you love God" (p. 84; *92*).

In such terms Lewis traces the degeneration of Orual's *storge* for Psyche in *Till We Have Faces*. Orual took the place of the mother Psyche never knew, and no child was ever better loved or more devotedly cared for. No terms seem adequate to encompass Orual's love: "I wanted to be a wife so that I could have been her real mother. I wanted to be a boy so that she could be in love with me. I wanted her to be my full sister instead of my half sister. I wanted her to be a slave so that I could set her free and make her rich" (p. 23). Psyche has the beauty, grace, and ease that Orual does not have, and Orual in some measure finds fulfillment in Psyche, as well as purpose and a return of love: truly she could mark her first sight of Psyche as "the beginning of all my joys" (p. 20).

In the very greatness and depth of her love—in its excess, one might say—are danger signs as well. For "this craving, of all love-cravings," Lewis warns, "easily becomes the most unreasonable."[3] *Storge* is a need-love, or acquisitive love, which gratifies the giver, and a gift-love, or unselfish love, as well—"but one that needs to give; therefore needs to be needed. But the proper aim of giving is to put the recipient in a state where he no longer needs our gift." *Storge* should work toward making itself unneeded, but, as a natural love, in itself it has no power to do so: "The instinct desires the good of its object, but not simply; only the good it can itself give. A much higher love—a love which desires the good of the object as such, from whatever source that good comes—must step in and help or tame the instinct before it can make the abdication. And of course it often does."[4] But it did not in the case of Orual, and the results in Chapter 7 are precisely what Lewis has described here.

The evidences of perverted *storge* abound. Orual *needs* assurance of Psyche's love and reacts sharply to any suggestion that Psyche's love is less intense than her own: "Why must she say bare *friends*?" (p. 69); "the parting between

29

her and me seemed to cost her so little" (p. 71). Orual needs
to feel needed, in the same old ways:

> And now [after Orual provokes feelings of fear in Psyche] she
> did weep and now she was a child again. What could I do but
> fondle and weep with her? But this is a great shame to write;
> there was now (for me) a kind of sweetness in our misery for
> the first time. This was what I had come to her in her prison
> to do. (p. 70)

And Orual wants Psyche to have only the good Orual gives
her. Psyche's assurance and strength irritate and even anger
Orual, not because Psyche is comforted but because she finds
that comfort apart from Orual: "Though the things she was
saying gave her (that was plain enough) courage and comfort, I grudged her that courage and comfort. It was as if
someone or something else had come in between us" (p. 75).
All the good in Psyche's life is to come from Orual, and all
her love is to be for Orual: "I did not want her to bring even
the Fox in now" (p. 73). When Psyche begs, "Oh, look up
once at least before the end and wish me joy. I am going to
my lover," Orual, in the throes of injured *storge,* snaps back,
"I only see that you have never loved me" (p. 76). Orual,
who should have been a source of comfort and encouragement to Psyche, ends up through her distorted natural love
being the opposite: "Had I not come to her to give comfort,
if I could? Surely not to take it away. But I could not rule
myself" (p. 72).

The source of Psyche's comfort instead was her longing,
or *Sehnsucht,* which was also a powerful force in Lewis's
life. Lewis defines it as "an unsatisfied desire which is itself
more desirable than any other satisfaction."[5] Momentary
experiences of satisfaction, through sudden encounters with
beauty in nature, literature, or music, or more often through
the memory of such encounters, only intensify the desire,
and the pain always associated with it. When Lewis refers
to it he uses such terms as "stab," "pang," and "inconsola-
ble," or calls it a "particular kind of unhappiness or grief,
[but] . . . a kind we want."[6] Unlike other desires, in which
pain arises from the absence of satisfaction, pain is inherent
in this desire—inherent because attainment of its object is

and remains inseparable from death, from death of self. Lewis puts it most directly in the chapter on Heaven in *The Problem of Pain:* "We need not suppose . . . that eternal life will not also be eternal dying. It is in this sense that, as there may be pleasures in hell (God shield us from them), there may be something not all unlike pains in heaven (God grant us soon to taste them)."[7] The object of this desire, also unlike other desires, is often unknown or mysterious: "It was a sensation, of course, of desire; but desire for what?"[8] Lewis's autobiography is the account of his search for the object of his longing, or "Joy," as he calls it there. He discovered at last that the longing was for union with God, and that longing is God's way of attempting to draw people to himself. It is God's way of preventing people from remaining satisfied with this world and forgetting that "our real goal is elsewhere."[9] As Lewis put it in *Christian Behaviour,*

> If I find in myself a desire which no experience in this world can satisfy, the most probable explanation is that I was made for another world. . . . I must keep alive in myself the desire for my true country, which I shall not find till after death; . . . I must make it the main object of life to press on to that other country and to help others to do the same.[10]

Such longing was a part of Psyche's being throughout her life. From the beginning, Orual reports, she "was half in love with the Mountain. . . . 'When I'm big,' she said, 'I will be a great, great queen, married to the greatest king of all, and he will build me a castle of gold and amber up there on the very top'" (p. 23). In her delirium when she was ill with the plague, "she talked most of her gold and amber castle on the ridge of the Grey Mountain" (p. 33). And now, because of that longing, she does not fear what the next day may bring:

> "I have always—at least, ever since I can remember—had a kind of longing for death. . . . It was when I was happiest that I longed most. It was on happy days when we were up there on the hills, the three of us, with the wind and the sunshine. . . . Because it was so beautiful, it set me longing, always longing. Somewhere else there must be more of it. Everything seemed to be saying, Psyche come! But I couldn't (not yet)

31

come and I didn't know where I was to come to. It almost hurt
me. I felt like a bird in a cage when the other birds of its kind
are flying home." (p. 74)[11]

The chapter's two themes, of perverted love and longing,
converge as Orual can only feel excluded and injured by
Psyche's expressions of a delight and comfort found outside
Orual: "The sweetest thing in all my life has been the longing—to reach the Mountain, to find the place where all the
beauty came from . . . my country, the place where I ought
to have been born" (pp. 75–76).

The chapter's themes blend two key influences on Lewis's
thinking, Platonism and Christianity, in a provocative way.
Plato, and Lewis, believed that human beings were made of
body and spirit, the former linked to the physical world, the
latter to the spiritual world of permanence and the Real; for
Plato (though not for Lewis), the spirit existed in the spiritual realm before being trapped in a physical body at birth,
from which it seeks to escape and return to the spiritual
world. Earlier Psyche mentioned that the Fox knew but did
not accept such a theory:

> "You know, Sister, he has sometimes let out that there were
> other Greek masters than those he follows himself; masters
> who have taught that death opens a door out of a little, dark
> room (that's all the life we have known before it) into a great,
> real place where the true sun shines and we shall meet—"
> (p. 73)

Plato regarded love, *eros,* as a desire, a longing. It is not
just a longing for wholeness in union with the other sex, as
Aristophanes suggests in the *Symposium,* but wholeness in
union with the Good forever. As Socrates puts it, "Love is
not for a half, nor indeed the whole, unless that happens to
be something good, my friend. . . . One must desire immortality along with the good—if love is love of having the good
for oneself always. It is necessary then from this argument
that love is for immortality also."[12] Because *Till We Have
Faces* is set prior to the birth of Christ, it would be anach-
ronistic to interpret Psyche's words as directly Christian.
But Psyche's references to her "gold and amber house" and
"the greatest King of all" who was going to build it for her

are surely anticipations of Christian truth—of a heavenly dwelling prepared by Christ the bridegroom for his bride the Church—and thus are more resonant and meaningful to the reader than they are to her. The Platonic love-longing for a return to the world of Ideas and the Christian longing for union with God reverberate together through Psyche's final expression of wistfulness: "Do you think it all meant nothing, all the longing? The longing for home? For indeed it now feels not like going, but like going back. All my life the god of the Mountain has been wooing me. Oh, look up once at least before the end and wish me joy" (p. 76).

Orual, however, is not open to such experiences, despite warnings against limiting her sources of knowledge. Thus Psyche tells her, "Sister, I have come to feel more and more that the Fox hasn't the whole truth. Oh, he has much of it. It'd be dark as a dungeon within me but for his teaching. And yet . . ." (p. 70; ellipsis in the original). She adds, "There must be so much that neither the Priest nor the Fox knows" (p. 72). Later Psyche is able to get beyond both Priest and Fox, as she says in telling Orual about her experience on the mountain:

> "The only thing that did me good . . . was quite different. It was hardly a thought, and very hard to put into words. There was a lot of the Fox's philosophy in it—things he says about gods or 'the divine nature'—but mixed up with things the Priest said, too, about the blood and the earth and how sacrifice makes the crops grow. I'm not explaining it well. It seemed to come from somewhere deep inside me, deeper than the part that sees pictures of gold and amber palaces, deeper than fears and tears. It was shapeless, but you could just hold onto it; or just let it hold onto you." (pp. 109–110)

The true knowledge does not come from the Priest's rituals, or the Fox's reasonings, or the images of Psyche's youth. It rests on what Lewis in a prefatory note to the book called "vision."[13] Orual, unable to go beyond the Priest or the Fox, is instead torn between them. She reflects on this later: "But I could not find out whether the doctrines of Glome or the wisdom of Greece were right. I was the child of Glome and the pupil of the Fox; I saw that for years my life had been

33

lived in two halves, never fitted together" (p. 151; see also p. 152). The two halves must come together if Orual is to find love, peace, and happiness, but they will do so only as she becomes the pupil of Psyche and is able to move beyond the limitations of both Glome and Greece.

V

Chapters 8–11:
Believing and Perceiving

Orual, bruised and sore from her father's beating, watches as Psyche is taken away, hideously costumed and painted. Orual is ill for a long time, and in her delirium dreams of Psyche doing some great wrong to her. She recovers, under the loving care of the Fox and her servants, to find that the drought is over, the plague and famine have ended, and the danger of invasion by Phars has passed. Orual wonders if the Great Offering was, therefore, effective, but the Fox assures her all this could be explained through natural causation. She decides she owes Psyche a proper burial and prepares to go to the Holy Mountain. Meanwhile, she relieves the emptiness of her existence by lessons in swordsmanship with Bardia. She journeys to the Holy Mountain with Bardia, repressing, out of her "duty" to grieve over Psyche, an urge to take joy in the beauties of nature along the way. They reach the mountain-top, but find only empty manacles—there is no sign of Psyche until, as they search about for clues, they come upon a paradisal valley where, across a river, they find Psyche herself. Psyche helps Orual cross the river, greets her joyfully, brings her food and drink, and relates her story: how West-wind himself took her from the mountain and put her down by "her" palace, where she was welcomed, served a feast, and bathed; at night her bridegroom came to her. When Orual stops her, however, and asks where the palace is, Psyche realizes Orual cannot see it; likewise, when Psyche served her wine and honeycakes, Orual tasted water and berries. A scene of tense conflict follows, and Psyche's conviction almost persuades Orual—but her need to possess Psyche holds her back. She protests, upon learning Psyche has not seen her husband, that she hates all this mystery and wonder and begs Psyche to return with her. It then begins to rain, and seeing Psyche get wet convinces Orual there is no palace—she commands

Psyche to come, but Psyche says she now must obey another and sends Orual away.

R UNNING through Chapters 8 and 9 are several different but related failures in perception. They begin with a failure to recognize the implications of allusions and archetypes and culminate in Orual's inability to perceive the realities of the world in which Psyche now lives. Two key allusions, misapplied by the King and Orual, occur at the end of Chapter 8: "Grandfather, I have missed being Iphigenia. I can be Antigone" (p. 86). In Greek mythology Iphigenia was sacrificed to Apollo in order that the winds would turn and the Greek fleet could set sail for Troy.[1] In *Till We Have Faces* Psyche is the Iphigenia figure, sacrificed for her country's good. Lewis uses the allusion to emphasize that she was *sacrificed;* in Apuleius's version of the tale she is not a sacrifice and that, as we shall see later, becomes an important difference. The allusion recalls the earlier occasion when the Fox used the story of Iphigenia to try to dissuade the King from allowing Psyche to be sacrificed:

> "Master," said the Fox, "I had not finished telling you. It is very true that a Greek king sacrificed his own daughter. But afterwards his wife murdered him, and his son murdered the wife, and Those Below drove the son mad."
> At this the King scratched his head and looked very blank. "That's just like the gods," he muttered. "Drive you to do a thing and then punish you for doing it. The comfort is I've no wife or son, Fox." (p. 58)

His comfort may be shortsighted. A few months after Psyche was sacrificed the King injures himself in a fall and dies shortly thereafter, not literally but at least symbolically killed by his own kin: "Some will say . . . that if I had murdered him indeed, I should have been no less impious than I was. For as he looked at me with fear, so I looked at him; but all my fear was lest he should live" (p. 202).

Antigone was a daughter of Oedipus, King of Thebes; she was sentenced to death by Creon, Oedipus's successor, because she performed burial rites for her brother after Creon had forbidden anyone to do so, on pain of death. Antigone has passed down through Western culture as a symbol of one who had to choose between the civil law and her moral duty, and who chose the latter though she died for doing so. Orual says that she can be an Antigone, but the comparison turns out to be ironic: Orual, too, will face a choice, between her own good and that of one she loves. But utterly unlike Antigone, she acts upon her own good, oblivious as she does so to both duty and moral codes.[2]

Archetypes—plot motifs, character types, or images which recur frequently in literature and mythology—appear throughout *Till We Have Faces*. Orual, for example, wondering what the new Queen will be like, reflects, "It wasn't only what Batta had said that frightened me; I had heard of stepmothers in plenty of stories" (p. 12). The cruel stepmother is a recurrent element in stories and fairy tales, because stepmothers—probably in many cases unkind to their stepchildren—were common when many women died in childbirth. Lewis slips this reference in partly to make us share Orual's feelings, partly for irony—Orual's stepmother turns out to be younger than herself, very small, and thoroughly frightened rather than frightening. But a deeper irony is buried here, one which will emerge later: Psyche will have a cruel and hateful "stepmother" in Orual herself.

Several important archetypes, whose significance Orual fails to recognize, appear at the end of Chapter 9. As Orual and Bardia search for Psyche on the mountain, they come to the edge of a cliff and "the sun—which had been overcast ever since we went down into the black valley—leaped out" (p. 100). The sun is a traditional symbol associated with the divine; it reminds one of Psyche's earlier reference to a Greek philosopher who contrasts our present life, "a little, dark room," with the life to come—"a great, real place where the true sun shines" (p. 73). As they look across the valley, it is described in the summer imagery traditionally associated with a paradise:

> The valley . . . was like a cleft in the Mountain's southern chin. High though it was, the year seemed to have been kinder in it than down in Glome. I never saw greener turf. There

> was gorse in bloom, and wild vines, and many groves of flour-
> ishing trees, and great plenty of bright water—pools, streams,
> and little cataracts. And when, after casting about a little to
> find where the slope would be easiest for the horse, we began
> descending, the air came up to us warmer and sweeter every
> minute. (p. 101)

That this is a paradisal world, the country of the gods, is
reaffirmed by another archetype: "There, not six feet away,
on the far side of the river, stood Psyche" (p. 101). A river
is traditionally a symbol of death or the dividing line between worlds—it is reflected in classical mythology by the
river Styx, which souls must cross to enter the underworld,
and in Christian thought by the river at the end of the
journey of life in John Bunyan's *The Pilgrim's Progress* and
by such hymns as "Guide Me, O Thou Great Jehovah" ("when
I tread the verge of Jordan . . ."). The archetypes prepare
us, then, for what Bardia utters a moment later when he
sees Psyche: "It is the bride of the god. It is a goddess"
(p. 102). Psyche has passed, through divine magic or death,[3]
into the world of the gods and is perhaps herself now one of
the immortals ("she was so brightface"—p. 102), though
Orual, as she fails to heed the archetypal signals, fails also
to recognize Psyche's new status.

Orual's imperceptiveness in comparing herself to Antigone and in neglecting the implications of the paradisal
archetypes foreshadows her inability to experience what was
present and evident to Psyche: "You can't see it. You can't
feel it. For you, it is not there at all. Oh, Maia [Psyche's "old
baby's name" for Orual[4]] . . . I am very sorry" (pp. 119–20;
ellipsis in the original). The scene, and point, are crucial to
the book: Lewis knew from the first time he read Apuleius
that this is "the way the thing must have been."[5]

Orual's inability to see the palace traces to the philosophical system she learned from the Fox—not just the rationalism but the materialism at its base. The Stoics differed
from earlier philosophers, especially Plato and Aristotle, by
their belief that nothing incorporeal exists: "The Stoics attempted to give a completely materialist explanation of
reality and the knowledge of reality. They maintained that

anything that was real was body."[6] It is only to be expected, then, that for the Stoics knowledge would derive directly from material objects: "The Stoics found the criterion of knowledge in sensuous impressions, which furnish the materials fashioned by reason . . . and affirm[ed] that every representation of an object implied the existence of the object itself."[7] Diogenes Laertius summarized it this way:

> The Stoics agree to put in the forefront the doctrine of presentation [impression] and sensation, inasmuch as the standard by which the truth of things is tested is generically a presentation. . . . For presentation comes first; then thought, which is capable of expressing itself, puts into the form of a proposition that which the subject receives from a presentation.[8]

The process of perception, thus of knowing, was described in physical terms. From the object proceed waves which strike upon the sense organs; the mind actively encounters or "assents to" this impact, and there is produced in the soul an effect like the imprint of a seal. Zeno needed an equally physical metaphor to describe the process:

> He then partly closed his hand, and so represented the response of the governing-principle to the impression: the mind assents to it. Having next made a fist he likened this to cognition ("grasping"). And finally, grasping his fist with the other hand he said: "This is what knowledge is like."[9]

Lewis was clear and definite about the Fox's background: "The Fox expresses *neither* Anthroposophy *nor* my views, but Stoicism."[10] If Lewis was knowledgeable and consistent in applying details, the Fox would hold the Stoic notions of substance, perception, and knowledge. That he does hold them is confirmed in Chapter 13, when Orual, upon her return to the palace, asks the Fox about sight and reality:

> "If I'd had my eyes shut, I would have believed her palace was as real as this."
> "But, your eyes being open, you saw no such thing."
> "You don't think—not possibly—not as a mere hundredth chance—there might be things that are real though we can't see them?"
> "Certainly I do. Such things as Justice, Equality, the Soul, or musical notes."

> "Oh, Grandfather, I don't mean things like that. .... Are there no things—I mean *things*—but what we see?"
>
> "Plenty. Things behind our backs. Things too far away. And all things, if it's dark enough." (pp. 141–42)

And Orual, as the Fox's pupil, accepts these notions as well; they underlie her attempts in Chapter 14 to convince Psyche that she does not know her husband because she has not seen him.

Such thinking, however, cannot account for the scene between Orual and Psyche, and the point of Chapters 10 and 11 is to establish the inadequacy of the Fox's theory of knowledge, even before Chapters 13 and 14 make use of it. The scene can be accounted for, and clarified, by ideas Lewis shared with his friend Owen Barfield, a way of thinking which the Fox and Orual resisted. Barfield begins with the point that seeing is not a simple process of "grasping," or "taking in," an external object in its physical "reality," its "matter": after all, things are "made" mostly of empty space. Rather, "seeing" is a complex process to which our minds and external objects both contribute: our visual faculty encounters the extended object; that meeting results in an image, or "appearance," or "phenomenon," and *that,* not "the thing itself," is what we "see"; as the Oyarsa of Perelandra puts it to Ransom, "You see only an appearance, small one. You have never seen more than an appearance of anything."[11] But we "see" the appearance only as the mind receives, sorts out, classifies, and recognizes the object. If we encounter something for the first time and aren't familiar with what it is, we can't really see it—we will receive an image, but we will not be able to interpret and thus perceive that image: thus, in *Out of the Silent Planet,* when Ransom first looked at the landscape of the planet Malacandra, "he saw nothing but colours—colours that refused to form themselves into things. Moreover, he knew nothing yet well enough to see it: you cannot see things till you know roughly what they are."[12] In Barfield's words, "I do not perceive any *thing* with my sense-organs alone, but with a great part of my whole human being. . . . When I 'hear a thrush singing,' I am hearing, not with my ears alone, but with all sorts of other things like mental habits, memory, imagination, feeling and . . . will."[13]

Lewis had studied the same philosophers as Barfield and knew that one does not see "the thing itself." In his teens he had summarized it as follows for his nonphilosopher friend, Arthur Greeves:

> Of course we all start with the idea that our senses put us in direct contact with reality—you think that your eyes are windows by which your brain "sees" the world. But science teaches you that your eye, or rather the nerve of your eye, is merely a telegraph wire. It's [sic] vibration produces a feeling in your brain which we call colour etc.: but what the Something at the other end which starts the vibration may be, of this no human being can have any conception. No increase of our sensory keenness, no microscope or telescope can put us in any direct relation with the Thing: we still remain dependent on this long chain of communications, travelling by vibration from atom to atom: and we can never have any proof that the sensation which it produces in our brain conveys any true idea of the external Thing.[14]

Lewis agreed with Barfield that one does not actually "see" objects; but he was suspicious of the psychological aspect of the process which chiefly interested Barfield, and of the subjective element that inevitably accompanies it. Thus the process as Lewis describes it is wholly physical, almost mechanical: there are wires, vibrations, and chains of communication. Ransom's becoming able to see strange objects on Malacandra was only like the automatically adjusting lens on a projector coming into focus. Lewis put his emphasis, through the thirties and forties, not on the process but on the *object,* even if direct knowledge of it is unattainable. Writing to Barfield in 1929, Lewis brings out the importance of the object through an analogy with economics:

> As it is impossible to conduct any developed economic operation in terms of the real wealth, so you cannot think without removing yourself from the thing really thought about to its counters or chits. But—just as the credit has no meaning apart from the wealth in the background—so the skeleton-conceptions live only in the light of the real which they represent: a thing v. different from them. It is therefore very necessary to go back now and then, either to an actual ex-

perience of the sort they abridge, or to the concrete imagination of such an experience.[15]

Because of this basic attachment to the object, Lewis would not say, with Barfield, that perception is in large part "dependent upon the percipient"[16]—it is simply *in* the percipient. Lewis, from his teen years through his forties, would not put much emphasis on Barfield's central point, that there is a subjective element in perception, that what a person brings to perception—the range of his or her experience, the state of emotions, the degree of attentiveness, the kind of training—will affect what one perceives. The mechanical nature of Lewis's approach to perception and the heavy emphasis on the object itself have affinities not with Barfield but with the Fox and Stoic ideas about perceiving.

Much of that changed for Lewis in his fifties. He came to accept Barfield's ideas about the importance of the perceiver, and a subjective element in perception. He embodies that change of emphasis in a key scene of *Prince Caspian,* written a few years before *Till We Have Faces.* The four children—Peter, Susan, Edmund, and Lucy—are brought back to Narnia to help put Caspian on the throne which has been usurped by Caspian's uncle, Miraz. With Trumpkin the Dwarf they start out confidently to join Caspian's forces at Aslan's How, relying on their knowledge of the forests and on their compass. At one point Lucy is sure she sees Aslan, beckoning them in a different direction:

> "Where did you think you saw him?" asked Susan.
> "Don't talk like a grown-up," said Lucy, stamping her foot. "I didn't *think* I saw him. I saw him."[17]

None of the others saw him, however, and, having not seen, do not believe her, so they continue on their own way—only to admit, by evening, that they chose the wrong route, wasted most of the day, and now must retrace their steps.

Aslan wakes Lucy that night and tells her she must "go back to the others now, and wake them up; and tell them you have seen me again; and that you must all get up at once and follow me."

"Will the others see you too?" asked Lucy.

"Certainly not at first," said Aslan. "Later on, it depends."
(pp. 126–27; Ch. 10)[18]

Lewis's use of the word "certainly" is striking. Reluctant as Lewis was to loosen his grip on the object as wholly determining perception, here he accepts a subjective aspect as simply the way things are. Thus, when Lucy wakes the others, they protest that they can't see Aslan—"because there isn't anything to see," says Susan; and they ask, "Why should Aslan be invisible to us? He never used to be" (p. 130; Ch. 11), not realizing that the change is in themselves and their relation to the lion. But they decide to go, and once they commit themselves by an act of faith (in Lucy, if not in Aslan), they gradually become able to see Aslan themselves.

In *Till We Have Faces,* as in the Chronicles of Narnia, Lewis suggests that belief, or even the will to believe, can be one of the factors that affect perception. Thus, as Orual sits on the steps of the god's house, her perceptual mechanism is not in a state which will enable her to experience it: "You can't see it. You can't feel it. For you, it is not there at all" (pp. 119–20). To Orual the cup of wine was water in Psyche's cupped hands, the fine honeycakes were mountain berries, Psyche's royal robes were nothing but rags. A similar scene occurs in *The Last Battle,* written only shortly before this work, where the Dwarfs are unable to experience the paradisal world all about them. "Can't you see?" Lucy asks. "Look up! Look round! Can't you see the sky and the trees and the flowers? Can't you see *me?*" But the Dwarfs, determined not to believe in such mysterious things, remain in the darkness of the Stable: to them sweet flowers are stable-litter, rich red wine is water from a donkey trough, and a glorious feast is hay, old turnips, and raw cabbage leaves. "They have chosen cunning instead of belief," Aslan explains. "Their prison is only in their own minds, yet they are in that prison."[19] Orual, too, is determined not to believe, lest it should—as indeed it would—make her act upon those beliefs and do things other than what she herself wants to do. Thus she protests, "I don't want it. I hate it. Hate it, hate it, hate it" (p. 124). Orual, her heart full of jealousy and unlove, wills not to see, and will not see, what would force her to give up her possessive hold on Psyche.

Orual's inability, or refusal, to perceive reality is reinforced by a motif of dreams. Dreams were always important to Lewis, in his life as well as his stories. In *Surprised by Joy* Lewis notes that he remembers "nothing earlier than the terror of certain dreams."[20] He writes to Arthur Greeves, "I wish you and your family would have the goodness to keep out of my dreams."[21] In his diaries he often mentions his dreams: "I dreamed that I was in our room at Little Lea . . ."; "I had a most horrible dream . . ."; "I had an unusually nasty dream connected with my father in the night"; "a curious dream in the night."[22] It is quite natural, therefore, that he should often use dreams in his stories: the hero of his early narrative poem *Dymer* has several dreams; *The Pilgrim's Regress* is a dream allegory and *The Great Divorce* a dream fantasy; Ransom, in the second chapter of *Out of the Silent Planet,* has a rather frightening dream of a garden and a wall and an attempt to scale it; and of course the "Dawn Treader," in its voyage to the end of the earth, encounters an island where dreams—"not daydreams: dreams"—"come true, . . . come to life, come real."[23]

Dreams appear in several forms, and have several functions, in *Till We Have Faces.* Orual dreams as she lies ill after her father beat her:

> Now mark yet again the cruelty of the gods. There is no escape from them into sleep or madness, for they can pursue you into them with dreams. Indeed you are then most at their mercy. . . . Finding me heart-shattered for Psyche's sake, they made it the common burden of all my fantasies that Psyche was my greatest enemy. All my sense of intolerable wrong was directed against her. It was she who hated me; it was on her that I wanted to be revenged. (pp. 80–81)

Fantasies, whether Psyche's "old dream of [her] gold and amber palace on the Mountain" (p. 109), or Orual's "impossible fool's dream" about being married to Bardia (p. 224), are referred to as dreams (see also pp. 129, 137, 152, 266, 282, and 295). "Dream" is frequently used in figures of speech:

"A sudden shock, like a vile dream"; "the last day, the eve of the battle, shows like a dream"; "now all the dreamlike feeling in me suddenly vanished"; "all the long years of my queenship shrank up small like a dream" (pp. 205, 211, 243, and 273).

Dreams contribute to the development of character and plot. Thus Orual's dreams about Psyche's ill-treatment of her bring to the surface her subconscious resentments and jealousy, though she does not recognize them for what they are. Dreams also anticipate and prepare the way for the visions Orual experiences near the end of her life. Blending the visions into an already established motif of dreams makes them seem more natural and acceptable than they would be if the many references to dreams had not already established a suitable tone.

More importantly, dream unites with the motif of sight in questioning the nature of reality. To Orual, Psyche's talk of her palace must be dreaming: "We're women, aren't we? Mortals. Oh, come back to the real world" (pp. 124–25). But Psyche suggests in reply that the mortal world, not her world, is the dream. As she was carried out of the palace on her way to the mountain, she now tells Orual, "I couldn't lift even a hand to wave to you. . . . And I thought it didn't matter much, because you too would wake up presently and find it was all a dream. And in a sense it was, wasn't it? And you are nearly awake now. . . . I must wake you more" (p. 106).

What, then, is reality—the mortal world back in Glome, or the world Psyche now inhabits? In *The Last Battle* Lewis uses Plato's idea that the present physical world is a transitory dream, while another, permanent and eternal world is the more real one. Professor Kirke declares,

> "That was not the real Narnia. That had a beginning and an end. It was only a shadow or a copy of the real Narnia, which has always been here and always will be here. . . . Of course it is different; as different as a real thing is from a shadow or as waking life is from a dream."[24]

So it is here: when Orual asks Psyche if what has happened to her is not just a dream, Psyche replies, "If it was a dream,

Sister, how do you think I came here? It's more likely everything that had happened to me before this was a dream. Why, Glome and the King and old Batta seem to me very like dreams now" (p. 112). She is now in the place of reality, the home she has longed for all her life. But it is a land Orual cannot even see: small wonder, then, that Orual feels "a sickening discord, a rasping together of two worlds, like the two bits of a broken bone" and that, "years after, I dreamed, again and again, that I was in some well-known place—most often the Pillar Room—and everything I saw was different from what I touched" (p. 120). Much, much later, after many experiences and much growth, Orual says the following about seeing and dreaming:

> For all I can tell, the only difference [between what men call real and what men call dream] is that what many see we call a real thing, and what only one sees we call a dream. But things that many see may have no taste or moment in them at all, and things that are shown only to one may be spears and water-spouts of truth from the very depth of truth. (p. 277)

But that point is much further along in her journey, and can be reached only when sight and reality need no longer be limited for her to the physical and the material.

Psyche said to Orual earlier, "Oh, Sister, you'd understand if you'd seen," and "Perhaps, Maia, you too will learn how to see" (pp. 111, 121). At this point Orual simply cannot see or understand the difference between dream and true Reality. Learning to see, although Orual is quite unconscious of the process as it goes on, is what the rest of the novel—and all of life—is actually about.

VI

Chapters 12–15:
Seeing and Knowing

ORUAL rejoins Bardia for food and rest, but, unable to sleep, she slips down to the river for a drink and has a moment's view of Psyche's palace—or imagines she does; she is full of uncertainty now and questions Bardia on the way home: he will say only that it seems Psyche must be bride to the Brute, but these are holy matters he doesn't pretend, or wish, to understand. Upon her return she tells the Fox of her adventure and questions him closely: he is convinced Psyche must have come under the control of one of the vagabonds who live on the mountain. Orual, torn between the reverent answer and the rational one, decides she must rescue Psyche at any cost. Taking with her a lamp, a roll of bandage, and a dagger, she returns to the mountain and tries unsuccessfully to convince Psyche that her lover is a monster. Orual then stabs her own arm to demonstrate the seriousness of her intent to kill Psyche and herself if Psyche will not look at her husband. To spare Orual's life, Psyche agrees. That night, from across the river, Orual watches as Psyche's lamp shines forth, hears a stern rebuke and then weeping, and sees a storm begin to lay waste the valley. As Psyche goes off, weeping, into the wilderness, a god appears to Orual and tells her, "You also shall be Psyche."

IN Chapters 12–15 the two earlier themes of possessiveness and blindness are blended in one of Lewis's most skillful alterations of Apuleius's tale. The theme of possessiveness was present as a continuing undercurrent through Chapters 8–11—in Orual's impression, during her illness, of some wrong or injury Psyche has inflicted on her; and in her protest against Psyche's separating herself from Orual: "Is it nothing to you at all that you are leaving me, . . .

turning your back on all our love?" (p. 125); but most of all in Orual's sense of hurt and then rage when Psyche tells her, "Dear Maia, I am a wife now. It's no longer you that I must obey" (p. 127). Orual's next line sums up the entire theme of distorted love: "I learned then how one can hate those one loves."

A key episode in the sight-blindness motif occurs later that night. Orual, unable to sleep, goes down to the river and—whether because her mental defenses are down, or because she drank water from the river in the gods' country, or for whatever reason, but *not* because she has come to believe—she has a momentary glimpse of Psyche's palace: "There stood the palace, grey—as all things were grey in that hour and place—but solid and motionless, wall within wall, pillar and arch and architrave, acres of it, a labyrinthine beauty" (p. 132).

Because its Gothic intricateness is unlike anything in Glome, Orual knows she can't be imagining it. She realizes she must ask forgiveness of Psyche and of her god for doubting; and she realizes Psyche now belongs to another world and is "far above me"—*if,* she thinks, "if what I saw was real." That thought recurs: "Perhaps it was not real." A moment later she can no longer see: "I looked and looked to see if it would not fade or change. Then as I rose (for all this time I was still kneeling where I had drunk), almost before I stood on my feet, the whole thing was vanished" (p. 133). Orual is left wondering if it was a "true seeing" or an illusion—it was, after all, only a momentary glimpse—and asks the reader to give judgment: "That moment when I either saw or thought I saw the House—does it tell against the gods or against me? . . . What is the use of a sign which is itself only another riddle?" (p. 133). The answer for Orual and the reader is contained in an earlier experience of Psyche. She had had only a momentary glimpse of West-wind: "Of course he was invisible again almost at once. I had seen him only as one sees a lightning flash. But that didn't matter" (p. 112). So too it could have been, should have been, for Orual.

But it was not, and the events which follow force one

to question Orual's motivations for her subsequent actions. Is it genuine uncertainty about the seeing that prevents her from telling the Fox about the glimpse of the palace through the mist? Is it genuine doubt that shapes her choice between the alternative explanations of Bardia and the Fox (p. 151)? Is it not rather the jealousy and possessiveness that are clear in her rationalizations a moment later: "For there was one point on which [Bardia and the Fox] agreed. Both thought that some evil or shameful thing had *taken Psyche for its own*. Murdering thief or spectral Shadowbrute—did it matter which?" (p. 151; italics added).

Orual tries further to rationalize her inclinations by asking herself, "What lover would shun his bride's eyes unless he had some terrible reason for it?" (p. 152). To this too she has the answer, if she would only recall and accept it. In the poem the Fox recited to Orual as a child, Aphrodite hides her immortal greatness before she comes to Anchises, not because she was hideous or fearsome, but because one must be made ready to come into the presence of a god. Psyche's experience as she related her story could have confirmed the point for Orual. She spoke of feeling ashamed in the presence of West-wind and the immortal servants: "Ashamed of looking like a mortal—ashamed of being a mortal"; for the difference between them is striking—"We, beside the gods, are like lepers beside us" (p. 111).[1] Embedded in the old Aphrodite-Anchises myth is a kernel of divine truth, a truth which reappears in Psyche's being forbidden to look upon her husband and again in the "till we have faces" motif of Part II, a truth which is available to all who are open to receiving it.

Out of the themes of possessiveness and blindness emerges the most profound and powerful of Lewis's alterations in the story Apuleius told. In Apuleius's version the two sisters deceived a simple, ignorant child by convincing her that her life would be in danger if she did not kill the monster who came to her by night. That account turns the sisters into unmitigated villains, almost criminals, and reduces one's esteem for Psyche, who lacks the intelligence to see through the obviously inconsistent argument. Lewis

changes this superficial and rather artificial scene of deception and intrigue to an intense and realistic psychological
struggle which reaches deep into the motives and self-
awareness of the two characters involved.

Convinced that Psyche's "husband" is a monster, natural or supernatural, Orual attempts to persuade Psyche,
using the arguments she herself found so convincing. She
argues first that there must be some logical reason why he
will not allow himself to be seen—"Nothing that's beautiful
hides its face" (p. 160). When Psyche replies confidently that
she knows he is no "salt villain," Orual uses her second
argument, that seeing is believing: "How can you know if
you have never seen him?" (p. 161). Psyche's reply, "How
could I not know?" (p. 162), reflects the culmination of a long
series of experiences. When she was shackled on the mountain and the rain came, "then I knew quite well that the
gods really are, and that I was bringing the rain" (p. 110).
She recognizes and responds to the rain as a "sign" from the
gods. Later that same sign is available to Orual, but she
ignores it: "I promised anything [the gods] might ask of me,
if only they would send me a sign. They gave me none. . . .
[Meanwhile] the rain drummed on as before" (p. 150). Psyche has a glimpse of West-wind and knows it is "he, not it"
(p. 112); she sees the palace and knows, because it is not the
gold and amber house she used to dream of, that she can't
be imagining it. When a mysterious voice says "Enter your
House," she doesn't rationalize it away; and when the servants lead her through the house, "though I could see no
one," she follows (p. 113). Because she believes, she can know;
but her knowledge is not dependent on seeing: it has a firmer
basis than that, in love or in Love:

> "Orual, how can you be so simple? I—how could I not
> know?"
> "But how, Psyche?"
> "What am I to answer to such a question? It's not fitting
> . . . it is . . . and especially to you, Sister, who are a virgin."
> (p. 162; ellipses in the original)

Orual's virginity, elsewhere a symbol of her barrenness, here
symbolizes the limitedness of her experience with love, so

different from Psyche's experience. Thus Psyche continues: "You do not think I have left off loving you because I now have a husband to love as well? If you would understand it, that makes me love you—why, it makes me love everyone and everything—more" (pp. 158–59). Orual knows "little of love" (p. 162) and nothing at all of such love: to hear of it can only intensify her anguish at no longer being the exclusive possessor of Psyche's affection. Because she knows so little of love, Orual thinks it can be *used*: she drives a dagger through her arm to demonstrate the seriousness of her determination to kill Psyche and then herself if Psyche will not put her lover to the test. To save not herself but Orual, Psyche capitulates and agrees to disobey her husband; she acts not out of fear and delusion, as does the Psyche in Apuleius's tale, but with full awareness of what she is doing and why: "I know what I do. I know that I am betraying the best of lovers and that perhaps, before sunrise, all my happiness may be destroyed forever. This is the price you have put upon your life. Well, I must pay it" (p. 166). And Orual acts not out of a conscious desire to destroy Psyche's happiness, as do the sisters in Apuleius's tale, but out of the remains of what once was her love and desire for the good of Psyche. Here we see the full extent of how distorted that love has become. In Orual's words,

> He made it to be as if, from the beginning, I had known that Psyche's lover was a god, and as if all my doubtings, fears, guessings, debatings, questionings of Bardia, questionings of the Fox, all the rummage and business of it, had been trumped-up foolery, dust blown in my own eyes by myself. (p. 173)

This becomes the central issue of Orual's legal brief: had the gods not withheld certain knowledge of themselves just long enough for Orual to force Psyche into destroying her happiness? This she now must believe to avoid having to accept blame herself. If so, the gods are unjust, and it is right for Orual to present a case against them, so that all will know of their cruelty and injustice.

But the decision to present her case comes later. At this point she has only the rather cryptic words the god speaks to her: "Now Psyche goes out in exile. Now she must hunger

51

and thirst and tread hard roads. Those against whom I cannot fight must do their will upon her. You, woman, shall know yourself and your work. You also shall be Psyche" (pp. 173–74). The gaining of such self-knowledge, of what it means that Orual also shall be Psyche, is the central theme in the rest of the book.

VII

Chapters 16–20:
Loving, Hating, Hiding

THE narrative now speeds up and these five chapters summarize perhaps forty years of Orual's life. Upon her return from the mountain, Orual hides what happened there from the Fox and decides henceforth to hide her face behind a veil. The King is injured in a fall, shortly thereafter, and lies dying, as does the old Priest: Bardia and the Fox, therefore, negotiate with Arnom, who will become Priest, to support the queenship of Orual. Orual solidifies her position as Queen by killing Argan, heir-designate to the throne of Phars, in single combat, thus saving Trunia, the heir by order of birth, and establishing friendship between the two nations. By plunging into the work of being Queen—and a very good one—Orual is able to crush her old personality and forget, most of the time, her past deeds and misdeeds.

*L*EWIS'S portrayal of Orual's character is sharpened and deepened, in Chapters 16–20, by a series of key motifs and images. First is the expansion of the theme of love to show in Orual's life distorted forms of the other two natural loves, *philia* and *eros*. Distorted *storge* is there, too, particularly as Orual, upon her return home, goes to Psyche's room and puts everything in it as it had been before all the sorrows began:

> The clothes that she had worn in the last year I burned . . .; but those she had worn earlier, and especially what were left of those she wore in childhood, and any jewels she had loved as a child, I hung in their proper places. I wished all to be so ordered that if she could come back she would find all as it had been when she was still happy, and still mine. (p. 183)

Orual, determined not to give up her ownership of Psyche ("when she was . . . still mine"), attempts to freeze her image and memory of Psyche at the desired point: it is an example of "what natural affection turns to in the end if it will not be converted," as Lewis put it in *The Great Divorce*.[1]

Orual's relationship with the Fox illustrates *philia* "going bad" in a similar way. Lewis defines *philia* as a deep, lasting friendship based on shared interests. There is a grandfatherly side to the Fox's relationship with Orual, and thus a strong element of *storge,* but there is also *philia,* for they are drawn together by their mutual interests: she shares his hunger for knowledge, and this forms the basis of one of the few friendships in her life. Because she has few friends, she comes to depend on the Fox, and to clutch at him in much the same way she did at Psyche. Thus, when she grants the Fox freedom before her fight with Argan, she is horror-struck and embittered by the thought that he might, now, return to Greece. Given no encouragement to go, and subtle pressure not to, he decides to stay, reluctantly and uncertainly. In that light it is particularly ironic—and particularly evil—that, having persuaded the Fox to stay, Orual herself later begins to neglect him: "I was too busy to be with him much" (p. 235). Always Orual considers her loves in terms of what they contribute to her, not what she should contribute to them. Later, Orual apologizes to the Fox for the possessiveness which she allowed to distort her love: "I knew at the time that all those good reasons you gave for staying in Glome after you were a freeman were only disguises for your love. I knew you stayed only in pity and love for me. I knew you were breaking your heart for the Greeklands. I ought to have sent you away. I lapped up all you gave me like a thirsty animal" (p. 296).

It is similar with Bardia and *eros.* Orual's relationship with Bardia includes a large measure of *philia,* growing out of their shared activity of swordplay and their shared interests in the governing of Glome. But this develops, for Orual, into at least a small measure of unrequited, frustrated, and inevitably distorted erotic love. Lewis defines *eros* as that special variety of sexual passion we call being in love. The first sign of it here is Orual's reaction when she hears that Bardia married for love (p. 146) and is ruled by his wife: "I was fretted by the thought of this wife, this petted thing, suddenly starting up to delay or to hinder" (p. 153). It appears again in Orual's irritation when the Fox makes denigrating comments about Bardia: "To hear Bardia called fool or barbarian angered me. (Bardia called the Fox Greekling and 'word-weaver' in return, but that never fretted me in the same way)" (p. 196). Her dislike of and jealousy over Bardia's attention to his wife (as on p. 222) lead to sexual fantasies: "The picture, the impossible fool's dream, was that all should have been different from the very beginning and he would have been my husband and Psyche our daughter. Then I would have been in labour ... with Psyche ... and to me he would have been coming home" (p. 224; ellipses in the original).

In *The Great Divorce* the possessive mother is told that God wanted her "merely instinctive love ... to turn into something better";[2] if natural love does not turn into something better, it inevitably becomes something worse—jealousy, possessiveness, a kind of hatred. So it is with Orual's loves for Psyche, the Fox, and Bardia. And standards of comparison, in parallel situations and contrasting reactions, are supplied to emphasize the self-centeredness and inadequacy of Orual's loves. When Orual returns from the mountain and refuses to tell the Fox all that went on there, he remarks sadly, "Well. You have a secret from me" (p. 180); he knows, as Psyche knew, that true love must be open, honest, and free, for when Orual suggested that Psyche's husband need not know Psyche had looked at him, Psyche replied, " 'You thought I would hide it? Thought I would not tell him?' she said, each word like the rubbing of a file across raw flesh" (p. 166). Later, when the Fox hears Orual's plan for combat with Argan, he "implored me with the same anguish I had felt when I implored Psyche [to return to Glome]" (p. 198). The striking thing, however, is that the next morning the Fox apologizes to her for treating love as a tool: "Daughter, I did badly last night. ... I was wrong to weep and beg and try to force you by your love. Love is not a thing to be so used" (p. 204). Such an apology, even such a thought, had never entered Orual's head. It is as Psyche commented earlier, "You know little of love" (p. 162).

Orual's early intimations of the inadequacy of her love and the hardships it caused lead to the second motif central to these chapters, that imaged by the veil. Veils appear first in the book at the time of the King's marriage, as a covering for Orual's ugliness. They arise next when Orual journeys to the sacred mountain with Bardia and wears a veil so that she will not be recognized. When she returns from her second journey to the mountain, she decides to "go always veiled": "It is a sort of treaty made with my ugliness" (pp. 180–81). What started out as a covering for physical ugliness and a disguise now becomes, symbolically, a way to cover her inner ugliness and to alter her self-identity, to hide and thus almost to bury her old and despised self.

The veil is a symbol—that is, it is itself (a literal veil in the action) and something more, but the more is always a group of possibilities radiating out from the central image. One is not, therefore, to look for "the one meaning" symbolized by the veil, but several meanings, some of which will of course be more satisfying or convincing than others. A variety of possibilities have been suggested by commentators on the story: that it stands for the queenship, for the flesh, for the barriers between herself and the gods. A veil is a conventional cultural and literary symbol, sometimes used as an emblem of modesty and decency—for this reason the Fox finds it rather barbaric that adult women in Glome do not wear veils (p. 197). Such qualities are important and valuable to the new identity Orual adopts, and the veil in part epitomizes the outward decorum and properness for which she is known as queen. It is an important biblical symbol of covering (for example, Exodus 34:33–35) which becomes a barrier to understanding or relationship (II Corinthians 3:13–16). But a veil also has been used conventionally as a symbol of shame and guilt: so Nathaniel Hawthorne used it again and again. And surely this is a very important dimension of Lewis's symbol.[3]

Beyond such direct and conventional symbolic meaning

for the veil, it also functions in *Till We Have Faces* as a symbol for symbolism. Like a veil, a symbol conceals in order to reveal: it conceals its meanings behind a literal image in order that they may be conveyed powerfully as they are grasped by the imagination. In a work which explores reason and imagination as a central theme, the veil suggests that the full value of symbol (and metaphor and myth) may be hidden, unrecognized by the overly rational mind, as Lewis failed to "see" it fully early in his life. And it suggests that *Till We Have Faces* itself reveals the full value of myth in conveying eternal and universal truths to the receptive heart and mind.

A key function of the veil is to symbolize Orual's new identity as the Queen, a third motif in this section. It begins when Orual negotiates with Arnom over the Crumbles, to get him to accept her claim to the throne, and when she decides to fight Argan: "Ever since Arnom had said hours ago that the King was dying, there seemed to have been another woman acting and speaking in my place. Call her the Queen; but Orual was someone different" (p. 199).

Lewis uses a series of symbols for Orual's efforts to repress her old identity: a door, death, a dam, and pregnancy. Thus, when Orual finishes restoring Psyche's room to its childhood state, she closes both a literal and a symbolic door: "I locked the door and put a seal on it. And, as well as I could, I locked a door in my mind" (p. 183). The symbol recurs in Chapter 20, with even stronger emphasis: "The Queen of Glome had more and more part in me and Orual had less and less. I locked Orual up . . . somewhere deep down inside me" (p. 226). Further symbols elaborate on the meaning of what she is doing to her personality. What she locks up, or dams up, to use another metaphor, are the feelings—love of Psyche, anger against the gods—associated with her earlier days:

> Sometimes at night, if the wind howled or the rain fell, there would leap upon me, like water from a bursting dam, a great and anguished wonder—whether Psyche was alive, and where she was on such a night, and whether hard wives of peasants were turning her, cold and famished, from their door. But

then, after an hour or so of weeping and writhing and calling out upon the gods, I would set to and rebuild the dam. (p. 184; see also p. 189)

But she wants not just to hold back but to push down the old Orual: there is to be reduction, not growth. The process is imaged as the reverse of pregnancy, as she lays her old personality to sleep deep inside herself: "It was like being with child, but reversed; the thing I carried in me grew slowly smaller and less alive" (p. 226). So, as Orual waits for her Father's life to end and her combat with Argan to begin, her thoughts are of death: "One part of me . . . said, 'Orual dies if she ceases to love Psyche.' But the other said, 'Let Orual die. She would never have made a queen' " (p. 211). And following the combat, the literal slaying of Argan becomes a figure for what will become of her old self: "I am the Queen; I'll kill Orual too" (p. 225). In light of all this, the wording of the first sentence of the third paragraph in the book is significant: "I *was* Orual the eldest daughter of Trom, King of Glome" (p. 4; italics added). She no longer is Orual; now, she is the Queen.

Orual clearly thinks of the accession to the queenship as marking a radical change in her life, in effect giving her a new identity. She notes the new direction in her life by speaking of it as embarking on a journey into a strange new land (p. 210) and comparing her victory over Argan to the loss of virginity: "I felt myself changed too, as if something had been taken away from me" (p. 220). The change is characterized by her stifling of the sensitive aspects of her personality, those traditionally labeled "feminine," in order to become an efficient and unemotional human machine: "My aim was to build up more and more that strength, hard and joyless, which had come to me when I heard the god's sentence; by learning, fighting, and labouring, to drive all the woman out of me" (p. 184). Thus, when Bardia treats her "more and more like a man" (p. 184), she is accomplishing her aim; but given the *eros* she feels toward Bardia, it is only natural that "this both grieved and pleased me."

A central element of Orual's new identity as the Queen is to be active and assertive. The queenship is "an art that left you no time to mope," and becomes Orual's effort to make herself "vanish altogether into the Queen" (p. 201). Thus as Queen she is always working, as judge, as administrator, always seeking ways to strengthen Glome:

> What did I not do? I had all the laws revised and cut in stone in the center of the city. I narrowed and deepened the Shennit till barges could come up to our gates. I made a bridge where the old ford had been. I made cisterns so that we should not go thirsty whenever there was a dry year. I became wise about stock and bought in good bulls and rams and bettered our breeds. I did and I did and I did. . . . (pp. 235–36)

It is in the light of all this activity that Arnom characterizes the Queen, after her death, as *"the most wise, just, valiant, fortunate and merciful of all the princes known in our parts of the world"* (pp. 308–9).

The activity in her new role, her devotion of her life to her role as Queen, leads into a fourth motif, that of sacrifice. As she leaves the city to meet Argan in combat, Orual remembers Psyche:

> Several lords and elders waited for us at the gate to bring us through the city. It's easy to guess what I was thinking. So Psyche had gone out that day to heal the people; and so she had gone out that other day to be offered to the Brute. Perhaps, thought I, this is what the god meant when he said *You also shall be Psyche.* I also might be an offering. (p. 216)

But she misapplies the comparison in thinking that she will die at Argan's hand. Actually, this going out to the combat field, as Psyche had gone out, epitomizes the way she will sacrifice her life for her country from this point on. The rest of her life she devotes to her people, filling her days with planning, administering, judging. Her identity as Queen, in fact, has substance only in activity:

> I did and I did and I did—and what does it matter what I did? I cared for all these things only as a man cares for a hunt or a game, which fills the mind and seems of some moment while it lasts, but then the beast's killed or the king's mated, and now who cares? It was so with me almost every evening of my life; one little stairway led me from feast or council, all the

bustle and skill and glory of queenship, to my own chamber
to be alone with myself—that is, with a nothingness. (p. 236)

Having eliminated Orual, her life has no meaning apart
from her work. Thus in one sense all that she does is for
herself, to fill the emptiness of her existence. But in another
sense she does all and gives all to her people: her life of toil
and suffering—physically in battle and mentally in deci-
sion-making—rather than death, becomes her sacrifice.

Her external identity can be altered by wearing a veil
and plunging into a life of activity, but her personal identity,
her own sense of inner ugliness, cannot so easily be ex-
punged by assuming a new name and role. Deeper down the
old sense of guilt and pain continue, biding their time. Orual
can cover her face with a veil, but she is reminded of her
guilt by the swinging chains of the well, which sound to her
like the weeping of a girl. She can build thick stone walls
around the well, as she can cover her face with a veil or
crush the Orual in her, and thus suppress her old being:
"For a while after that an ugly fancy used to come to me in
my dreams . . . that I had walled up, gagged with stone, not
a well but Psyche (or Orual) herself. But that also passed.
I heard Psyche weeping no more. The year after that I defeated Essur" (p. 235). The juxtaposition of the last two sentences suggests that she thinks she has succeeded: Orual is
dead, memories of Psyche permanently dammed up, the
Queen in control of Glome and of her life. But old guilt and
old identities will not remain repressed: they fester below
the surface, awaiting the lance which will release them,
which, in Orual's case, comes in the decisive final chapter
of Part I.

VIII

Chapter 21:
The Myth and the Retelling

ORUAL and several younger people undertake a progress, or journey, into Phars and then into Essur, combining the pleasures of travel with opportunity to consult with neighboring monarchs. In Essur they go to see a hot spring and plan then to return to Glome. As the others set up camp and prepare food, Orual wanders into the woods and comes upon a small white stone temple. A priest, for a few coins, offers to tell her the story of its goddess, Istra. The story is very much like that of Orual and Psyche, except that in the priest's tale, Istra's sisters were able to see Istra's palace, and they destroyed her happiness out of jealousy over her good fortune. Orual asks the priest where he learned all this, but he can only reply, "It's the sacred story," a story handed down to him as part of a fertility religion. Orual is greatly upset, for the story handed down seems wrong, for Orual wasn't jealous and she couldn't see the palace. Had she been able to, all would have been different. In order that things may be set right and the truth known, she determines to write an accusation against the gods as her own defense. She hurries back to Glome and begins to write what we have been reading so far, the twenty-one chapters of Part I.

CHAPTER 21, brief as it is, repetitive of the overall story as it may seem, actually is crucial to the success of Lewis's venture. As we said earlier, Lewis found in Apuleius a tale which, although called a myth, was not mythical—it lacks the mystery and power characteristic of true myth. Apuleius drew on folk motifs and archetypes which could have been—which even cried out to be—turned into myth, but he failed to imbue them with the imaginative and numinous qualities essential to myth. As Lewis retells the

61

story, it is important to notice that he inserts an extra step in order to bring out the basic mythical implications of the tale. The story told to Orual by the Priest of Essur becomes a middle level between Apuleius's telling and Lewis's retelling, needed to show what Apuleius could, perhaps even should, have developed but did not.

The excursion to see "a natural hot spring fifteen miles further to the west" is made on "the calmest day—pure autumn—very hot, yet the sunlight on the stubble looked aged and gentle, not fierce like the summer heats. You would think the year was resting, its work done. And I whispered to myself that I too would begin to rest" (p. 239). The setting is ironic, in terms of the unsettling revelations about to come, but also symbolic, since Orual, like the year, has reached her golden time, the time for a harvest of the wisdom which has been maturing over the decades. The setting introduces the seasonal archetype, which will be crucial to the story she is about to hear, as is the "journey" archetype (p. 239)—a journey of education into experience.

The story she hears is not, as she suspects, her own but the "sacred story," the archetype, on which her story rests. Inevitably, therefore, details of the Priest's story will be familiar to her. The black "band or scarf" tied around the head of the goddess's image in the temple is "much like my own veil, but that mine was white" (p. 241). Furthermore, as she listens to the Priest,

> to me it was as if the old man's voice, and the temple, and I myself and my journey, were all things in such a story; for he was telling the very history of our Istra, of Psyche herself— how Talapal (that's the Essurian Ungit) was jealous of her beauty and made her to be offered to a brute on a mountain, and how Talapal's son Ialim, the most beautiful of the gods, loved her and took her away to his secret palace. (p. 242)

Lewis turns Psyche into the goddess Apuleius worshipped, into Isis, originally a goddess of fecundity identified with Demeter,[1] and he uses that identification to indicate what Apuleius had missed, namely the theme of sacrifice: Istra in the Priest's tale is "offered to a brute on a mountain," not, like Apuleius's Psyche, given in marriage to "a dire

62

mischief, viperous and fierce" in obedience to Apollo's oracle. But for Orual, as she identifies with the story, two elements of the Priest's tale seem erroneous. First, he apparently mistakes the motivation of the sisters as jealousy rather than Orual's desire for the truth—and this is what incites Orual to the writing of Part I in her own defense. Second, he says that both sisters had visited Psyche and, more importantly, had seen her palace: "How," Orual writes in protest, "could any mortal have known of that palace at all? That much of the truth [the gods] had dropped into someone's mind, in a dream, or an oracle, or however they do such things. That much; and wiped clean out the very meaning, the pith, the central knot, of the whole tale" (p. 243).

Orual, however, preoccupied with the claim that the palace could be seen, misses "the very meaning, the central knot" of the Priest's account. She is not even listening until he gets to the part where "Talapal torments Istra and sets her to all manner of hard labours, things that seem impossible. But when Istra has done them all, then at last Talapal releases her, and she is reunited to Ialim and becomes a goddess. Then we take off her black veil, and I change my black robe for a white one, and we offer—" (p. 246). Here the seasonal archetypes Lewis planted earlier in the chapter reappear and transform Apuleius's pleasant tale into a pagan fertility myth: "But, Stranger," the Priest goes on when Orual asks if Istra has actually been reunited with her husband, "the sacred story is about the sacred things—the things we do in the temple. In spring, and all summer, she is a goddess. Then when harvest comes we bring a lamp into the temple in the night and the god flies away. Then we veil her. And all winter she is wandering and suffering; weeping, always weeping" (p. 246).

Orual concludes angrily that the Priest "knew nothing" (p. 246), but here in fact is the mythical significance Apuleius chose not to develop. By interrupting the Priest, Orual prevented him from completing his sentence with the word *sacrifices*. Inherent in the Cupid and Psyche story is what Lewis in "Myth Became Fact" called "the old myth of the Dying God";[2] it is, when its archetypal threads are traced back, one of "those queer stories scattered all through the heathen religions about a god who dies and comes to life again and, by his death, has somehow given new life to men."[3]

In missing the image of sacrifice, Apuleius neglected what is at the heart of the matter for Lewis, who brings out its importance later in the book when he has the Fox comment on the revolting blood sacrifices offered in Ungit's temple: "I never told [Orual] why the old Priest got something from the dark House that I never got from my trim sentences. . . . The Priest knew at least that there must be sacrifices" (p. 295). And Lewis knows that in the basic myth of Cupid and Psyche, there must be sacrifice, for it is in sacrifice that the old pagan religions anticipate God's fullest revelation of himself in Christ and God's requirement that his people also must sacrifice, must offer their bodies and lives "as a living sacrifice" (Romans 12:1) to God and to others.

Lewis saw, then, the failures of what Apuleius's tale was; but even more important to him was the inadequacy of what Apuleius's tale should have been, the insufficiency or incompleteness of paganism. *Till We Have Faces,* as a "myth retold," is actually a retelling of the Priest of Essur's tale, a retelling of Lewis's smaller retelling of Apuleius. Having, in the sacred story of the Priest, emphasized the theme of sacrifice, Lewis in *Till We Have Faces* points beyond pagan sacrifice to what it prefigures, the full embodiment of this theme in Christianity. Lewis earlier had put it this way: "If my religion is true, then these stories may well be a *preparatio evangelica,* a divine hinting in poetic and ritual form at the same central truth which was later focussed and (so to speak) historicised in the Incarnation."[4] The archetypes in the fertility myths of a dying god who returns to life, of an Istra who wears a black scarf through winter, are crucial to the Cupid and Psyche story because they convey a vital "gleam of divine truth."[5] Lewis explained that truth as follows in "The Grand Miracle":

> As soon as you have thought of this, this pattern of the huge dive down to the bottom, into the depths of the universe and

coming up again into the light, everyone will see at once how that is imitated and echoed by the principles of the natural world; the descent of the seed into the soil, and its rising again in the plants. . . . We all know about Adonis. . . . Christ *is* a figure of that sort. . . . The corn itself is in its far-off way an imitation of the supernatural reality; the thing dying, and coming to life again, descending, and re-ascending beyond all nature. The principle is there in nature, because it was first there in God Himself. Thus one is getting in behind the nature religions, and behind nature to Someone Who is not explained by, but explains, not, indeed, the nature religions directly, but that whole characteristic behaviour of nature on which nature religions were based.[6]

In retelling the Priest of Essur's tale, Lewis in *Till We Have Faces* takes us behind Istra, the nature goddess, to the Someone toward whom all such myths point: "We pass from a Balder or an Osiris, dying nobody knows when or where, to a historical Person crucified (it is all in order) *under Pontius Pilate*."[7]

Till We Have Faces is lifted far above the tales told by Apuleius and the Priest of Essur by the union of the theme of sacrifice with the love theme discussed in previous chapters. Sacrifice in *Till We Have Faces* is not just the death and rebirth of a pagan god or goddess, but the unselfish giving of self by individuals for others—Psyche going out to touch the sick and later offering herself on the mountain to end the drought; Bardia, the Fox, and Psyche disregarding their own good to promote Orual's; and Orual—unknowingly—spending her life for her country. Orual can find peace, forgiveness, and acceptance only as she sacrifices herself, her selfish demands and desires, and learns to give herself totally to others instead of requiring total devotion from them, a process completed in Part II.

The episode of the Priest of Essur is also crucial to the narrative strategy of *Till We Have Faces*. In recent years the concept of narrative has come under attack. Narrative sequence in history, for example, has come to be viewed by some historians as an interpretative, and thus somewhat artifical and subjective, pattern imposed upon discrete events. Louis Mink, for example, argues,

Life has no beginnings, middles, or ends; there are meetings, but the start of an affair belongs to the story we tell ourselves later, and there are partings, but only in retrospective stories are hopes unfulfilled, plans miscarried, battles decisive, and ideas seminal. Only in the story is it America which Columbus discovers and only in the story is the kingdom lost for want of a nail.[8]

According to this view, life is different from stories about life: only in retrospect does one see patterns and ends and causes. And such retrospective accounts are necessarily interpretative. As A. R. Louch says,

The notion of plot depends upon the choice of story. And this is very much a matter of what is emphasized, where the story begins, and where the historian chooses to end it. For what confers the aura of inevitability on the historical process is that the different episodes that carry the story forward are chosen in such a way as to *lead* to the circumstances with which the historian has chosen to end his tale. And he might have selected a different emphasis, a different starting point, a different conclusion. How we see the evolving process and how we understand the past will vary accordingly.[9]

For such thinkers, the description of a person's life is not an objective listing of events and places but a narrative in which events are related to each other in sequences which make them comprehensible and seem to make them meaningful.

Many twentieth-century literary figures have argued against any degree of meaningfulness in narrative: narrative, they say, is not subjective-but-meaningful, but inevitably falsifying. The French existentialist Jean-Paul Sartre, for example, has a character argue that to present life in narrative form always falsifies it.[10] The events in people's lives and in the world generally are wholly separate and unorderly; they lead nowhere; the course of things is random and "absurd." To put events and actions into a unified sequence, according to this view, is to impose in retrospect an order the events did not have as they were lived, and thus to falsify them. Many modern writers, therefore, have ceased to write sustained narratives. Their essays as well as their fiction—inevitably, since art reflects life—are made up of random fragments and images which readers are to experience as such, without imposing a logical or sequential pattern upon them.

What these people are arguing is that narratives—whether of the historian, or anthropologist, or economist, or theologian, or biologist, or biographer, or autobiographer—always and inevitably are subjective and somewhat artificial. The choice of starting point, end point, emphases, and connecting links give the "shape" to the story, not just the details or events by themselves. The issue facing those who write or read narratives is reliability: What limits the subjectivity? What supplies a norm or standard which makes a narrative meaningful rather than just arbitrary? This is not the place to explore the various answers which have been proposed; but we should notice how Lewis's narrative strategy anticipates the problem and supplies a solution.

Orual's story is just the kind to be open to charges of subjectivity. The story she tells is shaped considerably by the beginning point she selected, the point at which she intended to stop, and the things she chose to emphasize. Had she ended with Chapter 21, as she had planned, the narrative would have been very different from the one that includes Part II or that would have resulted had she been able to revise Part I, as she wishes she could. Chance, her own purpose, her knowledge and lack of it all enter into the narrative of her life. The story of her life would look quite different if Arnom had written it: his postscript to the book indicates that he would have begun differently, emphasized different details, aimed at a quite different goal. Is all storytelling, then, merely subjective and arbitrary? It is subjective—inevitably; one can never, in any enterprise, step out of oneself and be totally objective. Lewis seems to be aware of that here, as he might not have been earlier in his life, and to accept it and to use it, for that very subjectiveness leads to the ironies which are at the heart of the story. Something, however, must have seemed necessary to prevent it from appearing wholly arbitrary, and the tale told by the Priest of Essur becomes that something.

The chronology of events and the detail out of which a narrative is constructed place constraints on historical interpretation: they provide external criteria upon which to judge internal detail. The Priest of Essur's tale functions in a similar way in *Till We Have Faces*. Subjective as its account ultimately (and inevitably) may be, the Priest's own telling is utterly nonsubjective—he simply reports the "objective facts" of the "sacred story," and that is its effect in the book. It comes from outside the narrative (outside Orual's narrative, at any rate), verifies the chronology and detail used by Orual, and provides a standard for evaluating her interpretation of those details. It points to exactly what Orual did not want to recognize: that she could—or at least *did*—see the palace and that she was indeed jealous of her sister. By the introduction and careful placement of the Priest's tale, Lewis's story authenticates itself—from within itself it supplies the external standard needed to guard against total subjectivity. Thus Lewis's belief in the value of narrative is affirmed. There is an orderliness in the story of Istra, as there is in the story of Orual, and as there is in the lives of Lewis's readers—the first-person subjective narration of *Till We Have Faces,* framed and constrained by the Priest's tale, embodies this as a truth in a deeper, fuller way than Lewis's other, third-person stories can.

The key motifs of the book are drawn together here, near the end of Part I, in Orual's reaction to the Priest of Essur's story:

> It's a story belonging to a different world, a world in which the gods show themselves clearly and don't torment men with glimpses, nor unveil to one what they hide from another, nor ask you to believe what contradicts your eyes and ears and nose and tongue and fingers. . . . Now, instantly, I knew I was facing them—I with no strength and they with all; I visible to them, they invisible to me. . . . Well, I could speak. . . . The case against them should be written. (pp. 243–45)

The images—other worlds, veils, faces, invisibility—and the oppositions—seeing versus believing, Greece versus Glome, gods versus man—remind the reader of the central issues in the case Orual wrote. For Part I is that case against the gods; Part II presents the effects upon her of writing it.

IX

Part II, Chapters 1–4:
"Real Life is Meeting"

Chapter 1

AFTER her completion of the writing of Part I, Orual encounters a series of events which cause her to know herself much more fully than before, and force her in fairness to resume writing, to add a supplement on what more she has learned. From Tarin she learns of Redival's loneliness when Orual turned from her to the Fox and then to Psyche; and in an interview with Ansit she learns that out of her country's needs and her own distorted love she had made impossible demands on Bardia and virtually worked him to death.

THE brilliance of Lewis's achievement in *Till We Have Faces* emerges in Part II, in large measure from the way he returns to and incorporates the Cupid and Psyche myth into his own story. In the myth Psyche was set four tasks, or labors: sorting out a huge pile of seeds, gathering wool from the fleece of man-killing rams, fetching a cup of water from an inaccessible mountain river, and bringing Venus a box containing beauty from the underworld. If, as the god had said to Orual, "You also shall be Psyche," then Orual too must undertake these labors.[1] For Orual, they will be psychological rather than physical, yet even so they will be no less burdensome and full of anguish.

The first task, the sorting, the one treated in this chapter, comes with her writing. In the process of writing Part I, Orual dredged up old memories and confronted what she had for many years forced herself to forget. "I know so much more than I did about the woman who wrote it," she says of

Part I. "What began the change was the very writing itself. Let no one lightly set about such a work. Memory, once waked, will play the tyrant" (p. 253). As she writes, and as new events illuminate old ones, she begins to undergo mentally what Psyche, somewhere, was undergoing physically:

> So back to my writing. And the continual labour of mind to which it put me began to overflow into my sleep. It was a labour of sifting and sorting, separating motive from motive and both from pretext; and this same sorting went on every night in my dreams, but in a changed fashion. I thought I had before me a huge, hopeless pile of seeds, wheat, barley, poppy, rye, millet, what not? and I must sort them out and make separate piles, each all of one kind. Why I must do it, I did not know; but infinite punishment would fall upon me if I rested a moment from my labour. (p. 256)[2]

All this she is doing for herself, coming to know her motives and the results of her actions. But she is also, by the Way of Exchange,[3] helping Psyche, bearing some of Psyche's burden. In some of the dreams she becomes, as in the myth, "a little ant, and the seeds were as big as millstones; and labouring with all my might, till my six legs cracked, I carried them to their places" (p. 257).

The result of the sifting and sorting is the separation of what she thought she had been and done and suffered, from what actually had been the case. Specifically, she begins to learn about the quality of her own love, of her self-centeredness and failure to return in kind the love others extended to her. As she wrote about the early days with Redival, for example, she thought about activities they had shared, and how close they had been, and "how terribly [Redival] changed" (p. 254). From Part I one recalls how it had been:

> This was the beginning of my best times. The Fox's love for the child was wonderful; I guessed that long before, when he was free, he must have had a daughter of his own. He was like a true grandfather now. And it was now always we three—the Fox, and Psyche, and I—alone together. Redival had always hated our lessons and, but for the fear of the King, would never have come near the Fox. Now, it seemed, the King had put all his three daughters out of his mind, and Redival had her own way. (pp. 21–22)

Through Tarin, to whom Redival then had turned for companionship, Orual comes to realize that Redival had been excluded and left alone. As Tarin put it, "She used to say, 'First of all Orual loved me much; then the Fox came and she loved me little; then the baby came and she loved me not at all.' So she was lonely. I was sorry for her" (p. 255). Orual must admit, "I had never thought at all how it might be with her when I turned first to the Fox and then to Psyche" (p. 256). After all, Redival was beautiful and had golden hair—what more could she need?[4]

Nor had she thought about the nature of her relationship with Bardia until, after his death, she visited his widow, Lady Ansit. Ansit is, first, the vehicle by which Orual is informed of her greedy, possessive use of Bardia:

> "He had worked himself out—or been worked. . . . Five wars, thirty-one battles, nineteen embassies, taking thought for this and thought for that, speaking a word in one ear, and another, and another . . . , devising, consulting, remembering, guessing, forecasting. . . . The mines are not the only place where a man can be worked to death." (pp. 260–61)

Later, after Orual has had time to reflect, she realizes that the burdens she loaded on Bardia were caused less by the needs of the moment than by her possessiveness toward him: "For it was all true—truer than Ansit could know. I had rejoiced when there was a press of work, had heaped up needless work to keep him late at the palace, plied him with questions for the mere pleasure of hearing his voice. Anything to put off the moment when he would go and leave me to my emptiness" (p. 266).

Ansit also provides a touchstone, a basis for judging Orual, for Ansit knows that love must not clutch onto its object at all costs. When Orual asks why Ansit did not tell her that Bardia was fatigued and failing, Ansit replies, "Tell you? And so take away from him his work, which was his life . . . ? Make a child and a dotard of him? Keep him to myself at that cost? Make him so mine that he was no longer his?" (p. 264). But that, of course, is exactly what Orual has done—used people, devoured them, for her own benefit, rather than freeing and helping them to become themselves:

"Faugh! You're full fed. Gorged with other men's lives, women's too: Bardia's, mine, the Fox's, your sister's—both your sisters'" (p. 265). Ansit rightly sums up Orual's situation and a central theme of the work: "I begin to think you know nothing of love" (p. 264).

Chapter 2

Soon after the interview with Ansit, Orual takes part in a spring fertility ritual. As she sits in Ungit's house, awaiting the birth of the new year, she reflects on the meaninglessness of it all: Ungit devours the land, takes from all, but gives nothing. But then she watches a humble worshipper's comfort from sacrificing to Ungit and the people's joy in the general religious celebration. This leads into a dream in which she and her father descend far below the Pillar Room, where Orual looks in a mirror and sees Ungit. Having faced the ugly truth about herself, she tries to commit suicide, but is warned by a god not to do it.

This chapter describes a key confrontation, in Orual's mind, between the rational and the holy. Orual's mind rebels against the "dancing and feasting and towsing of girls" involved in the pagan rites, against the darkness and slaughtering and blood, against the devotion of lives and silver to the cause—all this, "and nothing given back" (pp. 269–70). Arnom seeks to reassure her by allegorical explanations of Ungit: " 'I think, Queen,' said he (his voice strange out of the mask), 'she signifies the earth, which is the womb and mother of all living things.' This was the new way of talking about the gods which Arnom, and others, had learned from the Fox" (pp. 270–71). And it is a way of talking which has persisted into the twentieth century. Why, asks Orual, should explanations of natural things like growth and clouds and rain be wrapped up in so strange a fashion? "Doubtless," replies Arnom, "to hide it from the vulgar" (p. 271). Orual says no more but reflects, "It's very strange that our fathers should first think it worth telling us that rain falls out of the sky, and then, for fear such a notable secret should get out . . . wrap it up in a filthy tale so that no one could understand the telling" (p. 271).

72

Orual's words echo those used by Owen Barfield, and after him Lewis, to reply to the naturalistic theory of myths. As Barfield put it,

> The remoter ancestors of Homer, we are given to understand, observing that it was darker in winter than in summer, immediately decided that there must be some "cause" for this "phenomenon," and had no difficulty in tossing off the "theory" of, say, Demeter and Persephone, to account for it.[5]

Barfield's description of such thinking as *"projecting post-logical thoughts back into a pre-logical age"* would fit Arnom as well as the twentieth century, where it is "extraordinarily widespread, being indeed taken for granted in all the most reputable circles." Such allegorical explanations take the heart and life out of myth—they are as inadequate as the allegorical readings of the story of Cupid and Psyche which Lewis felt impelled to revise.

That inadequacy is brought out particularly as a simple peasant woman, distressed and sorrowful, enters the temple, offers a pigeon as a sacrifice to Ungit, sinks down before the god, and weeps bitterly for a very long time. When she arises, she has received comfort and strength: "It was as if a sponge had been passed over her. The trouble was soothed. She was calm, patient, able for whatever she had to do" (p. 272). There is beauty in Ungit, a beauty she has always had, discernible to the eyes of humble faith.[6] Orual is struck in a new way by the woman's experience, and by the joy which filled the people as the priest enacted the new year's ritual—"every man and woman and the very children looking as if all the world was well because a man dressed up as a bird had walked out of a door after striking a few blows with a wooden sword" (p. 273). Rationalistic reservations and explanations ring hollow in the face of such experiences; Orual could have learned of their inadequacy from Psyche, long ago, but she was not ready then to hear and see the truth. Now, her certainty about her love for Bardia having already been cut from under her, yet another certainty, about the adequacy of reason, has been destroyed. And as he describes her experience, Lewis has also laid the foundation in Chapter 2 for the transition from paganism to Christianity to come in Chapter 4.

But Orual has more to learn before she is ready to meet the ultimate Truth. Resting in her chamber after the temple rituals, she opens her eyes to see—presumably in a dream—her father standing beside her and wonders, "How could I ever have thought I should escape from the King?" (p. 273). To get beyond her past she must go through her past, as everyone must; the past will not be ignored. Orual, specifically, cannot evade or ignore a crucial part of what made her what she is, a resemblance Psyche pointed out earlier: "You look just like our father when you say those things" (p. 40). Orual herself noticed a "fury—my father's own fury" (p. 118); and later she recognizes a meanness "like the snarl in my father's voice" (p. 290) in her accusation against the gods. She and her father descend from Pillar Room to Pillar Room below it—clearly symbolizing a psychological descent into herself:

> "Throw yourself down."
> "Oh no, no, no; no further down; mercy!" said I.
> "There's no Fox to help you here," said my father. "We're far below any dens that foxes can dig." (p. 275)

The play on the word "fox" in the final sentence links the latter half of this chapter to the first half. The level of understanding—into herself and her relation to the divine—for which she now is reaching lies beyond the scope of reason: it comes through what she calls "seeings." She has undergone a fundamental perceptual change: she now sees things in new ways. In the lowest Pillar Room hangs a mirror—the mirror Orual notes she had given to Redival when she became Queen of Phars (p. 274), which was also the time at which Orual had donned her veil and decided to suppress her old self and become the Queen. Now, pushed past her rational defenses, she must confront that old, and true, self: she looks in the mirror and sees the face of Ungit. Her mind takes details from her experience in the temple—her accusation that Ungit devours everything about her, her observation that Ungit had "no face" or a thousand ugly faces—and associates them with herself, thus admitting, and accepting, a truth about herself—about the possessiveness of her love—which confirms what she had so recently learned from Ansit.

> This vision, anyway, allowed no denial. Without question it was true. It was I who was Ungit. That ruinous face was mine. I was that Batta-thing, that all-devouring womblike, yet barren, thing. Glome was a web—I the swollen spider, squat at its center, gorged with men's stolen lives. (p. 276)

She had tried for years to hide, from others but especially from herself; now, having faced herself, her inner ugliness, in the depths of her being, she abandons her veil: "My disguise now would be to go bareface" (p. 278)—a crucial image, which Lewis had planned to use as the title for the book.[7] It gives emphasis to the theme of *truth*—of inner personal truth, unveiled, unforgotten—which is at the heart of the book. Thus she realizes that she is "ugly in soul" (p. 281), but, unable to accept that, she prepares to commit suicide. As she is about to fling herself into the water, a voice comes to her from beyond the river, as a voice came to her across the river after Psyche's palace was destroyed, the voice of a god telling her, "Do not do it. . . . Die before you die. There is no chance after" (p. 279). Only, in other words, by dying to self before she dies physically can she escape the spiritual death her ugliness of soul deserves.[8]

Chapter 3

Having recognized and accepted her ugliness, Orual decides to reform and thus achieve beauty of soul, symbolized by the golden fleece of wild, mighty rams. Her old habits and nature, however, crush her efforts at goodness as inevitably as the rams trample her in her efforts to seize some of their wool. She despairs of ever changing, ever achieving beauty, and thus holds fast to the one beauty left in her life, that she "had at least loved Psyche truly." In another vision, however, she is taken from a burning desert to a courtroom in a mountain where she presents her case against the gods and discovers that her love for Psyche too was distorted, filled with jealousy and possessiveness.

Lewis returns, in Chapter 3, to the four tasks of the ancient myth. In a dream or vision Orual sees across a river, in a country of the gods, a herd of rams of the gods and thinks, "If I can steal but one golden flock off their sides, I shall have beauty" (p. 283). Again what was in Apuleius's tale a physical labor has become psychological for Orual. As Psyche was required to seize a handful of golden wool, so Orual must attempt to "steal" beauty of soul through reform: "If I practiced true philosophy, as Socrates meant it, I should change my ugly soul into a fair one" (p. 282). She makes her best effort, crossing the river and approaching the rams, only to be trampled by them, and trying "to be just and calm and wise," only to discover "I could mend my soul no more than my face" (p. 282). The linking of soul and face here is important: by now Orual's physical ugliness has become a symbol of her spiritual poverty; her efforts henceforth will be to mend both at once. Again her suffering and anguish—as "their curled horns struck me and knocked me flat and their hoofs trampled me" (p. 284)—end up helping another. By attracting the rams to herself, she drew their attention from another woman (Psyche?) and caused them to run past thorn bushes from which the other was now gleaning golden wool: "She won without effort what utmost effort would not win for me" (p. 284). The thorns become a symbol of the suffering which Orual, as Psyche's surrogate, undergoes in order to fulfill the tasks.

Having attempted to achieve goodness and failed, having been told to die, without understanding how or why, Orual despairs. Her life now seems empty but must be lived on—in particular, her duties as judge must be carried on: "The dooms I gave, sitting on my judgement seat, about this time, were thought to be even wiser and more just than before; it was work on which I spent much pains and I know I did it well" (p. 285). Only one comfort had she left, that "however I might have devoured Bardia, I had at least loved Psyche truly" (p. 285). To renew her assurance in this one strength, she gorges herself on Part I, "reading over how I had cared for Psyche and taught her and tried to save her and wounded myself for her sake" (p. 285).

Her judging and her book mingle, in another vision, with the third task set for Psyche. She finds herself walking across a burning desert with an empty bowl which she must fill with the water of death—death to self—and bring back to Ungit (p. 286). After walking for a hundred years, enduring on Psyche's behalf the heat and sand, the physical task again turns to a psychological one, and she discovers that she is not carrying a bowl but her book, and that she is on her way to plead her case against the gods. A crowd of people drag and push and carry her to "a great black hole" which yawns before her and thence "into the dark inwards of the mountain, and then further and further in," until she reaches the judge (p. 288). That this is another descent into the depths of her own being, reminiscent of the descent into the Pillar Rooms with her father, is confirmed as she looks at the judge: "On the same level with me, though far away, sat the judge. Male or female, who could say? Its face was veiled. It was covered from crown to toe in sweepy black" (p. 289). On the opening page of Part I Orual complained that "There is no judge between gods and men" (p. 3), and again and again she wished for a judge to hear her (pp. 132, 151, 173, 248). Now the long-sought judge has appeared— herself. She must stand before herself, naked: "Hands . . . tore off my veil—after it every rag I had on" (p. 289). This is not more of the self-reformation she had attempted earlier: now the old Orual, the defenses she built up, the paltry accomplishments (her love for Psyche) which she relied on, are stripped away. It reminds one of Eustace Scrubb's futile attempts, in *The Voyage of the "Dawn Treader,"* to remove his dragon skin himself, and of his need finally to rely on someone else to do it for him.[9]

Orual, as plaintiff and judge, must read—and, even more important, listen to—her own complaint. The complaint reveals the depth of her jealousy and possessiveness, the fruits of her perverted *storge,* for she protests mainly against the gods' taking Psyche rather than killing her. "You know well that I never really began to hate you until Psyche began talking of her palace and her lover and her husband. Why did you lie to me? You said a brute would devour her. Well, why didn't it?" (p. 290). Orual must come to recognize that one did—she did: she is Ungit, gorged with her sisters' lives (p. 265). Her complaint, therefore, is not against the ugliness of the gods but against their beauty, used to lure and entice loved ones. "We'd rather you drank their blood than stole their hearts. We'd rather they were ours and dead than yours and made immortal" (p. 291). Her complaint is not against their obscurity but their attractiveness: "You'll say (you've been whispering it to me these forty years) that I'd signs enough her palace was real, could have known the truth if I'd wanted. But how could I want to know it?" (p. 291). Her complaint is not that the gods hide themselves but that they exist: "That there should be gods at all, there's our misery and bitter wrong. There's no room for you and us in the same world. You're a tree in whose shadow we can't thrive. We want to be our own" (p. 291). Her complaint echoes a line by George MacDonald—"The one principle of hell is—'I am my own' "—which Lewis quoted as the epigraph to the chapter "Checkmate," on his own conversion, in *Surprised by Joy*. "I was my own," Orual continues, "and Psyche was mine and no one else had any right to her" (pp. 291–92). Here is Orual's utter self-centeredness, naked and unavoidable. Here is why she must die before she dies. Here, she admits, "at last, was my real voice" (p. 292). And to a judge as perceptive and fair as she, she could only admit that her complaint had been answered—that it, in fact, had answered itself.

Chapter 4

As the trial ends, the Fox approaches, apologizes to Orual for misleading her, and shows her a series of living pictures in which Psyche undertakes the four tasks; the first three she completes easily, for another (Orual) bore the anguish for her. The fourth is of greater difficulty, because those who love her attempt to keep her from getting the casket with beauty for Ungit. She presses on, however, and gives the casket to Orual, who thus achieves beauty of soul in union with Psyche.

In Orual's complaint, in her realization of her own jealousy and self-centeredness, she is at last honest with herself. Now she is bareface indeed; the veil is completely lifted, the defenses gone; now she can both hear and be heard. Until, through honest self-searching and reflection upon her experiences, she reached that point, she could only protest vainly and argue defensively. As she puts it,

> I saw well why the gods do not speak to us openly, nor let us answer. Till that word [which has lain at the center of one's soul for years] can be dug out of us, why should they hear the babble that we think we mean? How can they meet us face to face till we have faces? (p. 294)

Lewis himself, in other works spread throughout his career, illuminates this key passage. In "Dogma and Science," written more than a decade before *Till We Have Faces,* he said,

> In the twinkling of an eye, in a time too small to be measured, and in any place, all that seems to divide us from God can flee away, vanish, leaving us naked before Him, like the first man, like the only man, as if nothing but He and I existed. And since that contact cannot be avoided for long, and since it means either bliss or horror, the business of life is to learn to like it. That is the first and great commandment.[10]

Learning to like it has, of course, been the business of the latter part of Orual's life. And in *Letters to Malcolm,* written several years after *Till We Have Faces,* Lewis further describes the same process:

> We are always completely, and therefore equally, known to God. That is our destiny whether we like it or not. But though this knowledge never varies, the quality of our being known can. ... Ordinarily, to be known by God is to be, for this purpose, in the category of things. We are, like earthworms, cabbages, and nebulae, objects of Divine knowledge. But when we (a) become aware of the fact—the present fact, not the generalisation—and (b) assent with all our will to be so known, then we treat ourselves, in relation to God, not as things but as persons. We have unveiled. Not that any veil could have baffled His sight. The change is in us. The passive changes to the active. Instead of merely being known, we show, we tell, we offer ourselves to view.[11]

By dropping her pretenses and defenses, Orual gains a "face," makes possible for herself a new, *personal* relationship to the divine: "By unveiling ... we assume the high rank of persons before Him. And He, descending, ... reveals that in Him which is Person. . . . The Person in Him . . . meets those who can welcome or at least face it. He speaks as 'I' when we truly call Him 'Thou.' "[12]

It is this personal relationship which the Fox now cites to set his former rationalism and the worship of Ungit apart from "the way to the true gods" (p. 295). The Fox appears in Orual's vision as her guide, much as Dante, in *The Divine Comedy,* uses Virgil, his symbol of reason, as his guide on his journey through Hell and Purgatory. It is not made clear whether the Fox is normally in a Limbo like that to which the Stoics are assigned in *The Pilgrim's Regress* — or whether, as he grew in old age to be less a philosopher and talked "more of eloquence and figures and poetry" (p. 235), he learned "the only means to . . . fulfilment" of his desires and now resides in heaven.[13] In any event, the Fox has changed—and that must challenge the reader to reassess his or her reliance on the rational. He now admits that he knew and should have told Orual that something was missing from his facile rationalism:

> "I never told her why the old Priest got something from the dark House that I never got from my trim sentences. . . . Of course, I didn't know; but I never told her I didn't know. I don't know now. Only that the way to the true gods is more like the house of Ungit. . . . The Priest knew at least that there must be sacrifices. . . . I made her think that a prattle of maxims would do, all thin and clear as water." (p. 295)

The Fox's words echo the old Priest's rebuke of Greek wisdom on page 50:

> "I, King, have dealt with the gods for three generations of men, and I know that they dazzle our eyes and flow in and out of one another like eddies on a river, and nothing that is said clearly can be said truly about them. Holy places are dark places. It is life and strength, not knowledge and words, that we get in them. Holy wisdom is not clear and thin like water, but thick and dark like blood."

And both reflect the distinction Lewis made elsewhere between "thick" and "clear" religions:

> By Thick I mean those which have orgies and ecstasies and mysteries and local attachments: Africa is full of Thick religions. By Clear I mean those which are philosophical, ethical

and universalizing: Stoicism, Buddhism, and the Ethical Church are Clear religions. Now if there is a true religion it must be both Thick and Clear: for the true God must have made both the child and the man, both the savage and the citizen, both the head and the belly.[14]

It is toward such a blend that Orual's dual heritage—from Ungit worship on the one hand, from the Fox on the other—is drawing her: a religion of sacrifice, with all that it entails, but of ethical demands as well, a religion very much like (though in the story prior to) Christianity. A passage from "Religion without Dogma?" summarizes it so pertinently that it deserves to be quoted at length:

> The traditions conflict, yet the longer and more sympathetically we study them the more we become aware of a common element in many of them: the theme of sacrifice, of mystical communion through the shed blood, of death and re-birth, of redemption, is too clear to escape notice. We are fully entitled to use moral and intellectual criticism. What we are not in my opinion entitled to do is simply to abstract the ethical element and set that up as a religion on its own. Rather in that tradition which is at once most completely ethical and most transcends mere ethics, in which the old themes of the sacrifice and re-birth recur in a form which transcends, though here it no longer revolts, our conscience and our reason, we may still most reasonably believe that we have the consummation of all religion, the fullest message from the wholly other, the living creator, who, if He is at all, must be the god not only of philosophers, but of mystics and savages, not only of head and heart, but also of the primitive emotions and the spiritual heights beyond all emotion. We may still most reasonably attach ourselves to the Church, to the only concrete organisation which has preserved down to this present time the core of all the messages, pagan and perhaps pre-pagan, that have ever come from beyond the world, and begin to practise the only religion which rests not upon some selection of certain supposedly "higher" elements in our nature, but on the shattering and rebuilding, the death and rebirth, of that nature in every part: neither Greek nor Jew nor barbarian, but a new creation.[15]

But such a religion also involves self-sacrifice, a total, personal commitment: in the Fox's terms, "They [the gods] will have sacrifice—will have man. Yes, and the very heart, center, ground, roots of a man; dark and strong and costly as blood" (p. 295). Lewis put it as follows in *The Problem of*

Pain: "[The soul's] union with God is, almost by definition, a continual self-abandonment—an opening, an unveiling, a surrender, of itself."[16] In *Letters to Malcolm* he adds: "We shrink from too naked a contact, because we are afraid of the divine demands upon us."[17] So it was, surely, with Orual—her veil was a defense against exposing her ugliness to herself and herself to Another. Behind her veil she could be her own; now, bare of face, she is ready to be Another's.

Having presented her case against the gods, Orual must come before the gods to hear if they will bring accusation against her. While she waits, the Fox shows her, in a series of living pictures, Psyche confronting the four tasks assigned to her—as she approaches them, Orual sees "in her face no such anguish" (p. 299) as she expected to see there; instead she sees ants separating the seeds, Psyche plucking tufts of wool from the brambles, and an eagle bringing a cupful of the water of death from the mountain. The Fox's explanation again brings the mythical together with the psychological and even the spiritual: "Another bore nearly all the anguish" (p. 300). One of the senses in which Orual "shall be Psyche" is that in living out her long, difficult, lonely existence as the Queen, Orual was bearing Psyche's burden in Psyche's place. It was Orual "who bore the anguish. But [Psyche] achieved the tasks" (p. 301). Lewis thus catches up what his friend Charles Williams believed to be at the heart of Christianity, the Way of Exchange. Williams took seriously the words of Paul, "Bear one another's burdens" (Galatians 6:2). As Christ bore the burden of sin, taking on himself the suffering due to humanity, so we are to take on ourselves the burdens of others. Lewis commented on Exchange in *Arthurian Torso*:

> We can and should "bear one another's burdens" in a sense much more nearly literal than is usually dreamed of. Any two souls can ("under the Omnipotence") make an agreement to do so: the one can offer to take another's shame or anxiety or grief and the burden will actually be transferred.[18]

This, of course, is a key element in, or even a definition of, *agape,* the love Christ brought for humanity to imitate from him: "By this we know love, that he laid down his life for us; and we ought to lay down our lives for the brethren" (I John 3:16).

Here, then, is that ultimate, selfless divine love which can and must transform the natural loves if they are to be and remain themselves. The entire theme of the loves, of the distortion of the natural loves into unlove unless they are converted by Love himself, is summed up, encapsulated, in the Fox's reply to Orual's question if Ungit is real. The Fox now speaks the language of myth—that he does so is ironic but also the most telling sign of his transformation; thus what he says cannot be rephrased adequately: myth must be received and experienced, not explained. The Fox tells Orual:

> "All, even Psyche, are born into the house of Ungit. And all must get free from her. Or say that Ungit in each must bear Ungit's son and die in childbed—or change. And now Psyche must go down into the deadlands to get beauty in a casket from the Queen of the Deadlands, from death herself; and bring it back to give it to Ungit so that Ungit will become beautiful." (p. 301)

The passage, in the richness of its myth-language, gathers together the book's central themes and shows their interrelatedness: the need for the rational and the "clear" to accept the numinous and the "thick" if the gods are to be known fully; the need for the natural loves (Ungit, possessiveness) to be sacrificed in total surrender ("die in childbed," "go down into the deadlands") and be thereby transformed by *agape* ("bear Ungit's son," "become beautiful") in order even to remain themselves; and the need to reject self-interest ("get free") in favor of action on behalf of others.

Now Psyche undertakes the fourth and last of her labors: going to the underworld to bring Ungit a box containing beauty, a task which Orual has been engaged in throughout the story as she went deep within herself to remove, or at least excuse, her ugliness of self and soul. Psyche begins her journey, a journey to achieve beauty of soul, the journey of her life, and Orual watches in the living pictures as first the people of Glome, then the Fox, and finally a woman-like figure, her left arm dripping with blood, try to distract or dissuade Psyche, try unsuccessfully to prevent her from completing that journey.

> The Fox and I were alone again.
> "Did we really do these things to her?" I asked.
> "Yes. All here's true."
> "And we said we loved her."
> "And we did. She had no more dangerous enemies than us. And ... this will happen more and more ... mother and wife and child and friend ... in league to keep a soul from being united with the Divine Nature." (p. 304)

The last five words sum up the fundamental purpose of human beings, that ultimate union with Love, with the divine, toward which their longings have been drawing them all their lives and toward which everything in *Till We Have Faces* has been pointing.

Orual's love has been converted and transformed; she has obeyed the god's instruction to die to self, which allows her self and her love to be infused by Love itself. Her words to Psyche reveal the change: " 'Oh Psyche, oh goddess,' I said. 'Never again will I call you mine; but all there is of me shall be yours' " (p. 305). With her jealousy and possessiveness goes her ugliness of soul: thus Psyche replies, "I have not given you the casket. You know I went a long journey to fetch the beauty that will make Ungit beautiful" (pp. 305–6). Since Orual is Ungit, she receives the box and receives beauty, of body and soul—not as something she achieved herself, as when she tried to change her face and mend her soul, but as a gift. So it is, slightly later, when she glances down at the courtyard pool, that she sees "two Psyches, the one clothed, the other naked" (p. 307), and finds the ultimate fulfillment of the god's words, "You also shall be Psyche."

First, however, Orual must meet Psyche's husband, who surely symbolizes Christ.[19] The theme of sacrifice, as Lewis introduces it to transcend Apuleius's tale and to fulfill what was latent in it, points toward the sacrifice of Christ. But in *Till We Have Faces,* set historically before his birth, Christ's death can only be anticipated. Thus the Fox is referring to the Incarnation when he talks of "that far distant day when the gods become wholly beautiful, or we at last are shown how beautiful they always were" (p. 304).[20] In humble faith which enables her to recognize divine beauty, to recognize that the divine jealousy and the demand for sacrifice are divine love, Orual can meet the most beautiful of the gods. She, having become like Psyche, also has an *anima naturaliter Christiana* [naturally Christian spirit].[21] And in that spirit, free of her veil, free from defenses and pretensions, now having a face (self), she is ready to meet the gods "face to face"; and the God she meets is Christ. Lifted out of this world and the temporal in her vision, she meets Christ in the timelessness of eternity, which is always "after" his redemptive activity, and finds salvation. The Christianization of the themes Lewis has been developing is completed on the final page of the book, as Psyche's husband comes to judge Orual:

> The air was growing brighter and brighter about us; as if something had set it on fire. Each breath I drew let into me new terror, joy, overpowering sweetness. I was pierced through and through with the arrows of it. I was being unmade. I was no one. ... I loved her as I would once have thought it impossible to love, would have died any death for her. And yet, it was not, not now, she that really counted. Or if she counted (and oh, gloriously she did) it was for another's sake. The earth and stars and sun, all that was or will be, existed for his sake. And he was coming. The most dreadful, the most beautiful, the only dread and beauty there is, was coming. The pillars on the far side of the pool flushed with his approach. I cast down my eyes. (p. 307)

The scene is very similar—in the encounter with something overwhelmingly, hugely other, in the total loss of self-ownership, in the utterly personal relationship—to the conversion scene in *That Hideous Strength*. The description there of Jane Studdock's response to the numinous, the divine, provides perhaps the best commentary on Orual's experience:

> A boundary had been crossed. She had come into a world, or into a Person, or into the presence of a Person. Something expectant, patient, inexorable, met her with no veil or protection between. ... There was nothing, and never had been anything, like this. And now there was nothing except this.

Yet also, everything had been like this: only by being like this had anything existed. In this height and depth and breadth the little idea of herself which she had hitherto called *me* dropped down and vanished, unfluttering, into bottomless distance, like a bird in a space without air. The name *me* was the name of a being whose existence she had never suspected, a being that did not yet fully exist but which was demanded. It was a person (not the person she had thought) yet also a thing—a made thing, made to please Another and in Him to please all others—a thing being made at this very moment, without its choice, in a shape it had never dreamed of.[22]

Orual has been shown at last how beautiful the true God always was, and to this experience her response can only be awe, reverence, worship, obedience, and love.

The book closes as it opens, by invoking the book of Job. Job repeatedly asks for a hearing: "But I would speak to the Almighty, and I desire to argue my case with God" (13:3). He pleads with God for an answer: "I would learn what he would answer me, and understand what he would say to me" (23:5). Eventually God does come, and he "answered Job out of the whirlwind" (38:1); he does not reason with Job, but bombards him with questions which demonstrate God's greatness and Job's finitude. Orual's closing words could well have been Job's: "I know now, Lord, why you utter no answer. You are yourself the answer" (p. 308). And Job's closing words could well have been Orual's: "I have uttered what I did not understand, things too wonderful for me, which I did not know" (42:3). Both works deal with alleged injustice in the universe; both present a case against God; and both agree that the case is refuted not by reason but by the nature of God. When God makes himself known, whether to Job, to Jane Studdock, or to Orual, the response is the same, a response Lewis believes must be the universal response to a true encounter with the Divine:

> I had heard of thee by the hearing of the ear,
>   but now my eye sees thee;
> therefore I despise myself,
>   and repent in dust and ashes.
>
>   (Job 42:5–6)

SECTION **II**

TILL WE HAVE FACES:
THE WORK IN CONTEXT

X

Poet of the Teens and Twenties: The Struggling Imagination

*O*NE way to come to know *Till We Have Faces* is close up, by reading the work attentively, taking into account its characters, structure, symbols, and themes. This way is necessary, and it must occur first, as it has in this study. But to understand and appreciate *Till We Have Faces* fully, it is necessary also to step back and view it from a distance, in the broader perspective of Lewis's works and life as a whole. It stands as the culmination of themes and images that appear throughout Lewis's previous works, but also as a striking contrast to earlier tendencies. The remaining five chapters of this book place *Till We Have Faces* in context. They offer a brief survey of Lewis's thought and works, focusing, for each decade, on a key work which has useful affinities to *Till We Have Faces* in theme or method—*Dymer, The Pilgrim's Regress, The Great Divorce, Surprised by Joy,* and *Letters to Malcolm.* They trace the ongoing tension in Lewis between reason and the imagination, and between reason and the self or the subjective, and the changes in Lewis's attitude toward them late in his life.

Owen Barfield, writing shortly after Lewis's death, mentions puzzling over what he terms the "individual essence" of his old friend: "I first met him in 1919, and the puzzlement has had to do above all with the great change that took place in him between the years 1930 and 1940— a change which roughly coincided with his conversion to Theism and then to Christianity."[1] Barfield sensed, beginning at that time, a studied effort by Lewis to direct his attention away from himself:

> At a certain stage in his life he deliberately ceased to take any interest in himself except as a kind of spiritual alumnus taking his moral finals. .... What began as deliberate choice became at length (as he had no doubt always intended it should) an ingrained and effortless habit of soul. Self-knowledge, for him, had come to mean recognition of his weaknesses and shortcomings and nothing more. Anything beyond that he sharply suspected, both in himself and in others, as a symptom of spiritual megalomania.[2]

Though Barfield comments that this change does not appear to be inevitably or even naturally connected with Lewis's conversion, it does seem to be quite directly related to two of Lewis's concerns at the time of his conversion: subjugation of pride and belief in moral law. About the time of his conversion, Lewis wrote to Arthur Greeves about pride, which he regarded as his "besetting sin": "There seems to be no end to it. Depth under depth of self-love and self admiration."[3] The solution is what Barfield wrote about, Lewis's keeping his attention directed toward things outside himself. About the same time Lewis came to accept the existence of moral order and the natural law—both of which are external and objective—and to recognize them as crucial to a proper understanding of life and the universe. These areas, both related to his conversion, involve a similar diminishing of the importance of the self and directing of attention toward external matters of greater importance than the self.

Barfield's concern—and I think it has not been given sufficient attention in considerations of Lewis's work—is that a consciousness of self, and of the inevitability of a degree of subjectivity, is necessary to proper understanding even of "objective" things, and that Lewis's failure to include self in his thinking was an inhibiting factor in his thought and work. Barfield does not indicate that this attitude changed later in Lewis's life. It appears to me, however, that for the final decade and a half of his life Lewis gradually shifted his emphasis to give fuller consideration to the self and the subjective, simultaneous with and related to an altered emphasis on reason and imagination, all of which leads to a noticeably different approach and tone in his later works.

Early in his life Lewis was pulled one way by rationalist tendencies, the other by romantic and imaginative ones. The rationalist grew out of home, family, and training. His father, for all his emotionalism, which so embarrassed Lewis, was a lawyer; his mother was a mathematician—both professions require and emphasize cool, clear-headed logic. His early training was classical, with the emphasis on rigor of thought and expression that implies. But it was the two years under the tutelage of W. T. Kirkpatrick, being prepared for the Oxford entrance exams that turned Lewis from a clear thinker to a thoroughgoing rationalist. Kirkpatrick—a nineteenth-century rationalist, fiercely logical except for his habit of exchanging his weekday suit for a nicer one on Sundays—taught Lewis that language was intended to promote knowledge and understanding: "The idea that human beings should exercise their vocal organs for any purpose except that of communicating or discovering truth was to him preposterous. The most casual remark was taken as a summons to disputation."[4] Lewis illustrates with an account of his initial conversation with Kirkpatrick after Lewis had remarked on the "wildness" of the Surrey scenery: " 'Stop!' shouted Kirk with a suddenness that made me jump. 'What do you mean by wildness and what grounds had you for not expecting it?' " After Lewis fumbled for a response, Kirkpatrick continued:

> On what had I based (but he pronounced it *baized*) my expectations about the Flora and Geology of Surrey? Was it maps, or photographs, or books? I could produce none. It had, heaven help me, never occurred to me that what I called my thoughts needed to be "baized" on anything. Kirk once more drew a conclusion—without the slightest sign of emotion, but equally without the slightest concession to what I thought good manners: "Do you not see, then, that you had no right to have any opinion whatever on the subject?" (p. 129; Ch. 9)

Knowledge, then, is to be grounded in sensory experience of the world or factual, "objective" data about it, and in reasonable reflection upon the data so obtained. As Lewis put it, such talk and such thinking were like "red beef and strong beer" to him (p. 131; ch. 9). He adopted Kirkpatrick's rationalism, his "ruthless dialectic" (p. 131; Ch. 9), and his habit of "talking for victory."[5]

The romantic tendencies arose from Lewis's response to nature and from his reading—his parents, he says, had no such romantic leanings: "Neither had ever listened for the horns of elfland" (p. 12; Ch. 1). The country he grew up in, Lewis notes, "had everything to encourage a romantic bent, had indeed done so ever since I first looked at the unattainable Green Hills through the nursery window" (p. 146; Ch. 10). Looking northeast from the Holywood Hills one saw Belfast and the Lough, with all the romance of the sea. South and east one saw a different, but equally attractive, world: "And having seen it, blame me if you can for being a romantic. For here is the thing itself, utterly irresistible, the way to the world's end, the land of longing, the breaking and blessing of hearts. You are looking across what may be called, in a certain sense, the plain of Down, and seeing beyond it the Mourne Mountains" (p. 148; Ch. 10). What from earliest childhood he had felt about the distant mountains was brought into focus by books: Longfellow's *Saga of King Olaf* and Arthur Rackham's drawings for *Siegfried and the Twilight of the Gods,* and other books as he discovered them, created a love of "northernness" and an intense longing for that which lay beyond the world he could know: "Instantly I was uplifted into huge regions of northern sky, I desired with almost sickening intensity something never to be described (except that it is cold, spacious, severe, pale, and remote)" (p. 23; Ch. 1). Rationalism and dialectic are not incompatible with romance, imagination, and myth: Plato, for example, combined them fruitfully and reached the highest levels of achievement in both. In Lewis the combination is less easy and, for a long while, less complete. Although he reaches very high levels in each, and unites the two in valuable ways, there remains a sense of perhaps an overcommitment to the dialectical which long prevents in practice the full understanding of myth Lewis advances in theory.

The tension between the rational and the romantic appears clearly in Lewis's early letters to Arthur Greeves, the short lyric poems collected in *Spirits in Bondage,* and the narrative poem *Dymer.* The letters to Greeves show his indulgence in romantic emotionalism side by side with a rationalist rebellion against religion and "illusion." They are dominated by the love of books, northern myth, and romantic longing which were the shared elements in their friendship. "Both knew the stab of Joy," Lewis wrote in *Surprised by Joy,* "and, . . . for both, the arrow was shot from the North" (p. 126; Ch. 8). Lewis mentions in one letter the "exalted" feeling he receives from reading Malory and goes on in his next letter to clarify what he means:

> Have you ever sat over the fire late, late at night when you are very drowzy & muddle headed, and it is no use trying to go on with your book? Everything seems like a dream, you are absolutely contented, and "out of the world." Anything seems possible, and all sorts of queer ideas float through your mind & sort of vaguely thrill you but only mildly & calmly. It is in this sort of mood that the quaint, old mystical parts of Malory are exactly suitable: you can read a chapter or two in a sort of dream & find the forests of "Logres & of Lyonesse" very agreeable at such a time—at least I do.[6]

Lewis's rationalism appears infrequently in these letters, largely because Greeves did not share Lewis's love of ideas and dialectic. Occasionally the rationalist comes through, often immediately after an emotionalist passage like that above, demonstrating the tension and diversity of Lewis's thinking at the time. The letter cited above continues,

> You ask me my religious views: you know, I think, that I beleive [sic] in no religion. There is absolutely no proof for any of them, and from a philosophical standpoint Christianity is not even the best. All religions, that is, all mythologies to give them their proper name are merely man's own invention—Christ as much as Loki. Primitive man found himself surrounded by all sorts of terrible things he didn't understand—thunder, pestilence, snakes etc: what more natural than to suppose that these were animated by evil spirits trying

to torture him. These he kept off by cringing to them, singing songs and making sacrifices etc.

The young Lewis, here, holds seriously the allegorical, post-logical naturalistic explanations of myth he would later undercut when they appear in the words of Arnom, the enlightened priest in *Till We Have Faces*. The letter goes on:

> Thus religion, that is to say mythology grew up. Often, too, great men were regarded as gods after their death—such as Heracles or Odin: thus after the death of a Hebrew philosopher Yeshua (whose name we have corrupted into Jesus) he became regarded as a god, a cult sprang up, which was afterwards connected with the ancient Hebrew Jahweh-worship, and so Christianity came into being—one mythology among many, but the one that we happen to have been brought up in.

One notes in all this Lewis's emphasis upon a lack of *proof* and his acceptance of it as "the recognised scientific account of the growth of religions." His thinking is, at this point, very much grounded in reason, realism, and materialism: "Of course, mind you, I am not laying down as a certainty that there *is* nothing outside the material world: considering the discoveries that are always being made, this would be foolish. Anything MAY exist: but until we know that it does, we can't make any assumptions."[7] And we would come to such knowledge only through the evidences of sense experience and experimentation and through conclusions drawn from logical inference.

There is a similar bifurcation and tension between rationalism and the romantic in Lewis's first book of poetry, *Spirits in Bondage,* published in 1919. Lewis was at this time a materialistic rationalist, as the letter to Greeves quoted above indicates; yet a dominant theme of this "Cycle of Lyrics" is a longing for a romantic world quite at odds with his epistemology. In one of the letters to Greeves, Lewis asserts that the themes of *Spirits in Bondage* are the malevolence of nature and the remoteness and essential goodness of God;[8] but the poems in fact seem to emphasize instead a rejection of conventional ideas about God, an appreciation and acceptance of the beauty of nature, and a longing to escape from the suffering caused by human cruelty to the comfort of a romantic paradise. The title itself reflects that ambivalence: the published title is a slight modification of Lewis's original choice, "Spirits in Prison," a biblical allusion (I Peter 3:19—"he went and preached to the spirits in prison") with Platonic overtones; it forms an ironic contrast to the rationalism and naturalistic realism Lewis professes to be his chief concern. In its "enlightened" rationalism on the one hand and deep sense of longing for a world of the spirit on the other, the collection provides an early and immature version of themes which would be treated much more satisfactorily in *Till We Have Faces*.

Rationalism is integral to Lewis's development of his themes, especially of the "Bondage" theme. The "Spirits" of the title are those of humankind, especially "The yearning, high, rebellious spirit of man" which has never rested, since life began, "From striving with red Nature and her ways."[9] The "Bondage" of the title refers to the imprisonment of that noble spirit in a world of cruelty, oppression, and evil, which constantly attempts to beat down and crush it. "In Prison," for example, is a protest against "the hopeless life that ran / For ever in a circling path / From death to death since all began" (p. 31). "Ode for New Year's Day," similarly, is not the celebration of newness and hope typical of poems for the new year; instead it affirms that there is no escape from the "red wrath" being poured upon this deformed world (p. 24). At one time the poet, like other people, raised his voice in prayer and complaint and cursing. Now, however, he knows better:

> I am grown wiser, knowing that our own hearts
> Have made a phantom called the Good, while a few years
> have sped
> Over a little planet. And what should the great Lord know of
> it
> Who tosses the dust of chaos and gives the suns their parts?
> (p. 25)

Whatever divine being exists is, somehow, at once a clock-maker god, who set the worlds in motion and withdrew, unhearing and uninterested, and an antagonistic god, who covers the sky with "clouds of God's hate" (p. 23). Such self-contradictory rationalism is much less convincing and insidious than the naturalism and benevolent humanism of the Fox's Stoic attitudes in *Till We Have Faces*.

The two themes of the collection, "Spirits" and "Bondage," are united in "De Profundis." The bondage results from the inescapable strength and malignity of the divine, who defeats whatever wisdom and joy human beings attain: "And suddenly the earth grew black with wrong,/ Our hope was crushed and silenced was our song" (p. 33). The only response more positive than to "curse our Master ere we die" is to assert human independence—"Yet I will not bow down to thee nor love thee"—and maintain the dignity of the human spirit: "Our love, our hope, our thirsting for the right,/ Our mercy and long seeking of the light,/ Shall we change these for thy relentless might?" (p. 34). One finds all of these sentiments in Orual, but deepened by Lewis's subsequent experience with life and as a writer.

Woven throughout the rationalism is a deep strain of romanticism, of romantic rebellion and of romantic longing for escape. The rebelliousness comes out particularly in "The Philosopher." It is clearly the poem of a youthful writer, unhappy with the state of the world and searching for encompassing answers to ultimate questions:

> Who shall be our prophet then,
> Chosen from all the sons of men
> To lead his fellows on the way
> Of hidden knowledge, delving deep
> To nameless mysteries that keep
> Their secret from the solar day!
> Or who shall pierce with surer eye
> This shifting veil of bittersweet
> And find the real things that lie
> Beyond this turmoil, which we greet
> With such a wasted wealth of tears?
> (p. 43)

It also shows the typical distrust of youths for the knowledge or answers of their elders, and—interestingly, from a rationalist—a romantic disenchantment with reason as a means of securing answers. The narrator asks if the prophet

being sought is an elder "In his solitary tower" with eyes
"dim and blind" (p. 44), and replies it is not.

> His monstrous books can never know
> The secret we would find.
> But let our seer be young and kind
> And fresh and beautiful of show,
> And taken ere the lustyhead
> And rapture of his youth be dead,
> Ere the gnawing, peasant reason
> School him over-deep in treason
> To the ancient high estate
> Of his fancy's principate,
> That he may live a perfect whole,
> A mask of the eternal soul,
> And cross at last the shadowy bar
> To where the ever-living are.
>
> (pp. 44–45)

"Seeing" here is a direct, almost intuitive knowledge, almost
Wordsworthian, available to the young and innocent in an
idealized world ("ancient high estate"). Wholeness comes
not through pure reason, or the union of reason and imagination, but through total commitment to the imaginative:
by such wholehearted embracing of the fancy, or imagination, one's life can become a "mask" revealing the eternal
soul. "Mask" here suggests not a barrier to or a hiding of
the truth, as it will in later works, but "an accurate reflection of." Similarly, the "shifting veil" in the earlier lines
suggests not rationalist barriers raised against sight but the
inevitable limitedness of the here and now, a rather contradictory image from one who purports to be a materialist and
rationalist.

Lewis himself, in the later poems of the collection, becomes in part such a young seer as the poem asks for. The
last section of poems, entitled "The Escape" (from "The
Prison House," title of the first section), concentrates on the
sweet desires experienced by romantic pilgrims as they long
for a romantic country far from such confines. The "Pro-
logue" to the entire volume places the emphasis not on imprisonment, but release. As singing of their homeland
enabled old Phoenician men sailing to the ends of the earth

to forget their toil and burden, so these poems will give comfort and courage to those who struggle through life desiring something better:

> In my coracle of verses I will sing of lands unknown,
> Flying from the scarlet city where a Lord that knows no pity
> Mocks the broken people praying round his iron throne,
> —Sing about the Hidden Country fresh and full of quiet green.
> Sailing over seas uncharted to a port that none has seen.
>
> (p. 8)

The "lands unknown" are either "somewhere, somewhere past the Northern snow" ("Song of the Pilgrims," p. 69) or "down the western ways" ("Hesperus," p. 95). Such lands are a "Country of Dreams!/ Beyond the tide of the ocean, . . . near to the end of day,/ Full of dim woods and streams" ("Death in Battle," p. 106). They are lands associated with fairies and other "lovely folk" ("World's Desire," p. 104), with "Immortal shapes of beauty clear" ("Ballade Mystique," p. 79), with "spirits that have . . . seen the bright footprints of God" ("Song," p. 74), and with "archangels fresh from sight of God" (" 'Our Daily Bread,' " p. 86).

Only glimpses of that "Hidden Country" enable one to go on through the prison house of life. In the most haunting and powerful poem in the collection, "Dungeon Grates," the poet reflects on the burden, the pain, "The nightmare march of unrelenting fate," and concludes,

> I think that he must die thereof unless
> Ever and again across the dreariness
> There came a sudden glimpse of spirit faces,
> A fragrant breath to tell of flowery places
> And wider oceans, breaking on the shore
> For which the hearts of men are always sore.
>
> (p. 40)

Such "sudden glimpses" are not the result of prayer, or fasting, or wisdom; rather, they are a reward given to the receptive romantic spirit:

> Only the strange power
> Of unsought Beauty in some casual hour
> Can build a bridge of light or sound or form
> To lead you out of all this strife and storm.
>
> (p. 41)

The experience of a sudden beam of "larger light" leaping out of beauty turns all the surroundings into gold and reveals a truth seven times more true than ordinary truth.

> For one little moment we are one
> With the eternal stream of loveliness
> That flows so calm, aloof from all distress
> Yet leaps and lives around us as a fire
> Making us faint with overstrong desire
> To sport and swim for ever in its deep—
> Only a moment.
>
> (p. 41)

It is but a moment, but it is enough: "We know we are not made of mortal stuff./ And we can bear all trials that come after,/... For we have seen the Glory—we have seen" (pp. 41–42). This is one of the fullest descriptions Lewis ever gave of the experience he later called "Joy"; it demonstrates impressively the strength and importance of the romantic strain in Lewis's life even at a time when he was training himself as a rationalist. It also illuminates the happiness and sustaining power Psyche received from her longings for the castle in the grey mountains of Glome.

Spirits in Bondage is uneven as a collection of poetry: there are a few gems, usually brief passages rather than entire poems. Its strength is expression of youthful emotions rather than handling of poetic skills. Its best quality as poetry is its visual imagery, as in "How He Saw Angus the God":

> —That little wood of hazel and tall pine
> And youngling fir, where oft we have loved to see
> The level beams of early morning shine
>   Freshly from tree to tree.
>
> Though in the denser wood there's many a pool
> Of deep and night-born shadow lingers yet
> Where the new-wakened flowers are damp and cool
>   And the long grass is wet.
>
> (p. 89)

The visualizing tendency Lewis calls attention to later as the heart of his imaginative ability was with him already as a youth. Despite weaknesses, however, the collection shows a great deal about Lewis's attitudes and experiences through his teens, particularly the tension between rationalism and romanticism, which stays with him through much of his life. At this point they are definitely in juxtaposition: the two appear in separate poems, pulling in opposite directions, and are in no sense moving toward a unity or even cooperation with each other.

That juxtaposition continues, in slightly altered form, seven years later, in the long narrative poem *Dymer*. *Dymer* was published in 1926, but Lewis worked on it for many years, beginning with a prose version in December 1916; it is of value, therefore, for the way it reinterprets themes and images of the previous decade in light of Lewis's positions in the mid-twenties. But it is of greater significance, in this study, for its anticipations of central themes, character types, and figures of speech in *Till We Have Faces*.

Dymer is a review and modification of Lewis's earlier romanticism, both the romantic protest and idealism and the romantic longing and emotional indulgence. The hero, Dymer, is engaged in a search for meaning and purpose, first by throwing off restraint and authority, and subsequently by pursuing "sweet desire." Both aspects of his search end in frustration and disillusionment. His example of rebellion is followed by others and unleashes a wave of anarchy and tyranny which appalls him when he learns about it. Sweet desire draws him to a paradisal wood and an encounter with a delectable maiden; but the harshness and evil of the world convince him that the longing created by natural beauty is a deception and a fraud. A narrow escape from death sobers and matures Dymer, and leads him to accept nature for the concrete reality she is and to conclude that the romantic worlds epitomized in his dream at the magician's house are only projections of his own fantasies and wishes. He realizes that his longings are not for nature but for the eternal Spirit, and he finds strength in the assurance that "the gods," unreachable and disinterested as they may be, do share all experiences of human beings, including woe and pain. Dymer is finally able to accept responsibility for his actions and to recognize that, having misused the time available to him, he must make some effort to "undo" what he has done amiss. In a type of death (it takes place in a graveyard), Dymer's spirit soars upward to a ruinous land in which he encounters a monster, the offspring of his union with the spiritual maiden earlier in the poem, engages willingly in combat with the monster, and is killed by it. His death, however, transforms the wasteland into a paradise and the monster into a god.

By the mid-1920s Lewis had rejected his earlier materialistic rationalism and had become an Idealist. This change led to changes in Lewis's thinking about the romantic, but did not eliminate or resolve the tension between it and the rational. The handling of romantic longing in *Dymer* reflects significant differences from *Spirits in Bondage*. As Dymer leaves the regimented society of the Perfect City, he enters a forest, hears music, and experiences a pang of longing: "So sharp it was, so sure a path it found,/ Soulward with stabbing wounds of bitter sound."[10] His encounter with the maiden in the darkness of "a world not made for seeing" (II, 28) is a coming upon "unsought Beauty in some casual hour" like that in the earlier "Dungeon Grates." But Lewis now regards the Western Garden imagery, so prominent in *Spirits in Bondage,* as illusory. The woods and paradisal palace of Cantos II and III are accentuated in the magical dreams of Canto VII: such places are lies, are only projections of inner romantic desires, and are ridiculed by the very spelling of "the good countrie" (VII, 23).[11] The longings themselves, for those who experience "whisperings at the heart, soul-sickening gleams / Of infinite desire" (VIII, 11), are not illusory, but they must point one past nature and illusory images to the world of pure Spirit. It was true Spirit that Dymer wooed and longed for when he thought he longed for nature and its "holiness" (VIII, 10). It was true Spirit he mated with in the sudden encounter with the maiden in the palace; he did not recognize what she really was, however, because she came in the shape he called for—as sensuous romantic experience rather than Truth—and because he did not ask her name, did not seek to know her as she really was (III, 10; VIII, 6). The emphasis on Spirit is an effort to eliminate romantic trappings while retaining a "deromanticized" longing, which strongly suggests a continued, and perhaps increasing, tension between the romantic and the rational.

Two passages in letters Lewis wrote to Arthur Greeves in 1918, though written a good deal earlier than the published version of *Dymer,* are helpful in getting hold of the attitudes and ideas Lewis put into the poem. The first was written about *Spirits in Bondage,* but it is in fact more applicable to *Dymer.* The theme of his forthcoming volume, Lewis tells Greeves, is mainly "the idea that I mentioned to you before—that nature is wholly diabolical & malevolent and that God, if he exists, is outside of and in opposition to the cosmic arrangements."[12] *Dymer,* more than *Spirits in Bondage,* develops the Platonic theme, or Lewis's adaptation of a Platonic theme, implicit in the earlier title and the ideas about nature expressed there. Dymer, like all humanity, is imprisoned within his mortal body; he must seek to become free of it, to keep his attention on higher things. But that effort is hindered by the world, especially by nature, which is "diabolical" in that its attractions and beauties create longings and satisfactions which invite one to be content with the world and this life. Natural evils—the disasters of storm and human brutality—convey the truth about nature's malevolence, from which God is separate and to which his goodness is opposed. It is a neat, abstractly satisfying means of dealing with the problems of suffering and evil in the world, and a good deal more sophisticated than the simple naturalism of *Spirits in Bondage.*

A few months later Lewis described to Greeves "The Redemption of Ask," a shortened, versified account of the Dymer myth.

> The main idea is that of development by self-destruction, both of individuals & species (as nature produces man only to conquer her [Nature], & man produces a future & higher generation to conquer the ideals of the last, or again as an individual produces a nobler mood to undo all that today's has done).[13]

The comments are applicable to the version of *Dymer* published some eight years later, so long as the evolutionary ring of "development" is not allowed to overshadow "by self-destruction." Lewis's real interest in the mid-1920s was not evolution but sacrifice, particularly the voluntary self-sacrifice found in the northern myths which he loved throughout his youth and which provide a context and set the tone for *Dymer*. Thus the epigraph taken from the collection of Icelandic runes entitled the *Hàvamàl* helps clarify the meaning of *Dymer*: "Nine nights I hung upon the Tree, wounded with the spear as an offering to Odin, myself sacrificed to myself."[14] The god Odin, in order to gain wisdom through acquisition of the magic runes, hanged himself on the ash Yggdrasil as an offering to himself, and wounded himself with his own spear. It is a symbolic enactment of the idea—central to *Dymer*—that development can be attained only by self-sacrifice and self-destruction.

Dymer unites the heroic individualism of the northern myths with an emphasis on personal responsibility which bears some resemblance to the ideas of Existentialism a decade or two later—though Lewis was in no sense an Existentialist, either then or later. One such parallel occurs when Dymer attempts to deny his responsibility for the anarchy which followed his rebellion: "What have I done? Wronged whom? I never knew./ What's Bran to me? I had my deed to do / And ran out by myself, alone and free" (V, 11). The poem implies, however, as Sartre will later, that to choose something as right for oneself assumes it would be right for others to choose that thing, too.[15] While Dymer is not responsible for what others do, he is responsible for the act of setting the example he did. Also, like the Existentialists, the poem affirms existence by virtue of choices made. The song of a lark symbolizes the voice of the world, "Of beings beyond number, each and all / Singing I AM. Each of itself made choice / And was" (V, 28). The poem holds that individuals, too, are determined by their choices and responsible for the choices they make, even if, or even though, no guidance is available for making those choices well: Dymer asks, "Must things of dust / Guess their own way in the dark?"; the maiden (Spirit) replies, "They must" (VIII, 12). And Dymer finally does accept such responsibility: "What would have been / The strength of all my days I have refused / And plucked the stalk, too hasty, in the green" (VIII, 16).

Having accepted responsibility for his choices and actions, Dymer also accepts, and is prepared to face, his destiny. The conclusion of the poem mixes Platonism and northern pessimism with the "existential" quality illustrated above. Having died repeatedly in spirit, through bad values and poor choices, Dymer at last approaches physical death, the time at which he will "cast [his] fetters" and leave this dream world (VIII, 19). Before that death, however, he feels himself capable of one heroic, though presumably fatal, act: "My course is run, / All but some deed still waiting to be done" (IX, 10). He must recognize the ruin he has made of his life and confront the monstrous spiritual nature he has created (given birth to) by his choices and actions. He does a noble deed and dies in the effort, but dies heroically, in keeping with the endings of northern myths. By sacrifice of himself to himself—in that the monster is his own off-spring—Dymer achieves a deed which ennobles Mankind and enables "great good" (IX, 35) to enter the world.

A careful examination of *Dymer* reveals a number of affinities with *Till We Have Faces*. First, the two works share basic imagery. The masks of the Priests and temple girls of *Till We Have Faces* are anticipated by the masks in the Magician's house and in Dymer's dream (VI, 13; VII, 28), and their antithesis, the frequent "unmaskings" which reveal things as they really are (IV, 6; VII, 26; and IX, 9). The image of the *veil* occurs often in the poem, though as a metaphor for illusion or delusion, not the rich symbol it becomes in the later work. Thus Dymer says, after his renewed experience with nature which makes him confident that he will remain henceforth free of illusions, "No veils should hide the truth" (VI, 2); and as a phantom of the maiden appears in his magic-induced dream a bit later, Dymer says, "Her sweetness drew / A veil before my eyes" (VII, 21).

Lewis also gives to Dymer many of the attitudes he

later gives to Orual. Dymer, unable to find the maiden and shocked by the actual carnage the example of his personal rebellion unleashed, sinks into despair and pessimism: "There stood the concave, vast, unfriendly night,/ And over him the scroll of stars unfurled" (V, 7). His heart is clouded by "deep world-despair" (V, 3), and he is repelled by the "Infinite malice" of nature (V, 14). He pours forth accusations against "the gods," very much like those of Orual: "And I suppose / They, they up there, the old contriving powers,/ They knew it all the time" (V, 9). Like Orual, Dymer curses and rejects the gods: "I have seen the world stripped naked and I know./ Great God, take back your world. I will have none / Of all your glittering gauds but death alone" (V, 15). In *Till We Have Faces* the allusions to Job put Orual and her accusations against the gods into proper perspective; *Dymer,* lacking such allusions, relies on simple irony to accomplish the same thing: throughout the world and universe, orderly patterns of action carry on as before, "And no one knew that Dymer in his scales / Had weighed all these and found them nothing worth" (V, 17). Dymer, like Orual, must come to realize that his indictment of the gods and justice is a projection of his inability to accept his own guilt. He must come to know himself and deal with what he has made of his life in order to understand his place in the order of things.

Basic character types in *Dymer* and *Till We Have Faces* are related as well. Psyche, with her almost otherworldly beauty and goodness, is parallel in some respects to the maiden who comes to Dymer in the palace. The sentry's description of the maiden could almost as well be applied to Psyche:

> Her ancient smile
> Made glad the sons of heaven. She loved to chase
> The springtime round the world. To all your race
> She was a sudden quivering in the wood
> Or a new thought springing in solitude.
>
> (IX, 12)

Dymer was searching for the Good, for Truth, for that divine Beauty which inspires the artist to paint and the poet to write. In meeting the maiden, he has found that for which he sought, though he does not realize it or seek to know her for what she is. After leaving her, he is prevented from returning to her by the hag, who is parallel in a number of ways to Orual as Ungit. The hag is described as "a dark mass" (III, 11), a many-breasted woman (III, 13), "the old, old matriarchal dreadfulness" (III, 23), and "that frightful woman shape" (VI, 18). The hag, like the maiden, is a true symbol, which cannot be fixed or limited to one specific interpretation. She may be a type of devouring female, a Lilith figure opposed to life and beauty, or she may be a projection of Dymer's own feelings, now passion-filled and possessive, which prevent a renewal of the innocence and openness of the initial encounter—but in any case the general similarity to Orual and Ungit is sharp and revealing.

More basic than such similarities in imagery and character, however, is the similarity of their myths. *Dymer* develops a personal myth which seems to have haunted Lewis for years, if not decades. Owen Barfield suggests that *Till We Have Faces* is a working out of the same myth: "Much later in ... *Till We Have Faces,* he seems to me to have succeeded in combining the old myth of Cupid and Psyche with this personal myth."[16] The personal myth to which he refers is that of a person engendering a monster which subsequently destroys its parent and is transformed through that sacrificial death. Thus Orual, early in her life, encounters the Good, the Beautiful, the True, embodied in Psyche; her efforts to possess Psyche, however, cut her off from Psyche and prevent their reunion. Through her possessiveness and jealousy, Orual gives birth to a monster, the ugly, jealous Orual of her natural self. She at last recognizes it as a monster of her own making and confronts it; she dies to it, and this death enables the monstrous Orual to be transformed into the beautiful, spiritual Orual who then resembles Psyche. The novel is a much richer, more mature, more aesthetically and imaginatively satisfying handling of the myth than *Dymer,* but it is essentially the same myth, a personal myth which grew over the decades and provides one of the strongest unifying threads in Lewis's life and works.

The development of this personal myth in *Dymer* has great power, and the similarities of the poem to *Till We Have Faces* are fascinating and instructive, but the work has significant weaknesses as poetry, especially weaknesses in metaphor.[17] It can safely be said that effective use of metaphor, the most imaginative of poetic figures, is essential to a poet and to fine poetry. What metaphors occur in *Dymer* are simple and trite, as the comparison of a glance to a small bird landing upon something, of time to an ocean, and of a task to a road, all in the opening stanza of Canto I:

> You stranger, long before your glance can light
> Upon these words, time will have washed away
> The moment when I first took pen to write,
> With all my road before me.

They are typical of the metaphors in the poem, decorative, adding to the diction, but not integral to the purpose of the poem. The figures which are integral, which carry the creative burden, are similes:

> He yawned, and a voluptuous laziness
> Tingled down all his spine and loosed his knees,
> Slow-drawn, like an invisible caress.

> (I, 9)

The similes are too frequent and call attention to themselves, but they are consistently more effective than the metaphors. The simile is generally considered less imaginative than metaphor—closer to analogy, with a more reasoned and calculated dimension, though in poets like Dante and Spenser the images in which a simile is elaborated, and even the comparisons themselves, are fresh and highly imaginative. But Lewis's similes are not those of Dante or Spenser (though his heavy reliance on similes in a narrative poem probably imitates them)—Lewis's have less naturalness, inevitability, and sensory effect than theirs, and give more sense of being thought out as illustrative material. Similar and related to the tension of reason versus the romantic in the content, therefore, is a tension between reason and the imagination in the style. Even here, in an early poem, Lewis does not seem to give free rein to his imagination. From early on, Lewis's imagination is held back, perhaps more than he himself ever realized, by deeply ingrained rationalistic tendencies and methods.

It is noteworthy, finally, that in *Spirits in Bondage* and *Dymer,* Lewis is writing about himself. The poems are in no sense allegorical, and Dymer is not Lewis in the same way that John in *The Pilgrim's Regress* is, but they do reflect Lewis's early searchings and sorting of values and ideas, including perhaps his own struggle to be a poet. Marjorie Milne identifies as a central motif "the poet's relation to his Muse." In Dymer's death and the apotheosis of the beast into a god, she suggests, the poet's (and thus, surely, Lewis's) "old romantic longings pass through the grave and gate of death and new and vital poetic powers are released."[18] There is as yet none of the reluctance to direct his attention to himself that Barfield saw arising in the next decade. By concentrating on experience as literary experience—on the form rather than the implications of what he is writing— he is able to write about himself, quite easily and naturally, without directing attention to himself. He will not accomplish that fully again until *Till We Have Faces.*

XI

Critic and Story-Writer of the Thirties: Imagination as Servant

THAT a major turning point in Lewis's intellectual and spiritual life occurred at the time of his conversion in the early 1930s is well known. Lewis affirmed, as is also well known, that an enlarged understanding of the relation of myth to Christianity played a crucial part in his conversion. That affirmation has sometimes been taken as evidence of a complete and abrupt change in attitude toward myth and the imagination and in their relation to reason. The evidence supplied by his works, however, does not support this. To understand Lewis's works of the 1930s requires recognition that the tension between reason and imagination continues after his conversion and that the place he allows to the imagination is limited at this point by his conception of the "objective."

A variety of forces came to bear upon the young atheist (or agnostic). His continuing unsatisfied longings, his readings in Christian authors, especially from the Middle Ages and the Renaissance, his growing belief in a moral law and therefore in a lawgiver, and his acquaintance and deepening friendships with men who were or were becoming Christians—all drew him to a belief in God. But there is a considerable distance between such Theism and Christianity. Part of the distance—the elimination of alternative possibilities—could be traversed intellectually. He reconstructs the situation in *Surprised by Joy*:

> There could be no question of going back to primitive, un-theologised and unmoralised, Paganism. The God whom I had

at last acknowledged was one, and was righteous. Paganism had been only the childhood of religion, or only a prophetic dream. Where was the thing full grown? . . . There were really only two answers possible: either in Hinduism or in Christianity. . . . But Hinduism seemed to have two disqualifications. For one thing, it appeared to be not so much a moralised and philosophical maturity of Paganism as a mere oil-and-water coexistence of philosophy side by side with Paganism unpurged. . . . And secondly, there was no such historical claim as in Christianity.[1]

It was the remaining distance—which required him to deal with such matters as sacrifice and substitution—that caused him difficulty. His rationalism appeared to give him no grounds for handling such nonrational elements of Christianity.

At this point occurred a key episode in Lewis's life, a long, late-night conversation with J. R. R. Tolkien and "Hugo" Dyson on Saturday, 19 September 1931. The effect of that conversation can hardly be overstated: it was a turning point in Lewis's journey toward Christianity. He wrote to Arthur Greeves, twelve days later, "I have just passed on from believing in God to definitely believing in Christ—in Christianity."[2] But the episode must be examined closely if its effects upon his imaginative and literary life are to be assessed accurately.

In recounting the conversation to Greeves, Lewis begins: "What has been holding me back (at any rate for the last year or so) has not been so much a difficulty in believing as a difficulty in knowing what the doctrine *meant*." His problem, then, was not one of accepting the truth or reality of Christianity, but one of relevance: "What I couldn't see was how the life and death of Someone Else (whoever he was) 2000 years ago could help us here and now." Lewis had become convinced intellectually of the existence of God and the historicity of the gospel accounts, and the need for help from outside to change the direction of one's life. But he was not yet able to embrace the "thick" element of Christianity, the mysterious but central parts about "propitiation," "sacrifice," and "the blood of the Lamb." His friends persuaded him to accept those elements with the imagination and the emotions, if not with the mind:

> Now what Dyson and Tolkien showed me was this: that if I met the idea of sacrifice in a Pagan story I didn't mind it at all: again, that if I met the idea of a god sacrificing himself to himself (cf. the quotation opposite the title page of *Dymer*) I liked it very much and was mysteriously moved by it: again, that the idea of the dying and reviving god (Balder, Adonis, Bacchus) similarly moved me provided I met it anywhere *except* in the Gospels. The reason was that in Pagan stories I was prepared to feel the myth as profound and suggestive of meanings beyond my grasp even tho' I could not say in cold prose "what it meant."

Notice that myth is restricted to areas of meaningfulness; it does not convey knowledge of how Christ's life and death can help one here and now, but enables one to appreciate its power and beauty. What sets Christianity apart from other myths, however, is not its power or meaning, but the factual, historical, "real" elements in it—Lewis seizes on the fact that it is *knowable* as well as meaningful:

> Now the story of Christ is simply a true myth: a myth working on us in the same way as the others, but with this tremendous difference that *it really happened*: and one must be content to accept it in the same way, remembering that it is God's myth where the others are men's myths: i.e. the Pagan stories are God expressing Himself through the minds of poets, using such images as He found there, while Christianity is God expressing Himself through what we call "real things." Therefore it is *true,* not in the sense of being a "description" of God (that no finite mind could take in) but in the sense of being the way in which God chooses to (or can) appear to our faculties. The "doctrines" we get *out of* the true myth are of course *less* true: they are translations into our *concepts* and *ideas* of that wh. God has already expressed in a language more adequate, namely the actual incarnation, crucifixion, and resurrection. Does this amount to a belief in Christianity? At any rate I am now certain (a) That this Christian story is to be approached, in a sense, as I approach the other myths. (b) That it is the most important and full of meaning.[3]

Christianity embodies the meaningful in the knowable. Reason and the imagination are separate avenues to, on the one hand, knowledge of and, on the other hand, the meaning

of "the actual incarnation, crucifixion, and resurrection."
The talk with Tolkien enabled Lewis to recognize the mythical element in Christianity, to accept that element as completing the cognitive; now, comfortable with its meaning,
Lewis can put his faith in the God who expressed himself
in the incarnation, crucifixion, and resurrection as well as
in creation and the moral law, and become a Christian.

The need expressed in the letter to reconcile myth with
"real things" calls attention to an intriguing aspect of Lewis's
thinking, which remains a part of the tension between
reason and the imagination for many years. As Lewis, after
his conversion, became ever more convinced of the importance of an objective approach to truth and values, he en-
deavored to convey the utter reality and the unambiguous
clarity of the objective by depicting it in concrete imagery
or metaphors. Such an approach could have unified imagination and reason in his thinking, as the imagination provides a "picture" which enables the reason to grasp more
firmly what the objective is. That unity is not attained at
once, however, because of Lewis's resistance against attention to the self or to a subjective dimension in apprehending
the objective, and because of his tendency to treat the con-
cretized objective not as image but as fact, thus received by
the reason rather than the imagination. Let it be clear that
Lewis never relaxed even slightly his belief in the reality
and importance of objectivity; but he did change his way of
thinking about the objective and its representations. The
physical and mechanical manner of his depiction of the objective in the thirties and forties conveys an absoluteness
and rigidity of attitude and interpretation which, in the fifties, he abandons for an approach which softens his attitudes and allows for more subjectivity and flexibility.

The emphasis on concreteness appears first in the twenties, as a part of Lewis's Idealism, particularly in his attention, in his criticism, to "real things" in literary texts. That
was the point of a paper on *The Faerie Queene* he delivered
to a discussion-class at Oxford in the fall of 1922, as Nevill
Coghill recalls it: in the paper Lewis gloried not in the

meaning of the allegory but in its details—its dragons, giants, knights, dwarfs, and sorceresses.

> He rejoiced as much in the ugliness of the giants and in the beauty of the ladies as in their spiritual significances, but most of all in the ambience of the faerie forest and plain that, he said, were carpeted with a grass greener than the common stuff of ordinary glades; this was the *reality* of grass, only to be apprehended in poetry: the world of the imagination was nearer to the truth than the world of the senses, notwithstanding its palpable fictions. . . . He needed the Greek word γάνος [brightness, sheen, gladness, joy, pride] to express the radiance of the reality of the greenness of Spenser's groves and glades, lawns, hills, and forests. It was like the Platonic idea of greenness, a spiritual reality.[4]

Notice the lack of emphasis on the *literary work* as object: that is not Lewis's kind of objectivism. He was not a part of the New Critical movement which began in America during the 1920s as a reaction against biographical criticism. Lewis, unlike Cleanth Brooks or Allen Tate, did not write close readings of individual texts, analyzing structure, word choice, imagery, figures, and tone to demonstrate the unity of artistry and theme. His interest throughout his career was, rather, in the "real things" seen through the text.

Lewis's criticism, like that of the New Critics, reacted against biographical criticism. He confronted it directly in a paper on "The Personal Heresy in Poetics," read to the Martlet Society in 1930 and published in 1933. In it he attacks the assumptions, whether implied or explicit, that "poetry must be the expression of . . . personality" and that "to read poetry means to become acquainted with the poet."[5] Lewis's position is that awareness of the writer behind the poem is not part of the imaginative experience of reading the poem. "The poet" is an abstraction constructed after the fact as one thinks back on the poetic experience; and even the abstraction so constructed is severely limited, drawing upon only those parts of the author involved in making the poem. There can be, Lewis holds, "poetry without a poet" (p. 18)—poetry which grew out of an oral tradition, for example. And all poetry should be read as "poetless poetry" (p. 18).

My interest here is less in Lewis's approach as literary theory than in its reflection of his emphasis on "real things" and his disinterest in selves—his own and the "personalities" of others. For part of what bothers Lewis in "personal" criticism is the subjective element it introduces into poetry:

> The personal theory will hold that the consciousness in question is that of the poet, considered as an individual, contingent, human specimen. Mr. Smith sees things in one way; Mr. Jones sees them in another; Mr. Wordsworth sees them in a third. What we share in reading Wordsworth is just Wordsworth's point of view as it happens to exist in him as a psychological fact. . . . (p. 15)

For Lewis, poetry is important and valuable to the extent that it is universal, not individual and subjective:

> It is absolutely essential that each word should suggest not what is private and personal to the poet but what is public, common, impersonal, objective. The common world with its nights, its oaks, and its stars, which we have all seen, and which mean at least *something* the same to all of us, is the bank on which he draws his cheques. (pp. 20–21)

One finds those universal qualities by giving attention not to the text itself but to the "real things" seen through the text—seen in a new way, for that is the value of poetry. "I myself, in reading [Herrick's 'Upon Julia's Clothes'], became conscious of silk in a new way. . . . The only experience which has any claim to be poetical experience is an apprehension, not of the poet, but of silk" (pp. 10–11).

Here, however, a troublesome aspect arises. Lewis is developing an "objective," "depersonalized" theory of poetry, one in which attention is fixed wholly on the essence of things and away from emotional or contextual attachments personal to the poet: "What is used for the poem is the significance which [things] have for every one; their objective characteristics as real elements in the drama of history" (p. 22). Attention is to be on "the thing itself," not an individual perception of the thing. But Lewis grants that the poem does not show the thing itself, only an image of it: "It may be true that what I am aware of in reading Herrick's poem is silk, but it is not silk as an object *in rerum natura*.

I see it as Herrick saw it" (p. 14). Lewis does not seem fully aware of the implications of that concession: one cannot have the kind of simple "objectivity" Lewis desires as a support for his "objective" view of reality. One cannot escape a subjective element in writing poetry, in reading it, or even in the very perception of "real things." It is an understanding Lewis begins to take into account in the fifties, and it gives *Till We Have Faces* depth and resonances his earlier work lacks. At this point, however, he avoids that subjective element by treating images as if they were objects *in rerum natura,* in spite of his qualification, and by assuming a sort of "readerless poetry" as a corollary to "poetless poetry."

Lewis's handling of imagery in poetry is related to the tendency in his early works to image Reality in concrete terms. That tendency appears here also, in his sentence "The first *object* presented to me is an *idea* of silk" (p. 10; italics added). Lewis's attempt to convey the externality of truth brings him dangerously close to Positivism's claim that only the sensory is real, though Positivism, ironically, seeks to deny the position Lewis was affirming. The same tendency is evident in a review of *Taliessin through Logres:* he writes that "Byzantium," in the poem, "is an imaginative net to catch that single, utterly concrete constituent of experience which has no name and which we come to know by using the symbol Byzantium."[6] Of course the constituent of experience he refers to is "concrete" only metaphorically; but the "utterly" denies the metaphor. As paradox, it works quite nicely; I suspect, however, that Lewis was not conscious of the paradox, or even of the metaphor itself, so intent was he on conveying the realness of the thing about which Williams wrote. Similarly, in the tenth of his radio talks, Lewis wrote that "the whole mass of Christians are literally the physical organism through which Christ acts."[7] He deleted "literally" when the talks were reprinted as *Mere Christianity*[8] and later apologized for its use, calling it "a vile journalistic cliche";[9] the problem caused by the word is less its hackneyed quality than its reliance on "concreteness" to convey reality. Such images may be an effect of Lewis's platonism, or his vividly visual imagination, or they may be rhetorical devices. In any case they tend to oversimplify the "objective" and to complicate the issue of how such reality is known.

Lewis does not discuss reading explicitly in "The Personal Heresy," but an objective, quasi-mechanical approach to reading is definitely implied as the standard of "good reading." The reader is to take in the objects imitated in the poem with as little personal interaction as possible; the metaphor he adopts later, of "receiving" the poem, like a radio set receiving signals, captures his sense well. In this essay he adopted the metaphors of a window and of eyeglasses—they are used for the poet rather than the poem, but the implications are the same for the act of reading:

> The poet is not a man who asks me to look at *him*; he is a man who says "look at that" and points; the more I follow the pointing of his finger the less I can possibly see of *him*. . . . To see things as the poet sees them I must share his consciousness and not attend to it; I must look where he looks and not turn round to face him; I must make of him not a spectacle but a pair of spectacles. (p. 15)

Behind such metaphors and such a conception of reading is the tendency to concretize the "objective" and to isolate it from the subjective element which is inevitably part of the acts of reading and perception. A reviewer of *The Personal Heresy* points out the ultimate inadequacy of Lewis's approach to reading: "To suggest, as Mr. Lewis does, that the personality is merely something like a window through which the writer looks upon the world, is to create an unnecessary and insoluble problem by enforcing a cleavage, tolerable only to abstract epistemology, between the subject and the object."[10] Such a cleavage between subject and object, between "seer" and "perceived," does not appear in *Till We Have Faces*—that is crucial to the handling of the key episodes of the work. But it will continue to be reflected in Lewis's metaphors for two decades more before he finds the conception inadequate.[11]

Several of Lewis's early literary essays are technical or textual, helping establish accurate literary texts, but those that are critical reflect the theory introduced in "The Personal Heresy." They often direct attention to the object presented by the work: love in Donne's poetry,[12] metals in *The Merchant of Venice*,[13] death in *Hamlet*,[14] and courtly love in the allegorical poetry of the Middle Ages.[15] Where they do not emphasize the object which the poem makes one see, they help one see things—such as the "medievalness" of *Troilus and Criseyde*, alliterative poetry, fifteenth-century heroic verse, the epic, and Christian theology[16]—the way the poet and the poet's contemporaries saw them. Lewis's finest achievement as a literary scholar, *The Allegory of Love*, deals with literature of the Middle Ages, an ideal subject for one who wanted to work "objectively." Much of the poetry is anonymous; where authorship is known, little biographical information is available, and what is available is not of a kind to encourage speculation about the personality of the writer. Attention, therefore, must be directed toward the work. And the work is so far removed from twentieth-century life that response is quite naturally directed toward the universal images and themes Lewis preferred.

The tension between reason and imagination evident in the early poetry and the emphasis on the concreteness of reality shown in the early criticism are reflected also in Lewis's first published narrative work, *The Pilgrim's Regress*, which appeared in 1933, only two years after the conversation with Tolkien and Dyson. *The Pilgrim's Regress* is an allegory embodying an autobiographical account of Lewis's own religious and intellectual pilgrimage toward his recent experience with Christianity. But it is more than just personal: it is in part a sketch of the cultural and philosophical landscape of the late nineteenth and early twentieth centuries and in particular of those attitudes and movements which Lewis saw as antithetical to Christianity.

The Pilgrim's Regress is the account of a journey to salvation, and especially of the role of longing, "sweet desire," *Sehnsucht*, what Lewis later came to call "Joy" but here calls Romanticism, in the pursuit of that journey. *Sehnsucht* supplies the underlying unifying structure for the narrative and is Lewis's chief interest, as the book's epigraph indicates: "As cold waters to a thirsty soul, so is good news from a far country."[17] The central character, John, experiences "Sweet Desire" in his youth, and his life thereafter is a quest westward, to locate the island which is his personal image of the object of his desire. Along the way he experiments with a series of substitutes for that real object of desire: lust (brown girls), romantic poetry (Mr. Halfways), and the frivolity of the twenties (the Clevers); each of these objects soon reveals its falsity, but John takes each as further evidence that something real must exist as the true object of his desire, and presses on to find it.

More dangerous to John than the false objects, however, are those philosophies which would explain away his longings and induce him to abandon his quest. In these the allegory presents a brief survey of late nineteenth- and early twentieth-century philosophical movements, each summarized pithily and creatively in the words or conduct of a character or group of characters. There is nineteenth-century rationalism (Mr. Enlightenment), which uses scientific explanations to dismiss religion and longing; Freudianism (the Spirit of the Age), which accounts for his longing as wish-fulfillment; cultured worldliness (Mr. Sensible), which tames religion and turns it into a civilizing virtue; counter-romanticism (Mr. Neo-Angular, Mr. Neo-Classical, and Mr. Humanist), which rejects spiritual and emotional experiences generally as "graceful veil[s] of illusion"; and Philosophical Idealism, which covers more of the facts than any system John had yet encountered, but which calls John's quest and search for a real or personal object of desire only picture-writing or beautiful metaphors which must be appreciated for their beauty, not mistaken for reality.

As John decides to live by Idealism and to accept the Absolute, philosophy turns into religion and a personal god, and he becomes a Theist. History then shows John that there was really a divine element in his romanticism all along—that it, along with moral law and elements of pagan mythology, are means God uses to draw people to himself. John yields up his struggle against Mother Kirk (Christianity), dives into her pool (symbolic of baptism, death of self), and emerges, reborn, to discover that the object of his longings is not really an island but the heavenly home of his early religious training. He must, therefore, regress—must go back to the East, must live out his Christian life among the people and ideas he had moved through on his way to Christianity, until he reaches the river of physical death, which will finally unite him with that which he desired all along.

The Pilgrim's Regress resembles *Till We Have Faces* in a number of ways. Masks are used in both stories, and those in *The Pilgrim's Regress* can help illuminate those of *Till We Have Faces*. Masks in *The Pilgrim's Regress* are the symbol of conventional religious attitudes and practices. When John first meets the Steward, symbol of the clergy or church officialdom, they have a good talk about fishing tackle and bicycles. "But just when the talk was at its best, the Steward got up and cleared his throat. He then took down a mask from the wall with a long white beard attached to it and suddenly clapped it on his face, so that his appearance was awful. And he said, 'Now I am going to talk to you about the Landlord' " (I, i). Later, when John and his family escort his Uncle George toward the river of death, they all put on masks which enable them to handle the situation, except Uncle George: "They wanted to put a mask on Uncle George, but he was trembling so that it would not stay on. So they had to see his face as it was; and his face became so dreadful that everyone looked in a different direction and pretended not to see it" (I, iii).[18] One is reminded of the mask worn by the Priest of Ungit, of his temple girls with "their faces painted till they looked like wooden masks" (p. 42), and of Psyche on her way to the Sacred Mountain, "her eyes, peering out of the heavy, lifeless mask which they had made of her face" (p. 80). The image in both works depicts the proper approach to the gods as impersonal, through the set formulas of organized religion in its least lively and living form, and in both cases that way is shown to be limited and inadequate. Lewis affirms that one must encounter the gods in a personal way, face to face; and one cannot do so while wearing masks of conventionality, deception, or pride.

Thus John in *The Pilgrim's Regress*, like Orual in *Till We Have Faces*, must remove his clothes, emblems of his

defenses and reliance upon himself: "He began, nevertheless, to take off his clothes. They were little loss to him, for
they hung in shreds, plastered with blood and with the grime
of every shire from Puritania to the canyon: but they were
so stuck to him that they came away with pain and a little
skin came with them" (IX, iv). Like Orual, he must present
his true self, without pretenses or defenses, in order to establish a genuine relation with God. And as in *Till We Have
Faces* a key theme is that acceptance by God requires dying
"before you die." John approaches Mother Kirk with the
words, "I have come to give myself up" (IX, iv). He is told
he must dive into the water; he must not jump and thus rely
on himself, but let go of himself, "abandon all efforts at self-
preservation." In the previous chapter he confronted Death
and was told "the cure of death is dying. He who lays down
his liberty in that act receives it back" (IX, iii). Now he must
act upon what he was told, and in diving, in dying to self,
he, like Orual, finds new life.

Also, in both *Till We Have Faces* and *The Pilgrim's Regress,* the central personality in the story is divided between
two characters who must be brought together. The rational
but especially the emotional aspects of the central person-
age of *The Pilgrim's Regress* are represented by John, while
his moral aspect is embodied in the character Vertue: these
are the personal equivalents of Sweet Desire and the Rules,
of the Pagans and the Shepherds [Israel]. On the personal
and the general levels, the two must be unified; so History
instructs John: "The truth is that a Shepherd is only half a
man, and a Pagan is only half a man, so that neither people
was well without the other. . . . And even so, my son, you
will not be well until you have overtaken your fellow trav-
eller [Vertue] who slept in my cell last night" (VIII, viii).
Thus in both books a central aim is to show the need for
combining desire and reason in the religious experience. In
Till We Have Faces Orual must unite Psyche's longings with
the clarity of thought and understanding they learned from
the Fox. That this was also Lewis's theme in *The Pilgrim's
Regress* is indicated by the subtitle: *An Allegorical Apology
for Christianity Reason and Romanticism.* In the Preface he

added later he says that the "lived dialectic [of pursuing Desire beyond its false objects to the true one], and the merely argued dialectic of my philosophical progress, seemed to have converged on one goal; accordingly I tried to put them both into my allegory which thus became a defence of Romanticism (in my peculiar sense) as well as of Reason and Christianity."[19] That union occurs in *Till We Have Faces* also.

Differences between the two books are equally striking and in some cases even more important than the similarities. One difference involves *seeing*. Sight is an important motif in *The Pilgrim's Regress,* but its handling is based on Lewis's emphasis at that point on a nonsubjective approach to reality. As in *Till We Have Faces,* one character may see something which another character does not: "When [John] sat of an evening with his father and mother, a brown girl, visible only to him, would sidle in and sit at his feet" (I, vi). The girl is visible only to him because she is an illusion, a sexual fantasy which he now must fight against constantly, a barrier to perceiving reality. The same thing is true after John and Vertue reach the extreme West and begin their return journey. "I should warn you of one thing," their Guide tells them; "the country will look very different on the return journey" (IX, vi). It will look different because their vision of reality previously was blocked by "veils" of illusion like those of *Spirits in Bondage* and *Dymer.* Veils are used repeatedly in *The Pilgrim's Regress* to distract attention from the subjective, to suggest that perception is a mechanical process, which can be disrupted by "external" means. Thus Humanist talks of throwing a "graceful veil of illusion" over the truths of Mr. Sensible and the giant (VI, iv), and thus the Divine voice says that pagan myth "is the veil under which I have chosen to appear even from the first until now" (IX, v). Lewis, in guarding against a very real danger in subjectivity, puts emphasis on the constancy of the object—objects can be perceived as they really are so long as fantasies or delusions do not hinder one's sight, as they had hindered John's and Vertue's previously. Now, the Guide tells them as they set out, "you are seeing the land as it really is" (X, i), with the "veils" removed. And as Vertue looks for Mr. Sensible's house, Slikisteinsauga explains, "It is just as it was when you passed it before, . . . but your eyes are altered. You see nothing now but realities" (X, ii). What they had seen before were illusions, or appearances which deceived them; those now have been stripped away so that they apprehend "the real shape" of things, as Lewis put it in the running headline he added to the 1943 edition to explain the allegory.[20] He acknowledges that impediments to sight are possible, but not that a subjective element is inevitably involved.

A second major difference between *The Pilgrim's Regress* and *Till We Have Faces* is that the emphasis in the earlier work is on the acceptance of Christianity by the understanding and the will; myth and imagination are much less important than they will be in *Till We Have Faces*. *The Pilgrim's Regress* is, of course, an apology for Romanticism as well as Reason, but longing appears as that which draws John to the place or person from whom he can learn the truth. Intellectual barriers are removed systematically and first Theism, then Christianity, become convincing and unavoidable. The very form of the work suggests that Lewis's ultimate faith, at this point, is in the intellect. He writes in allegory, which of all literary forms has the greatest tendency to rely on the intellect for completion of its meaning and effect. In his Preface Lewis does assert that "when allegory is at its best, it approaches myth, which must be grasped with the imagination, not with the intellect."[21] But Lewis's allegory is far from the best; he is unable to embody his material in images and events sufficiently to make it directly apprehendable by the imagination. His real faith is in explanation, in intellect, so he depends on long passages of philosophical discussion to convey the book's themes. To some extent, of course, the failure to rely sufficiently on images and symbols may be attributed to lack of experience in writing prose fiction. But ability and approach cannot be entirely divorced from inclination. Lewis chose to write allegory, one assumes, partly because he was dealing with allegory regularly as he worked during that time on *The*

Allegory of Love; but he also chose it because it seemed the best vehicle to do what he wanted to do, to convey what he wanted to say, and we must conclude, then, that the emphasis on intellectual acceptance of the truth was central to that purpose.

That his attitude toward imagination and myth was more limited in *The Pilgrim's Regress* than it later became is confirmed by the neglect in *The Pilgrim's Regress* of a theme central in *Till We Have Faces,* the theme of sacrifice. It is not that the theme had not yet assumed importance to Lewis: he made it a central theme of *Dymer,* before his conversion, and he identified it as a turning point in the conversion itself. Its neglect in *The Pilgrim's Regress* is a further evidence that Lewis's emphasis in this work is on the intellect. Despite all the definitions and clarifications of Romanticism in the added Preface, despite the importance of Sweet Desire in drawing John from his home and to salvation, Lewis's emphasis in his first effort to communicate publicly about his conversion is on the journey to the acceptance of Theism, a largely intellectual process. The remaining distance, that covered by acknowledgment of the place of sacrifice and substitution, which as he learned from Tolkien and Dyson are best dealt with through myth and received through the imagination, is neglected in *The Pilgrim's Regress*—in striking contrast to *Till We Have Faces,* where just those aspects are emphasized. In *The Pilgrim's Regress,* as Kathryn Lindskoog puts it, "Reason is a great heroine";[22] she is by no means a villainness in *Till We Have Faces*—Psyche herself, who embodies longings and divine insight, acknowledges the importance of the Fox's approach: "It'd be dark as a dungeon within me but for his teaching" (p. 70). But Reason does not have the strong influence on form, style, and tone in *Till We Have Faces* that it has in *The Pilgrim's Regress.*

A further confirmation of Lewis's limitations on myth at this point appears in the book's explicit remarks on myth. As John goes through the caverns of death to self, Wisdom appears to him to say that this adventure is only figurative, only an enactment of the old myths of descent and ascent,

death and rebirth. He is answered by the voice of Mother
Kirk, or more likely of Christ himself:

> "Child, if you will, it *is* mythology. It is but truth, not fact: an
> image, not the very real. But then it is My mythology. The
> words of Wisdom are also myth and metaphor: but since they
> do not know themselves for what they are, in them the hidden
> myth is master, where it should be servant: and it is but of
> man's inventing. But this is My inventing, this is the veil
> under which I have chosen to appear even from the first until
> now. For this end I made your senses and for this end your
> imagination, that you might see my face and live. What would
> you have? Have you not heard among the Pagans the story
> of Semele? Or was there any age in any land when men did
> not know that corn and wine were the blood and body of a
> dying and yet living God?" (IX, v)

Lewis's distinction in the second sentence is perplexing, for
a decade later, in "Myth Became Fact," he would write, "What
flows into you from the myth is not truth but reality."[23]
Either Lewis was being unusually careless with terminology, or there is a shift in emphasis, a clarification or refine-
ment in his thinking about myth, between the mid–1930s
and the mid–1940s. The evidence, considered chronologi-
cally, points to the latter. The passage in *The Pilgrim's Regress* closely resembles the letter to Greeves, which was
written only two years earlier and thus provides a better
basis for understanding *The Pilgrim's Regress* than does an
essay written ten years later. There is, for example, the
same distinction between God's myth and men's myths, and
a striking similarity in wording between "the way in which
God chooses to (or can) appear to our faculties" and "the veil
under which I have chosen to appear even from the first
until now." Most importantly, however, in the letter to
Greeves as in *The Pilgrim's Regress,* the emphasis is on the
truth of myth. It is not truth as abstract formulations, the
way it is used in the later essay, so the two positions are not
contradictory. But there is a definite and deliberate asser-
tion that myths are not just falsehoods or errors, perpetrated
by pagans; rather, myth contains truth and is one of the
means by which God reveals himself to the world. Later, in
reflecting back on his schooling, Lewis says that he was

taught the pagan myths were utterly false, "a mere farrago of nonsense." "No one ever attempted to show in what sense Christianity fulfilled Paganism or Paganism prefigured Christianity."[24] In his writings about myth following his conversion, Lewis seems intent on countering that misconception. As yet there is no attempt to describe myth as a "tasting" of Reality, as there will be in "Myth Became Fact"; first must come the emphasis on the value and acceptability of myth because of its basis in truth.

That this was his intent comes out explicitly in a long footnote on myth in *Miracles*. It was written, apparently, in 1943 or 1944, about the same time as "Myth Became Fact," though it retains the emphases of *The Pilgrim's Regress*. Lewis specifies that myth cannot be dismissed in the terms his schoolmasters had used: "Myth in general is not merely misunderstood history . . . nor diabolical illusion . . . nor priestly lying." Rather, myth is "a real though unfocussed gleam of divine truth falling on human imagination." It is one of the means God used to reveal himself: the mythology of the Hebrews was "the mythology chosen by God to be the vehicle of the earliest sacred truths."[25] Less than a year later, Lewis writes that myth is related to reality, not truth; but there he has moved on to deal with a different threat, that of abstraction, and "truth" is used in a different sense from that in the letter to Greeves, *The Pilgrim's Regress, Miracles,* and "Is Theology Poetry?"[26] The point is that he has moved on—there is a definite shift of attention, a growth of conception, from the earlier emphasis on myth as revealing truth, to the later emphasis on myth as affording a "taste" of reality.

Lewis's linking of truth with myth derives directly from his manner of imaging the "objective." Myth, in the terms of *The Pilgrim's Regress,* is neither "fact" (the scientific or historical—dealt with by reason) nor "the very real" (the concrete—apprehended by the senses); it is, rather, "truth" or "an image"—to be grasped with the imagination. The distinctions, the relationships, the implied lower status of myth, since it is "but truth" and only "an image," are difficult to reconcile with Lewis's later ideas. But Lewis is driven to all this by "concreteness." "Reality" is superior to "meaning" and "image" because reality exists, whether it has meaning for anyone or not, whereas an image is but a reflection of the "real"; and reason ranks above imagination because the former deals with "real things," the latter only with images. Myth, therefore, remains limited: it is a veil, something one must ultimately get past if one is to experience reality.

The conclusion of the passage in *The Pilgrim's Regress* also is similar to the letter to Greeves: for salvation one needs both "real things" ("the actual incarnation, crucifixion, and resurrection") and myth (which shows the significance of those things). And both are emphasized by the Divine voice's words: "For this end I made your senses [to see and taste real corn and wine] and for this end your imagination [to bring out their significance, that they are the blood and body of a dying and yet living God]." All this, "that you might see my face and live": that you might accept the incarnation, crucifixion, and resurrection as the complete revelation of God and be saved. The final phrase contains a biblical allusion, to Exodus 33, where Moses was talking to God on Mount Sinai: "Moses said, 'I pray thee, show me thy glory. . . .' [The Lord] said, 'you cannot see my face; for man shall not see me and live' " (vv. 18, 20). Lewis's alteration of the biblical phrase seems to reflect the difference between the Old Testament situation and that which follows the incarnation. Before the incarnation God appeared behind the veil of myth, as he hid his full glory from Moses: "And the Lord said, . . . 'I will cover you with my hand until I have passed by; then I will take away my hand, and you shall see my back; but my face shall not be seen' " (33:21–23). Lewis's "see my face" suggests the fuller knowledge of God available, through myth and fact, after the incarnation. There are close similarities between "that you might see my face and live" and "how can they meet us face to face till we have faces": the imagery is the same, both draw upon the tradition of the danger confronting a mortal who comes into the presence of a god, and both allude to the same chapter in Exodus.[27] The similarities demonstrate the continuity of central elements of the *Till We Have Faces* myth throughout Lewis's life. But the differences are equally important. The emphasis in the earlier passage, in its allegorical form as well as in the ideas expressed, is on understanding, on the "seeing," in keeping with Lewis's sense of myth at the time. The emphasis in the later one, however, is on the experience, the "meeting," the "tasting" of Reality central to the broader and more adequate conception of myth he developed later.

The conversation with Tolkien and Dyson, important as it was to Lewis's conversion, did not resolve the tension between reason and imagination. Lewis continued, after his conversion as before it, to appreciate the imagination greatly, but to put his final trust in reason. Thus, although Lewis enjoyed reading fantasies, plunging into imaginative worlds wholly different from and separate from our world, he held back, in his own stories, from the commitment to the imagination required for pure fantasy. So it was in *The Pilgrim's Regress*; so it is also in the first book of his "space trilogy," *Out of the Silent Planet*. It enables one to visit, imaginatively, the strange region of Malacandra, "in search of such beauty, awe, or terror as the actual world does not supply," which made stories of fantasy or science fiction appealing to Lewis.[28] In this case a character with the moral and social presuppositions of our world encounters a world with different assumptions and values, a world which is truly a community, where beings very different from each other are able to cooperate and live in harmony. The narrative, however, is not left to convey those themes on its own. The conceptual truths which underlie the story are spelled out in statement form, in the account of the war in heaven at the time of Satan's rebellion[29] and in the extended conversation between the Oyarsa and Weston, with Ransom as interpreter.[30] Lewis's perhaps unconscious penchant for and ultimate reliance upon the conceptual comes through as he comments on the story to a correspondent: "Any amount of theology can now be smuggled into people's minds under cover of romance without their knowing it."[31] The emphasis on the imaginative as *useful* to the conceptual stands in striking contrast to the method of Tolkien, and to Lewis's own later method in *Till We Have Faces*.

Tolkien, in his important essay "On Fairy-Stories," glories in the imagination's "freedom from the domination of observed 'fact.' " The quality Tolkien called Fantasy, or the imaginative in its fullest sense, creates

> images of things that are not only "not actually present," but which are indeed not to be found in our primary world at all, or are generally believed not to be found there. . . . That the images are of things not in the primary world (if that indeed is possible) is a virtue not a vice. Fantasy (in this sense) is, I think, not a lower but a higher form of Art, indeed the most nearly perfect form, and so (when achieved) the most potent.[32]

Tolkien stresses that separateness because he believed that the farther stories are removed from our world, the better they can convey "a sudden glimpse of the underlying reality or truth."[33] Thus Tolkien carefully distanced his stories from the worlds of everyday reality and wrote pure fantasy, never allegory. Lewis avoids such a total removal from our world, because of his attachment to "everyday reality or truth," embodied for him in the "objective." Tolkien also held an objective view of truth, but he did not need to embody the objective in something from the knowable world to give it stability, as Lewis seems to in his early stories: thus Lewis turns to allegory, with its overt pointers to our world; or uses human characters and earthly departure points to ground his story in the "knowable" world; or includes expository passages to assure that intended significance not be lost.

Valuable as Lewis regarded myth, and great as was the appeal of imagination to him, he was unable to give himself to it fully. His early grounding in rationalism and his need for the stability of the "object" create a tension in him between reason and the imagination, and a constraint upon the imaginative, not in theory but in practice. That he will use the rational without the mythical but not the mythical without the rational shows, if not a preference for the latter, at least a greater trust in it, which will increase in the apologetic works of the 1940s before it is reversed in *Till We Have Faces* in the 1950s.

XII

Apologist of the Forties: Reason as Master

*T*HE 1940s were a richly productive period for Lewis. In addition to twelve books, there were scholarly essays, regular contributions to religious periodicals, book reviews, prefaces, poems, scholarly talks, talks to the Royal Air Force, radio talks, sermons, letters to newspapers and magazines—and a growing correspondence. A survey of the entire output would not be pertinent to the interests of this book. Rather, this chapter will demonstrate Lewis's increasing skill at and commitment to the use of reason in the apologetic books of the period, and, at the same time, point to an important enlargement of his ideas about myth and the place of the imagination. Imagination and reason intermingle throughout the decade—some of his most carefully reasoned pieces are also strongly imaginative, in language and conception, and the imaginative writings always rely also on reason. But an element of tension remains, as evidenced by the narrative works, particularly *The Great Divorce*. The increasing confidence in the power of reason in the forties dramatizes how great the change to an imaginative emphasis in the fifties was, even as the increasing interest in and broadened understanding of the mythical prepares for that shift.

Because reason contributed significantly in drawing Lewis to Christianity, it is not surprising that Lewis's early emphasis in writing about Christianity is in the field of apologetics, reasoned efforts to demonstrate the truth of the faith. The three major apologetic works display growing skillfulness in the handling of dialectic, and increasing reliance upon dialectic as a method. Each of the three presents an argument on its specific topic—suffering, guilt, miracles—but each also offers a proof of the existence of God, and it is the latter particularly that shows a growing confidence in the adequacy of reason. In a letter to Dom Bede Griffiths in 1938, Lewis wrote, "As to whether reason can rigorously prove God and immortality, what is one to say? I do not remember to have seen a proof that appeared to me absolutely compelling, but that may be only *my* reason or the writer's reason: At any rate it is obvious that pure reason, in human beings, is very often in fact not convinced."[1] In spite of that, he puts increasing effort into such proofs and eventually speaks of them, in *Miracles,* as if they were entirely compelling.

The tone of the case presented in *The Problem of Pain* is quite in keeping with the comments of that letter. In the opening chapter, which presents the case, Lewis states, "In what follows it must be understood that I am not *primarily* arguing the truth of Christianity but describing its origin."[2] He goes on to discuss the numinous and the universal moral law, the combination of the two in the Jews, and the union of that background with the historical events surrounding the life of Christ; he then mixes in some hard argument:

> The fourth strand or element is a historical event. There was a man born among these Jews who claimed to be, or to be the son of, or to be "one with," the Something which is at once the awful haunter of nature and the giver of the moral law. The claim is so shocking—a paradox, and even a horror, which we may easily be lulled into taking too lightly—that only two views of this man are possible. Either he was a raving lunatic of an unusually abominable type, or else He was, and is, precisely what He said. There is no middle way. If the records make the first hypothesis unacceptable, you must submit to the second. (pp. 11–12)

The passage may well be "arguing the truth of" rather than just "describing"; perhaps the disclaimer itself, that it is *primarily* describing rather than arguing, is itself a rhetorical ploy, designed to help cover the gap reason cannot fill. Lewis makes the best case he can, but knowing that reason alone is insufficient to establish the existence of God, he carefully acknowledges that the case is not intended to be sufficient.

As he moves on to deal with pain itself, he uses reason and argument to meet and deal with a problem which long had haunted him: "If God is *good,* why does he allow so much suffering in the world?"[3] He proceeds to clarify the nature of God's power and of his goodness, and reconciles them with the existence of pain as a part of a fallen world and as a means of drawing people away from the false appeal of that world: "We can rest contentedly in our sins and in our stupidities. . . . But pain insists upon being attended to. God whispers to us in our pleasures, speaks in our conscience, but shouts in our pains: it is His megaphone to rouse a deaf world" (p. 81; Ch. 6).

The procedure is highly systematic, with orderly outlines—numbered series of the various types of love and of the different explanations used by people to deal gently with the reality of wickedness, for example—and carefully shaped arguments. Because of its systematic nature and its inclusiveness, extending to a chapter on hell, another on heaven, and one on animal pain, the book is a valuable source of, even introduction to, Lewis's ideas on and approaches to a wide range of issues. It contains many moving, beautifully written passages, like the one quoted just above. And it anticipates *Till We Have Faces* a number of times, as in its lengthy discussion of death to self ("to surrender a self-will inflamed and swollen with years of usurpation is a kind of death"—p. 79; Ch. 6) and its repeated use of the "veil" image: "No doubt Pain as God's megaphone is a terrible instrument; it may lead to final and unrepented rebellion. But it gives the only opportunity the bad man can have for amendment. It removes the veil; it plants the flag of truth within the fortress of a rebel soul" (p. 83; Ch. 6).

There is very little use, yet, of the analogies which later become almost the defining characteristic of his apologetic style. Through example, authority, and explanation, he simply tries to lay out a convincing case, a case which will make a reader "see" and thus accept the truth.

The logical approach is strong also in the first series of radio talks Lewis delivered on the BBC in 1941 and subsequently published in *Broadcast Talks*.[4] His explicit purpose in those talks is to convey to a twentieth-century audience a sense of guilt or sin. It was in these terms that he described his proposed topic to Dr. James W. Welch of the BBC:

> I think what I mainly want to talk about is the Law of Nature, or objective right and wrong. It seems to me that the New Testament, by preaching repentance and forgiveness, always *assumes* an audience who already believe in the Law of Nature and know they have disobeyed it. . . . The first step is to create, or recover, the sense of guilt. Hence if I give a series of talks I should mention Christianity only at the end, and would prefer not to unmask my battery till then.[5]

A few years later, in an essay entitled "Difficulties in Presenting the Christian Faith to Modern Unbelievers," he returned to the same issue:

> The [second] greatest barrier I have met [in presenting the Christian Faith to modern unbelievers] is the almost total absence from the minds of my audience of any sense of sin. . . . The early Christian preachers could assume in their hearers, whether Jews, *Metuentes* or Pagans, a sense of guilt. . . . Thus the Christian message was in those days unmistakably the *Evangelium*, the Good News. It promised healing to those who knew they were sick. We have to convince our hearers of the unwelcome diagnosis before we can expect them to welcome the news of the remedy.[6]

Although he mentions, in the essay, the need for "awakening the sense of sin" in people, his method in *Broadcast Talks* is not to create feelings of guilt in his listeners. Rather, he seeks to demonstrate in logical fashion the need for repentance in human beings over their failure to live in accord with their knowledge of the right and wrong they know exists.

The method he employs in pursuing that purpose is empirical and logical. He begins with observation (listen "to the kind of things [people] say," like " 'that's my seat, I was there first' ") and proceeds to inference: "It looks . . . very much as if both parties had in mind some kind of Law or

Rule of fair play or decent behaviour or morality or whatever you like to call it, about which they really agreed. And they have" (p. 9; Bk. I, Ch. 1). This Rule of Right and Wrong is a real thing, outside of and separate from human beings and not simply made up by them: "A real law which we didn't invent and which we know we ought to obey" (p. 24; Bk. I, Ch. 4). That failure to obey perfectly puts human beings at odds with whatever power is behind the universe and made up the law. Only when Lewis reaches this point is he willing to bring in Christianity and admit that to be his "real subject":

> Christianity simply doesn't make sense until you've faced the sort of facts I've been describing. Christianity tells people to repent and promises them forgiveness. It therefore has nothing (as far as I know) to say to people who don't know they've done anything to repent of and who don't feel that they need any forgiveness. It's after you've realised that there is a real Moral Law, and a Power behind the law, and that you have broken that law and put yourself wrong with that Power— it's *after* all that that Christianity begins to talk. (p. 32; Bk. I, Ch. 5)

In his letter to Dr. Welch, Lewis wrote, "In modern England we cannot at present assume [a sense of sin], and therefore most apologetic begins a stage too far on."[7] His central purpose in the first half of *Broadcast Talks* is to go back to the prior stage and lay the proper foundation for further evangelization.

A secondary purpose in the talks, however, is readily discernible: he uses the existence of moral law as a basis not only for bringing out the reality of sin, but also for a proof of the existence of "a Power behind the law." The proof begins with the existence of an objective moral law: "It begins to look as if we'll have to admit that there's more than one kind of reality; that, in this particular case, there's something above and beyond the ordinary facts of men's behaviour, and yet quite definitely real—a real law, which none of us made, but which we find pressing on us" (p. 23; Bk. I, Ch. 3). It moves then to the origin or source of that law: either the universe and its moral laws just happened by chance, or there is something behind them, something "more like a mind than it's like anything else we know," something which is "conscious, and has purposes, and prefers one thing to another" (pp. 27, 24; Bk. I, Ch. 4). That Something appears "in me as a law urging me to do right and making me feel responsible and uncomfortable when I do wrong" (p. 27; Bk. I, Ch. 4). From the universe and from the moral law, one should conclude that there is a Lawgiver and that the Lawgiver is a being "intensely interested in right conduct—in fair play, unselfishness, and decency" (p. 30; Bk. I, Ch. 5).

Surely Lewis was as aware then as a year or two earlier of a gap which reason cannot bridge, but the argument, or rhetoric, does not allow for it explicitly, as it did in *The Problem of Pain*—on the contrary, it seeks to distract attention from such a gap. This appears first in the movement from law to Lawgiver. The existence of an inner moral sense, after being used as the proof for existence of a universal moral law, is used also as the evidence of a Lawgiver: "The only way in which we could expect [a Power behind the law] to show itself would be inside *us* as an influence or a command trying to get us to behave in a certain way. And that's just what we do find inside us" (p. 26; Bk. I, Ch. 4). Thus the argument is this: if there were a Power behind the law, it would be evident within us as an inner moral sense; there is evidence of such an inner moral sense; so there must be a Power behind the law. But such reasoning assumes what it must prove. The existence of an inner moral sense, though it may be evidence for a universal moral law, is not in itself evidence of anything concerning the origin of that law.

To say this is not to deny or diminish the value of the radio talks as a whole. Lewis's initial purpose, of awakening a sense of personal moral responsibility in the modern world, is as timely and necessary in the 1980s as it was in the 1940s, if not more so. His exposition of the atonement, of various facets of Christian ethics, and of the transforming power of Christianity in the three series which follow is clear, powerful, and memorable. Perhaps one needs only to assume, as one reads the argument for the existence of God, that the qualifiers in the letter to Griffiths and in *The Prob-*

lem of Pain are operative here as well: it will then appear not as a proof for God, but as a valuable instance of the use of reason to do as much as reason can do, and should do— even must do—in supporting belief in God. The failure to make such qualifiers explicit may be a result of compression due to time constraints, or simply Lewis's thinking that they would be taken for granted. Or it may be a signal that he is beginning to regard them as less necessary because of his increasing confidence in the adequacy of the proofs he presents. *Miracles* suggests it may well be the latter.

Miracles also has a two-level argument, for the existence of God and for the possibility of miracle, but in this case the two are closely intertwined: the latter position is based upon the former one. The interdependence is clear from the definition of miracle: "An interference with Nature by supernatural power."[8] The reliance on reason is heightened by this interdependence, and by the philosophical nature of the issue: Lewis stresses that it is a study "preliminary to historical inquiry" (p. 13; Ch. 1). It is not an attempt to prove that miracles have actually occurred historically, but an effort to clear away obstacles which hinder or prevent belief in the miraculous: "The result of our historical enquiries ... depends on the philosophical views which we have been holding before we even began to look at the evidence. The philosophical question must therefore come first" (p. 12; Ch. 1). Because the proof for God is not a supplementary issue but the foundation upon which the central investigation rests, Lewis is forced to a greater emphasis upon reason here than in his earlier apologetic works.

The central difference between *Miracles* and the two earlier apologetic works is its detailed refutation of Naturalism. Its inadequacy was assumed, or mentioned, in the others, but not demonstrated successfully, as it is here in what Lewis called "The Self-Contradiction of the Naturalist." Naturalism believes that Nature is independent and self-existent, "a vast process in space and time which is *going on of its own accord*" (p. 16; Ch. 2)—and that "nothing else exists" (p. 19; Ch. 2). But, Lewis goes on, if anything else exists which has an independent existence, Naturalism

134

would be refuted. And, for Naturalists to argue the truth of Naturalism is, in fact, evidence of the existence of one such thing, reason: "All possible knowledge . . . depends on the validity of reasoning, . . . and we must not believe in anything inconsistent with its validity" (p. 26; Ch. 3). But Naturalism is based on such an inconsistency, for it ascribes nonrational origins to rationality: thought is merely a product of physical processes within the Total System, which "is not supposed to be rational" (p. 28; Ch. 3). Lewis concludes that the position of the Naturalist is self-contradictory:

> Each particular thought is valueless if it is the result of irrational causes. Obviously, then, the whole process of human thought, what we call Reason, is equally valueless if it is the result of irrational causes. Hence every theory of the universe which makes the human mind a result of irrational causes is inadmissible, for it would be a proof that there are no such things as proofs. Which is nonsense. (p. 28; Ch. 3)

To posit a theory by which the universe is known is thus to grant that reason exists on its own, independent of Nature. And since existence "on one's own" means what Supernaturalists attribute to God, reason must be a product of "an eternal, self-existent rational Being, whom we call God" (p. 36; Ch. 4). That such a Being exists, however, does not mean that there would necessarily be "interference with Nature" by that Being. The rest of the book—after a supplementary refutation of Naturalism on the basis of moral judgments and a handling of difficulties—argues for the possibility and propriety of such interferences.

It is a tight and carefully articulated argument, much more thorough, subtle, and precise than a summary can indicate. But it too leaves the unavoidable gap, for Lewis does not actually establish in positive terms the existence of reason, which is the foundation of his proof of God. The entire argument builds on the self-contradictoriness of developing a theory by which to know the universe without granting the independent existence of reason. But perhaps it cannot be known: Skepticism remains, at least in theory, a possible alternative to Naturalism and Supernaturalism. The case leaves open the possibility that the Total System of Naturalism is indeed all that is, but that we could not know it or know anything about it. Lewis shows that Naturalism can offer no substantive arguments against reason; but a negative proof is not the same as a positive one. Thus when he says "If any thought is valid, such a Reason must exist . . ." (p. 36; Ch. 4), we are inclined to accept the conditional clause as self-evident, but it has not been proved.

I mention what appears to me a gap in Lewis's discussion not to undermine or disparage it as an argument: its value to readers does not depend on the absence of such a gap. My interest, rather, is what his failure to acknowledge such a gap suggests about Lewis himself at that point. He makes claims for reason here which exceed those he makes elsewhere. In Chapter 3, for example, there is his perplexing claim, quoted above, that "all possible knowledge . . . depends on the validity of reasoning." This contradicts Lewis's acceptance, in other works, of authority and revelation as means of knowledge,[9] and it clashes with Chapter 6, where mystical knowledge is allowed as a source of knowledge about God (p. 52). There are, later, further unqualified expressions of confidence in the adequacy of his approach: "I do not maintain," he notes in Chapter 4, "that God's creation of Nature can be proved as rigorously as God's existence" (p. 42); and in Chapter 6 he reminds the reader that "Human Reason and Morality have been mentioned not as instances of Miracle . . . but as proofs of the Supernatural" (p. 54). All this suggests that in the course of writing *Miracles* Lewis became so enrapt in the case he was developing and, momentarily, so captivated by reason itself that he forgot about its limitations and believed he had constructed the "absolutely compelling" case he had earlier despaired of. If that is correct, it would help account for the sense of surprise and defeat attributed to him when the case was attacked by another Christian; but it would also suggest the possibility of an element of satisfaction, almost of pride in his achievement, shortly to be humbled: an experience which could well have enriched the writings on Christianity in the decade ahead.

About the same time Lewis was involved in thinking

through the closely reasoned argument of *Miracles,* he was also giving a great deal of thought to myth, out of which came the altered emphasis and enlarged perspective of his valuable essay of 1944, "Myth Became Fact." The new perspective was not a sudden realization that Christianity combines the mythical and the historical: that goes back as far as the letter to Greeves and is stressed in *Miracles* and "Is Theology Poetry?" The new element seems to have grown out of his reflection upon a real or imagined dispute with a real or imaginary "Corineus," a spokesman for the modernist view that the old mythological elements of Christianity should be dropped so that Christians will focus instead on the theological "essentials." As Lewis's earlier perspective was a response to those who dismiss myth as error or falsehood, so the perspective in "Myth Became Fact" is a response to those who dismiss myth as outdated imagery which detracts from the enduring principles which underlie it. It is not that he has rejected the perspective of *The Pilgrim's Regress:* he still would insist that myth is truth, not falsehood; nor is the approach in "Myth Became Fact" wholly new: what he now emphasizes was implicit in his previous statements, but had not yet crystallized, and its deeper, richer significance had not yet become apparent to him.

He begins, in "Myth Became Fact," by asserting that without the mythical, religion lacks the element which enables one to *experience* it as reality: "It is the myth which is the vital and nourishing element in the whole concern. . . . It is the myth that gives life. Those elements even in modernist Christianity which Corineus regards as vestigial, are the substance: what he takes for the 'real modern belief' is the shadow." To emphasize myth's expansiveness and vitality, Lewis contrasts it with the limitations of intellectual inquiry. "Human intellect is incurably abstract. . . . Yet the only realities we experience are concrete—this pain, this pleasure, this dog, this man. While we are loving the man, bearing the pain, enjoying the pleasure, we are not intellectually apprehending Pleasure, Pain or Personality."[10] This is certainly not new for Lewis: it is a restatement of what he adopted from Samuel Alexander's *Space Time and De-*

ity,[11] and had stated in his writing a number of times.[12] But he now applies it more directly to the realms of reason and imagination: "This is our dilemma—either to taste and not to know or to know and not to taste—or, more strictly, to lack one kind of knowledge because we are in an experience or to lack another kind because we are outside it. As thinkers we are cut off from what we think about; as tasting, touching, willing, loving, hating, we do not clearly understand."[13]

As at least a partial resolution of this dilemma, Lewis turns to myth considered not as a form containing truth but as an embodiment of imaginative experience. That also is not entirely new: as far back as "The Personal Heresy" one can find him discussing the imaginative experience in reading poetry. If there is a difference between the two essays, it is a matter of emphasis, or greater precision—but there does seem to be a shift, signaled by a difference in metaphor: in "The Personal Heresy" poetry, through the imagination, enables one to "see" universal objects; in "Myth Became Fact," myth enables one, through the imagination, to "taste" reality. In the earlier essay Lewis asserted that "see" is used for "apprehension," in a nonintellectual sense; but the metaphor, in Lewis, can never be totally disassociated from intellect. Just before the footnote disclaiming intellectual overtones for the metaphor, Lewis used sight imagery both ways in the same sentence: "I see that 'liquefaction' is an admirably chosen word; but only because I have already found myself seeing silk as I never saw it before."[14] And although by "universal objects" Lewis meant the utterly Real, the metaphors could allow it to seem abstract, particularly when one such "object," which the poet causes us to see in a new way, is "the age and mystery of man."

Because of these intellectual and abstract overtones, I think, Lewis does not use the metaphor "see" in "Myth Became Fact"—the word does not appear even once, in striking contrast to its frequent use elsewhere. Lewis uses instead the metaphor of "taste" and emphasizes its distance from the abstract: "When we translate [state the principle of a myth] we get abstraction—or rather, dozens of abstractions.

What flows into you from the myth is not truth but reality (truth is always *about* something, but reality is that *about which* truth is), and, therefore, every myth becomes the father of innumerable truths on the abstract level." Even more important than the shift of metaphor is the resulting difference in his use of Alexander's terminology, a use which has the potential for resolving the tension between reason and imagination. The previous references had juxtaposed knowing and experiencing, the outside view and the inside one, "contemplating" and "enjoying." The "tasting of reality" seems to unite them, for in receiving the myth one *experiences* a *principle:* "In the enjoyment of a great myth we come nearest to experiencing as a concrete what can otherwise be understood only as an abstraction."[15] In his previous references to Alexander's ideas, Lewis emphasized the separation and incompatibility of contemplation and enjoyment: "You can see any eyes rather than the pair you see with, and if you want to examine your own glasses you must take them off your own nose";[16] now he suggests one way in which they might be united.[17] Myth, in a sense, combines the outside view and the inside view, contemplation and enjoyment, in a single act. The metaphor he uses for characterizing myth at the end of a key section of "Myth Became Fact" highlights that reconciling potential: "Myth is the isthmus which connects the peninsular world of thought with that vast continent we really belong to. It is not, like truth, abstract; nor is it, like direct experience, bound to the particular."[18] Thus myth has the potential for joining the outside view with the inside view, contemplation with enjoyment, and the rational with the imaginative.

The potential for reconciliation is there, but such a reconciliation does not yet appear as accomplished fact. In the stories of the early and mid–1940s statement of principle exists side by side with the imaginative depiction of experience offered by the story as story, with an element of tension between them. Lewis continues to be careful not to leave imaginative modes to themselves, without expository or dialectical devices for conveying theme. This is not to say that imaginative achievement is lacking, or insignificant—

it is certainly there, and of highest quality, particularly in *Perelandra*—but to indicate the continuing limits Lewis placed, perhaps unintentionally or even unconsciously, on the imaginative mode.

Nowhere did Lewis create a more richly imaginative world than in the second book of the "space trilogy": the tastes, sounds, and sights of Perelandra create in the reader, as they did in Lewis,[19] a sense of longing, of sweet desire, for the world his imagination had created:

> At long last he reached the wooded part. There was an undergrowth of feathery vegetation, about the height of gooseberry bushes, coloured like sea anemones. Above this were the taller growths—strange trees with tube-like trunks of grey and purple spreading rich canopies above his head, in which orange, silver, and blue were the predominant colours. Here with the aid of the tree trunks, he could keep his feet more easily. The smells in the forest were beyond all that he had ever conceived. To say that they made him feel hungry and thirsty would be misleading; almost, they created a new kind of hunger and thirst, a longing that seemed to flow over from the body into the soul and which was a heaven to feel.[20]

And nowhere except in *Till We Have Faces* is he as successful in setting before us "an image of what reality may well be like at some more central region."[21] The reader, like Ransom, feels that here the mythical is very much being achieved: "If a naked man and a wise dragon were indeed the sole inhabitants of this floating paradise, then this also was fitting, for at that moment he had a sensation not of following an adventure but of enacting a myth."[22] But even here Lewis is not content to leave the imaginative unaided by the conceptual. The heart of the book—not the most memorable aspect, but the dominant part in terms of length and placement—is an extended philosophical-theological discussion between the unfallen queen of the planet, Weston, who tempts her to sin, and Ransom, who defends her and helps her to retain her purity.

The reliance upon the conceptual in *That Hideous Strength* is readily evident. The imaginative appears in the narrative—a theological thriller, in the Charles Williams mold rather than the fantasy-romance of the previous volumes—and in the Williams-like spirit world which surrounds and penetrates ours. But the burden of the book is the exposure and defeat of evil and the conversion of the two central characters, Jane and Mark Studdock. The exposure of evil and instruction in the good are achieved largely through exposition of ideas, often in the kernel ideas of what later became such essays as "Vivisection" and "The Humanitarian Theory of Punishment,"[23] and in stimulating and engaging mini-essays, like William Hingest's demolition of sociology:

> That's what happens when you study men: you find mare's nests. I happen to believe that you can't study men, you can only get to know them, which is quite a different thing. Because you study them, you want to make the lower orders govern the country and listen to classical music, which is balderdash. You also want to take away from them everything which makes life worth living, and not only from them but from everyone except a parcel of prigs and professors.[24]

The conversions of Mark and Jane in no sense involve the mythical—his comes through exposure to disproportion, which gives rise somehow to a sense of its opposite, the sweet, the straight, the "Normal"; that sense grows increasing solid, becomes personal, and ends up as awareness of the divine. Jane's acceptance of God grows out of her personal relation to and experience with Ransom, and through the convincingness of the arguments he propounded to her.

Of particular importance in showing the continued tension between reason and imagination is *The Great Divorce*. It uses imagination strikingly, in story, in sketches of character, and in the imaging of Reality. But all of this is done in a work whose appeal to the head outweighs its imaginative appeal to the heart and the emotions.

The Great Divorce, like *The Pilgrim's Regress,* is a dream poem, but it is not a dream allegory: rather than using material images to stand for immaterial qualities (a slough for despondency), it uses material images to stand for supernatural matters and offers a fine example of what Lewis called "sacramentalism."[25] Thus the story uses realistic details of a bus, a city, a meadow, and ordinary people to depict hell, heaven, and the choices and attitudes that determine the ultimate destinies of persons in their life journeys. The story tells of a group of ghosts on a day's outing from hell paying a visit to heaven: a holiday there is an alternative to visiting earth to haunt houses or accommodate mediums. Unlike these other alternatives, this journey can be permanent: the ghosts may remain in heaven if they really desire to.

The story focuses on the choices the ghosts from hell face and on the efforts of old acquaintances now in heaven to persuade them to stay. Each of the ghosts, to stay in heaven, would have to get beyond and outside his or her self; each must heed the call to "fix your mind on something not yourself."[26] All have "something they insist on keeping, even at the price of misery" (p. 64; *69*). The fate of one or two is left unclear, but most of the others choose to return to hell: throughout their lives their choices pointed them toward and prepared them for hell—now they can desire nothing else. One ghost, however, asks to be purged of his lust and turns into a heavenly creature. It is not that he is given a second chance after death: as Lewis puts it in *The Problem of Pain,* "I believe that if a million chances were likely to do good, they would be given. But a master often knows, when boys and parents do not, that it is really useless to send a boy in for a certain examination again" (p. 112; Ch. 8). Rather, in life he desired good but was plagued and defiled by lust, and he went to a place of purging rather than directly to heaven. Now, cleansed of his faults, he is ready to enter the presence of God.

The Great Divorce handles several of the themes which appear later in *Till We Have Faces*. The theme of longing, *Sehnsucht,* is important. It was emphasized by the title of the work when it was published serially in *The Guardian* as "Who Goes Home?", a phrase shouted by the policeman on duty through the lobbies and corridors of the House of Commons when it has concluded a session and is about to close its doors.[27] The phrase also invokes "the idea of the spiritual world as *home* . . . —the feeling that you are coming *back* tho' to a place you have never yet reached,"[28] which

Psyche experienced throughout her life. The original title enhanced the irony when the Big Man refuses to accompany his former employee into deep heaven and says, "If they're too fine to have me without you, I'll go home. ... That's what I'll do. ... I'll go home. I didn't come here to be treated like a dog. I'll go home" (p. 34; *36*). Even without that title, one thinks of longing when one reads of the mountains: "Very far away I could see what might be either a great bank of cloud or a range of mountains" (p. 29; *29*). These are, of course, the originals, the "forms" or "ideas," of the mountains which Psyche sees and longs for in Glome. Thus the artist ghost, when he was still alive and before he became interested in paint for its own sake, was able to catch "glimpses of Heaven in the earthly landscape" and through his paintings he enabled others to see the glimpses, too: "It is from here that the messages came" (p. 73; *80*). Here too they signify that toward which one's longings really are directed: "Every one of us," the spirit of MacDonald tells the narrator, "lives only to journey further and further into the mountains" (p. 66; *72*).

The theme of love is developed in *The Great Divorce* in very much the same way as in *Till We Have Faces*. There is the same warning about the natural loves: "They all go bad when they set up on their own and make themselves into false gods" (p. 84; *93*). Details surrounding the domineering wifely ghost and Pam, the possessive mother ghost, closely resemble those characterizing Orual, as indicated previously in Chapter IV. There is the same attention to the evil of manipulating others by playing on their pity. The Tragedian used it so throughout his life, as Orual did in attempting to force her will upon Psyche. Sarah Smith's reply would apply to Orual as much as to her husband: "Pity was meant to be a spur that drives joy to help misery. But it can be used the wrong way round. It can be used for a kind of blackmailing" (pp. 107–8; *117*). And there is the same emphasis on the need for divine love, *agape,* to infuse and convert the natural loves if they are to be saved: "He wanted your merely instinctive love for your child ... to turn into something better. He wanted you to love Michael as He

143

understands love. You cannot love a fellow-creature fully till you love God" (p. 84; *92*).

And *The Great Divorce,* like *Till We Have Faces,* focuses on the theme of death to self. To attain heaven, one must be freed from self: "Every state of mind, left to itself, every shutting up of the creature within the dungeon of its own mind—is, in the end, Hell" (p. 63; *69*). Only if one dies to self before dying, before one's choice is fixed on the self, can one find salvation. Thus it is so important, at the end of the story, that the story-teller is only dreaming and has not yet died physically: there is yet time for him to conquer self before he dies. The theme of the natural loves—of the need for their conversion by divine love and their potential as precursors to love of God—is tied nicely to the die-before-you-die theme: "Every natural love will rise again and live forever in this country: but none will rise again until it has been buried" (pp. 88–89; *97*).

The themes of *The Great Divorce,* then, resemble in many respects the themes of *Till We Have Faces.* Equally significant, however, is a particular contrast, the difference in the handling of sight imagery. Throughout the apologetic works sight is used regularly in Plato's sense of intuitive understanding. This meaning is made explicit in *Miracles:*

> I believe that the primary moral principles on which all others depend are rationally perceived. We "just see" that there is no reason why my neighbour's happiness should be sacrificed to my own, as we "just see" that things which are equal to the same thing are equal to one another. If we cannot prove either axiom, that is not because they are irrational but because they are self-evident and all proofs depend on them. (pp. 43–44; Ch. 5)

The metaphor of "sight" in *The Problem of Pain* is closely linked with the reason: "Everyone who stops to think can see that when we meet the enemy this neglect is going to cost every man of us his life" (p. 52; Ch. 4). Similarly, "I have been aiming at an intellectual, not an emotional, effect: I have been trying to make the reader believe that we actually are, at present, creatures whose character must be, in some respects, a horror to God, as it is, when we really

144

see it, a horror to ourselves" (p. 55; Ch. 4). It is used similarly in *Broadcast Talks:* "And when you've grasped that, you will see that what this man said was, quite simply, the most shocking thing that has ever been uttered by human lips" (p. 50; Bk. II, Ch. 3); or, "Another way of seeing that the Moral Law is not simply one of our instincts is this" (p. 14; Bk. I, Ch. 2). As Lewis gained experience as an apologist, he began to use analogies to help readers "see" the point he is making. They appear occasionally in *The Problem of Pain* and the first series of radio talks, and frequently thereafter. Analogy creates an image—thus it appeals to the imagination; but the formation of analogical comparisons is mostly an intellectual process. Here too imagination cooperates with reason, but still in *serving* reason, as it does in *The Pilgrim's Regress* and the Ransom trilogy.

The Great Divorce takes that cooperation a significant step further in its handling of sight imagery. Throughout the work, "see" is used again and again in a number of different senses. It is used literally, of course: the fashion-conscious lady ghost says, "How *can* I go out like this among a lot of people with real solid bodies? . . . They'll *see* me" (p. 56; *61*). But mostly "see" is used as a metaphor. Sometimes it means, figuratively, to "meet": "My dear boy, I'm delighted to see you" (p. 35; *38*). There is "see" as to "perceive": "Ye see it in smaller matters," George MacDonald says to the narrator (p. 66; *71–72*). There is "see" as "find out, discover": Sarah Smith says to her husband, "I am full now, not empty. I am in Love Himself, not lonely. Strong, not weak. You shall be the same. Come and see" (p. 104; *113*). There is "see" as "understand": "Oh—I see" (p. 73; *79*), or "Go away! Can't you see I want to be alone?" (p. 55; *60*), or "If you'll only wait you'll see that isn't so" (p. 103; *113*).

That Lewis is aware of the word and deliberately developing its significance is confirmed by his playful and multiple uses of it, as with the Big Man and the disillusioned world traveler. The Big Man uses "see" as a habit of speech, for emphasis—"But I done my best all my life, see?" (p. 31; *33*)—at the same time that he admits he does not "understand": "And what I don't see is why I should be put below a bloody murderer like you. ... I don't see myself going in the same boat with you, see?" (p. 32; *34*). The world traveler says, "I guess I've seen about all there is to see." He "likes to see things for himself," and everything he sees ends up "not worth looking at." Thus he does not "understand" why there was so much excitement about Heaven: "Well, I don't see what all the talk is about" (pp. 49–50; *54–55*).

As "see" recurs in the story, it establishes itself as an important structural and thematic motif. It is noteworthy that all this "seeing" and "understanding" occurs in a place where, as the traveler complains, the fruit is so solid that ghosts cannot eat it, the water so hard they cannot drink it, and the grass so sharp they cannot walk on it. They are experiencing Reality, where truth is as firm and touchable as the apples and raindrops. It is a place where thoughts themselves have solid qualities, where one can "see an unheard-of idea trying to enter his little mind" (p. 103; *112*), where one can round a bend and "see" an explanation (p. 45; *48*), and where one can "see" an absurdity (p. 106; *115*). This world, then, is the source of the objective truth and the "Real Law" whose "concreteness" Lewis had long been attempting to convey, often through sight images. "The light, the grass, the trees ... were different; made of some different substance, so much solider than things in our country that men were ghosts by comparison" (p. 27; *28*). Here is the "otherness," the solidity, of the utterly Real—of Heaven, of God, of Truth, of Value.

Thus *The Great Divorce* in some instances retains the earlier intellectual emphasis in its uses of sight imagery, but in other instances goes beyond it. Lewis attempts to give an additional sense to "see"—the significance of "taste" in "Myth Became Fact." That significance stands in direct and deliberate contrast to the abstract. Says one heavenly Spirit, "We know nothing of speculation [here]. Come and see. I will bring you to Eternal Fact, the Father of all other facthood" (p. 42; *44*). This "seeing" would be the original, the model, of which the imaginative experience of reality is the echo: "When you've grown into a Person," the artist is told, "there'll be some things which you'll see better than anyone else. One of the things you'll want to do will be to tell us about them. But not yet. At present your business is to see. Come and see. He is endless" (pp. 73–74; *80*). One should notice, however, that even here the "see" image is not adequate: Lewis shifts metaphors in the next sentence: "Come and *feed*" (italics added). And in the fullest statement of the "experience of reality" theme, he does not use "see" at all: "Hitherto you have experienced truth only with the abstract intellect. I will bring you where you can taste it like honey and be embraced by it as by a bridegroom" (p. 41; *43*).

Although *The Great Divorce* talks of tasting reality, it does not itself offer such a taste, for it is not myth: its effect is to convey a message, not to give an imaginative experience. Chad Walsh sums it up well when he writes, "In its thin, serious way it preaches a sermon that reaches the will and the heart as well as the intellect."[29] But the attempt in *The Great Divorce* to use sight for such an experience stands as a major step toward the use of pure myth in *Till We Have Faces*, and toward the union of imagination and reason in the fifties and sixties.

XIII

Autobiographer of the Fifties: Reason and Imagination Reconciled

*T*HAT a major change in Lewis's life occurred during the years 1929–1931 is readily granted. But I want to suggest that another turning point of major significance occurred in the 1940s. It is a change evidenced by a lessening of the strong reliance on reason which had come to mark his thinking in the mid-forties, and a much greater use of and confidence in the imagination than before. It is a change which enabled Lewis to write about himself, and, as a result, to write about others, in his fiction, in a new and more effective way.

The change can be attributed to a number of causes, any one of which would have been insufficient by itself to bring it about. One can be assigned to a particular time and place. As the last chapter shows, Lewis's apologetics had placed increasing confidence in the ability of reason to establish the existence of God, a confidence shown most strongly in the highly rationalistic methods of the early chapters of *Miracles*. Eight months after the publication of *Miracles,* its methods were challenged in a public debate by G. E. M. Anscombe, then already a well-known and impressive philosopher—and a Catholic. At a meeting of the Socratic Club in Oxford on 2 February 1948, Miss Anscombe attacked the methods of the crucial third chapter of the book. In the mode of analytic philosophy, she focused on what she called Lewis's imprecision or confusion in his use of the key terms in his argument: "I am going to argue that your whole thesis is only specious because of the ambiguity of the words 'why,' 'because,' and 'explanation.' " She proceeded to analyze his arguments for the validity of reason and the incongruity of a naturalist asserting the validity of reason on naturalistic grounds, and concluded, "I do not think that there is sufficiently good reason for maintaining the 'naturalist' hypothesis about human behaviour and thought. But someone who does maintain it, cannot be refuted as you try to refute him, by saying that it is inconsistent to maintain it and to believe that human reasoning is valid."[1]

The adequacy and effectiveness of Miss Anscombe's attack are still being discussed.[2] But the issue of whether Miss Anscombe "won" the debate seems less important than the effect the encounter had on Lewis. According to his friends, Lewis felt depressed and defeated: Derek Brewer reports that Lewis's talk, at lunch in a pub a few days after the meeting, "was all of the fog of war, the retreat of infantry thrown back under heavy attack."[3] Particularly striking, apparently, was the fact that the attack came not from an atheist but from a fellow-Christian, who therefore did not oppose Lewis's conclusion but questioned his method of arriving at it. The effect of the experience apparently was to alert Lewis to something his friends, according to Humphrey Carpenter, had warned him of much earlier: "Charles Williams, listening to his wartime broadcasts, had expressed serious reservations about his tendency to make Reason the primary basis for belief in God, while Tolkien was aware of Lewis's too close reliance on supposedly infallible dialectics."[4] Clearly the encounter with Miss Anscombe did not shatter his belief in reason: he in no way repudiated the apologetic works and, later, revised the third chapter of *Miracles* to avoid the difficulties Miss Anscombe had pointed out. Equally clearly, however, there is a movement away from apologetics after the forties which, combined with his broadened approach to myth, suggests that Lewis has reassessed his earlier heavy reliance upon reason.

A second cause was the effort to put into practice the expanded conception of myth Lewis arrived at in the mid–1940s. This effort is partially attributable also to the influence of Tolkien: the cumulative effect of two decades of listening to and reading Tolkien's stories and poems must account at least to some extent for Lewis's deepened interest in and expanded vision of what myth can undertake and achieve. It is also partially attributable to Lewis's continuing concern about the effect of abstraction. In "Myth Became Fact" he described abstract knowledge as useful, but less vital than myth. A year or so later, in 1945, he went further, to warn of a danger in the development of abstract formulas in apologetics. An apologist who is focusing on arguments for the existence of God cannot at the same time be tasting the reality of God:

> I have found that nothing is more dangerous to one's own faith than the work of an apologist. No doctrine of that Faith seems to me so spectral, so unreal as one that I have just successfully defended in a public debate. For a moment, you see, it has seemed to rest on oneself: as a result, when you go away from that debate, it seems no stronger than that weak pillar. That is why we apologists take our lives in our hands and can be saved only by falling back continually from the web of our own arguments, as from our intellectual counters, into the Reality—from Christian apologetics into Christ Himself.[5]

If there is a danger for the writer of apologetics, it would seem there could be a related danger for readers of apologetics. A person who overindulged in apologetic works, in preparing an arsenal of defenses for the faith, could do so at the cost of a living experience with Christ himself. Such thinking, I believe, reinforced by the Anscombe dispute, led Lewis to ask himself if perhaps he should move on to another mode of writing about Christianity. His turning to myth is not a rejection of his earlier mode, but an effort to go beyond it and to offer a reader not "knowledge" of God but a "taste" of Divine Reality. That effort was at least partially successful in the Chronicles of Narnia[6] and entirely so in *Till We Have Faces*.

A third cause of the change, perhaps the most important, is an acknowledgment that an element of subjectivity is inherent in perception, and that a degree of self-consciousness is necessary to sound understanding. His movement away from an almost mechanical approach to the objective, and from his lack of interest in the self, is surely a result of his friendship with Barfield and years of talking about "consciousness," the central element of Barfield's thought. Recent studies also discuss the influence of Lewis's growing relationship with Joy Davidman, whom he married in 1956. Her effect is suggested in a poem he wrote apparently to her:

> Only that now you have taught me (but how late) my lack.
> I see the chasm. And everything you are was making
> My heart into a bridge by which I might get back
> From exile, and grow man.[7]

The lines suggest that the chasm, the sense of exile, the way in which he was less than fully man, was a lack of balance between heart and head. They show an ability at this point, helped along by his relationship with Joy Davidman, to give attention to himself and to write about himself. Consciousness of self, and of self as a necessary aspect of perceiving, thinking, and imagining, is a factor that shaped Lewis's works in the last decade of his life, particularly *Surprised by Joy*, which was crucial in preparing the way for *Till We Have Faces* and the subsequent books.

When Lewis previously had told the story of his conversion, in *The Pilgrim's Regress*, he could do so only at a distance, through allegory and an everyman character named "John." The pilgrimage John undertakes is clearly Lewis's own journey toward Christianity, but Lewis wished to maintain a sense of separation from his material, perhaps to increase the sense of objectivity about what he says. In the 1950s, in *Surprised by Joy*, he tells essentially the same story, but close-up, in the first person—although he fears the account will be "suffocatingly subjective."[8] That Lewis now can give attention to himself and not only use but take rhetorical advantage of a subjective approach is the key element in the success of this and many of his later books.

In *Surprised by Joy* Lewis is looking back on events and feelings of twenty to fifty years earlier; this will inevitably involve reconstruction of events and choices of detail dictated by what seems important to his purposes in the fifties and to the kind of book he is writing. Lewis himself calls attention to the retrospective nature of the account. He writes, for example, "My real life—or what memory reports as my real life—was increasingly one of solitude" (p. 18; Ch. 1). Not just that thought, however, but the entire account is the report of memories—inevitably incomplete and unconsciously altered by later perspectives—and of partial reconstruction. The opening of Chapter 2, for example, illustrates the latter.

> *Clop-clop-clop-clop* . . . we are in a four-wheeler rattling over the uneven squaresets of the Belfast streets through the damp twilight of a September evening, 1908; my father, my brother, and I. I am going to school for the first time. We are in low spirits. (p. 29)

The present-tense description of his first departure for school in a four-wheeler is surely a reconstruction, a telling of what it must have been like rather than exactly what it was. There is a rather clumsy shift of tense and point of view, at the beginning of the chapter, to signal that this bit is "story"—with the implied suggestion that the rest, that which is not told in narrative fashion, is objective recounting. A bit later in the chapter he mentions that "the flats of Lancashire in the early morning are in reality a dismal sight; to me they were like the banks of Styx" (p. 30). The second clause is a later reflection, with apt and resonant allusion, but the past tense verb ("were like") makes it seem as if it were an expression of his immediate reaction. I do not mention these examples to challenge the accuracy and fairness of Lewis's memory. Surely the incidents were very much like what he describes, and one must allow an autobiographer, like a poet, a bit of poetic license. But such poetic license involves subjectivity. Thus Lewis will sometimes present a distant and recollected detail as an assured and objective truth, as when he recalls the first metaphysical argument he ever took part in: "I have forgotten which side I took though I know that I took it with great zeal" (p. 37; Ch. 2). Does he know it (now) because he remembers the episode or its emotional imprint so clearly, or because— knowing the kind of person he always has been—that was the way it must have been?

Lewis, then, was aware that *Surprised by Joy* was retrospective and subjective. But there is some cause to wonder if he was aware of how subjective it was. Some episodes, for example, are presented as objective and universal, though they are clearly personal and subjective. Such is his account of boyhood:

> For boyhood is very like the "dark ages" not as they were but as they are represented in bad, short histories. The dreams of childhood and those of adolescence may have much in common; between them, often, boyhood stretches like an alien territory in which everything (ourselves included) has been greedy, cruel, noisy, and prosaic, in which the imagination has slept and the most un-ideal senses and ambitions have been restlessly, even maniacally, awake. (p. 73; Ch. 5).

Is boyhood almost always so? The following sentence, "In my own life it was certainly so," suggests that he regards his case as part of a universal pattern rather than acknowledging that his experience was the basis for the generalization.

Lewis also realized that a work such as this inevitably involves selectivity. Thus he notes, "I pass over a holiday in Normandy (of which, nevertheless, I retain very clear memories) as a thing of no account" (p. 21; Ch. 1). It is safe to assume that much else was passed over as well. The stated principle for inclusion of details appears in the next sentence: "If it could be cut out of my past I should still be almost exactly the man I am." That may generally account for what is included, but it probably does not account for the amount of detail given in particular instances. Oldie's school is described, in Chapter 2, because it helped shape Lewis's development and character; he would indeed have been a different man if he had never attended the school. But the amount and kind of detail reflects the fact that he is his father's son. In Chapter 1 Lewis described his father's love of "wheezes," or anecdotes, told by acting "all the characters in turn with a free use of grimace, gesture, and pantomime" (p. 12). Is not the depiction of Oldie just such a "wheeze"?

> He called his class up and asked questions. When the replies were unsatisfactory he said in a low, calm voice, "Bring me my cane. I see I shall need it." If a boy became confused Oldie

flogged the desk, shouting in a crescendo, "Think—Think—
THINK!!" Then, as the prelude to execution, he muttered, "Come
out, come out, come out." When really angry he proceeded to
antics; worming for wax in his ear with his little finger and
babbling, "Aye, aye, aye, aye. . . ." I have seen him leap up
and dance round and round like a performing bear. (p. 34;
ellipsis in the original)

The detail is not crucial to the central purpose, but the anec-
dotalist in Lewis could not resist, and was reluctant to
stop: "I must restrain myself. I could continue to describe
Oldie for many pages; some of the worst is unsaid" (p. 35).

A different sort of selectivity, and subjectivity, enters
with his decision to include the sentence, later in the chapter, "My father must not bear the blame for our wasted and
miserable years at Oldie's" (p. 36). All that has been said on
that page and the preceding one, even the rather weak disclaimers, puts the blame just there. Lewis says much in
Surprised by Joy about his difficulties with his father, but
he by no means says it all—the antipathies ran very deep.
Reflecting back on Oldie's, he writes, "If the school had not
died, and if I had been left there two years more, it would
probably have sealed my fate as a scholar for good" (p. 39).
The language suggests that Lewis might well be using the
chapter to express, perhaps unintentionally, some of the bit-
terness the experience, and the lack of awareness on his
father's part, engendered in him.

A similar motivation, surely, lies behind his account of
his public school experiences. It is difficult to justify the
long, detailed, intense accounts of "bloodery" and pederasty
in Chapter 6, and even much of Chapter 7, on the grounds
that they clarify Lewis's development and character in any
significant sense. Chapter 6 says comparatively little about
Lewis. The point of it and Chapter 7, that Malvern College
(he calls it "Wyvern") made him a Prig, that "the Public
School system had thus produced the very thing which it
was advertised to prevent or cure" (p. 104; Ch. 7), could have
been made more briefly and believably. Lewis is aware that
this account is personal, for in the middle of Chapter 8 he
admits, "My brother had liked Wyvern as much as I loathed

it" (p. 122). But he takes pains rhetorically, in this instance, to minimize its subjectivity. Several pages in the first half of the chapter are devoted to contrasting his and his brother's factual precision with their father's subjective distortions of what they say. The effect is to heighten the sense of accuracy and objectivity in what Lewis recalls about Malvern. So does his effort to explain away his brother's positive response to the school:

> He had gone there straight from Oldie's and I from a preparatory school where I had been happy. No school in England but would have appeared a heaven on earth after Oldie's. Thus in one of his first letters from Wyvern my brother communicated the startling fact that you could really eat as much (or as little) as you wanted at table. To a boy fresh from the school at Belsen, this alone would have outweighed almost everything else. But by the time I went to Wyvern I had learned to take decent feeding for granted. (p. 122)

The school had "appeared" a heaven on earth to Warren, in other words, but in reality it was the hellish place Lewis described. Although he realizes that *Surprised by Joy* as a whole is subjective, he seems to have difficulty admitting that this particular portion is subjective and that the school might not have been as bad as his situation and reaction made it seem to him. His brother later persuaded Lewis he was wrong about some details; Lewis had included them, apparently, because he regarded them as accurate and significant.[9] But an equally important reason for their inclusion might stem from the fact that he admittedly "loathed" the school. When he mentions that at Malvern an "orgiastic" dimension entered his imagination, he explains it as follows: "It was perhaps unconsciously connected with my growing hatred of the public school orthodoxies and conventions, my desire to break and tear it all" (p. 111; Ch. 7). It appears that, perhaps unconsciously, he devotes a chapter and a half to just such a breaking and tearing of it all.

Thus the selection of details or emphasis is at times governed by Lewis's purposes at the time of writing, purposes he may not always have been fully aware of, not just by the demands of accurate reporting. So it is, I believe, with the theme of imagination. What he now calls the "imaginative" side of his life was always an important factor in his life, but he did not, previously, use that term often in referring to it. Longing, or "sweet desire," in earlier works is regularly identified with the term "romanticism." Neither of the two main statements about *Sehnsucht,* or longing— the Preface added to *The Pilgrim's Regress* in 1943 and the 1941 sermon "The Weight of Glory"—associates it explicitly with "imagination." The Preface to *The Pilgrim's Regress* spends two pages clarifying various meanings of romanticism before specifying that "what I meant by 'Romanticism' when I wrote the *Pilgrim's Regress* ... was a particular recurrent experience which dominated my childhood and adolescence and which I hastily called 'Romantic' because inanimate nature and marvellous literature were among the things that evoked it."[10] The experience obviously involves the imagination, but it doesn't seem to have occurred to Lewis to mention that. It is striking, therefore, that he not only mentions it in *Surprised by Joy* but includes a deliberate pattern of references linking "Joy" with "imagination."

The first reference to imagination occurs in the paragraph which leads up to the first occurrences of longing: "It will be clear that at this time—at the age of six, seven, and eight—I was living almost entirely in my imagination; or at least that the imaginative experience of those years now seems to me more important than anything else" (p. 21; Ch. 1). "Now seems" cannot be ignored. It is a reminder that the account does not necessarily record the terms and emphases Lewis used at ages six, seven, and eight, or in his thirties, but those of the 1950s, when he was writing *Surprised by Joy*. The linking of imagination with Joy continues. At Oldie's, "there was also a great decline in my imaginative life. For many years Joy (as I have defined it) was not only absent but forgotten" (p. 40; Ch. 2). When he wrote *The Pilgrim's Regress* he would have said in my "romantic life"; now he uses "imaginative" for the same quality. In his discussion of the school he calls Chartres, imagination is made one side of a dichotomy: "My secret, imaginative life began to be so important and so distinct from my outer life that I almost have to tell two separate stories" (p. 79; Ch. 5). It begins to be contrasted with the rational when he goes to Kirkpatrick's: "Though I could never have been a scientist, I had scientific as well as imaginative impulses, and I loved ratiocination. Kirk excited and satisfied one side of me" (p. 131; Ch. 9). Its fullest expression, two chapters later, brings out an element of tension:

> Such, then, was the state of my imaginative life; over against it stood the life of my intellect. The two hemispheres of my mind were in the sharpest contrast. On the one side a many-islanded sea of poetry and myth; on the other a glib and shallow "rationalism." Nearly all that I loved I believed to be imaginary; nearly all that I believed to be real I thought grim and meaningless. (p. 161; Ch. 11)

The terms and emphasis are, of course, those of the fifties. The subjectivity and retrospectiveness of the account are unavoidable. He might have felt the same tension in the twenties, but he did not make it explicit earlier. In particular, he did not previously use such terms as "glib and shallow" with rational activity. It might be well to reflect, then, upon the context in which these changes in terminology and, to some extent, attitude were taking place.

The emphasis on giving explicit attention to and mention of the imagination appears elsewhere in the early 1950s. He begins to write about the imaginative process involved in his own writings: "I have never exactly 'made' a story. With me the process is much more like bird-watching than like either talking or building. I see pictures. Some of these pictures have a common flavour, almost a common smell, which groups them together. Keep quiet and watch and they will begin joining themselves up."[11] The very fact that he focuses such attention on himself as writer may well be significant. In another essay he emphasizes that his Narnia stories grew out of the imagination, not out of cognitive or thematic purposes:

> Some people seem to think that I began by asking myself how I could say something about Christianity to children; then fixed on the fairy tale as an instrument; then collected infor-

mation about child-psychology and decided what age group
I'd write for; then drew up a list of basic Christian truths and
hammered out "allegories" to embody them. This is all pure
moonshine. I couldn't write in that way at all. Everything
began with images; a faun carrying an umbrella, a queen on
a sledge, a magnificent lion.[12]

A few years later he reveals that his earlier stories likewise
began with visual images: "All my seven Narnian books,
and my three science fiction books, began with seeing pictures in my head."[13] Surely all this is not a new insight for
Lewis—he did not suddenly, in the fifties, come to realize
that *Perelandra* grew out of mental images. But he had not
previously cared to direct attention to himself and talk about
inner processes, and he had not felt it important to stress
the imaginative aspects of his work. Now he does. Thus, in
a letter to the Milton Society of America in the mid-fifties,
he goes out of his way to highlight the imaginative and even
to cite it as a unifying quality of his lifework:

The list of my books which I send . . . will I fear strike you as
a very mixed bag . . . (but) there is a guiding thread. The
imaginative man in me is older, more continuously operative,
and in that sense more basic than either the religious writer
or the critic. It was he who made me first attempt (with little
success) to be a poet. It was he who, in response to the poetry
of others, made me a critic, and, in defence of that response,
sometimes a critical controversialist. It was he who after my
conversion led me to embody my religious belief in symbolical
or mythopeic forms, ranging from *Screwtape* to a kind of theol-
ogised science fiction. And it was of course he who has brought
me, in the last few years, to write the series of Narnian stories
for children; not asking what children want and then endeav-
ouring to adapt myself (this was not needed) but because the
fairy tale was the genre best fitted for what I wanted to say.[14]

This, like *Surprised by Joy,* is retrospective: he now sees
the imaginative as central, because of the context in which
he is writing in the fifties.

Behind this new attention to the imaginative stand a
decreased dependence upon the rational, shaken as it was
by the encounter with Miss Anscombe, and an increased
confidence in the imagination. Through his theorizing about
myth, reinforced by his experiments with the mythical in
the Narnian Chronicles in the years following, he came to

realize that he had unnecessarily limited the role of the imagination, that he could entrust to it a larger role than he previously had. Having reached this new appreciation of the imaginative, it is only natural that as he looked back over his life, he should begin to recognize that it had, after all, been very important to him all along, more important and influential than he had realized. And it is only natural that he should begin to use terminology and to emphasize qualities which, on the one hand, highlight the place imagination had filled in his life in the past, and, on the other hand, play down the rational. As he looked back across his life, he concluded that what he had previously regarded as primarily a tension between the romantic and the rational, or faith and science, or the "other worldly" and "this worldly," was also a tension between the imagination and reason; and he recognized that, while the earlier tensions had been resolved by his conversion in the early 1930s, the tension between imagination and reason lingered on, and even intensified, until it reached a breaking point in February 1948. His subsequent efforts to pick up the pieces culminated in the paired works *Surprised by Joy* and *Till We Have Faces*.

The tension seems to be resolved in *Surprised by Joy* itself, at the end of Chapter 11, when imagination becomes the key term in his description of the effect that reading *Phantastes* had upon him. Previous visits of Joy were reminders of another world which left this world drab and unappealing in contrast.

> But now I saw the bright shadow coming out of the book into the real world and resting there, transforming all common things and yet itself unchanged. Or, more accurately, I saw the common things drawn into the bright shadow. *Unde hoc mihi?* In the depth of my disgraces, in the then invincible ignorance of my intellect, all this was given me without asking, even without consent. That night my imagination was, in a certain sense, baptised; the rest of me, not unnaturally, took longer. I had not the faintest notion what I had let myself in for by buying *Phantastes*. (pp. 170–71)

This sounds as if it resolves the tension, as if imagination has won out over intellect, and Lewis was content that it should seem so, for it is a satisfying place, rhetorically, to leave the matter. His imagination was "saved" from the directions his romanticism was taking him, toward Magic and the Occult, and was directed by MacDonald to the glory of everyday experiences and the everyday world—a crucial preliminary step toward his later acceptance of Christianity. The succeeding chapters trace the further contributions of longing and of his reading, the influence of friends, and the force of logic, all of which lead to an acknowledgment that the Reality he has tasted is the God of Christianity. That the tension between imagination and intellect continued after his conversion is not a part of this story, the story of the influence of Joy upon his life, and he has no reason to go on. And he would have been unable to go on, at this point or in this literary form, to tell of a harmony between intellect and imagination which was yet to be achieved.

The subjectivity and selectivity in *Surprised by Joy* seem to have opened the way for Lewis to write *Till We Have Faces,* his next book, in which full unity of reason and imagination at last were achieved. As Lewis had before attempted to tell the story of his conversion objectively and at a distance, so had he also attempted much earlier an objective account of the story of Cupid and Psyche, but had been unable to find the right "form" for it. Now the right form comes to him, and it is no coincidence that it is fictional autobiography. All of Lewis's earlier stories are related by third-person or first-person narrators whose accounts are objective and reliable. Orual's account of her life, like Lewis's account of his own in *Surprised by Joy,* is retrospective, subjective, and selective. It is striking, then, that suddenly he is able to complete successfully two stories he had long sought to tell but had been unable to: his own story and that of Cupid and Psyche. That he can now tell them, the one as pure autobiography and the other as pure myth, is perhaps the best evidence of a second major change in his life, and of the nature of that change.

As he finds himself able to tell the two stories, he finds they actually are one. The story of Orual, which resembles the myth in *Dymer* and develops most fully the themes of *The Pilgrim's Regress* and *The Great Divorce,* is also the story of *Surprised by Joy*. Each is a story of consciousness, and of the achievement of wholeness through sacrificial death; and each is the story of Lewis himself. In the earlier attempt at autobiography, the character closest to Lewis himself was John, the pilgrim, in search of the object of the longings which had haunted him throughout his life. In *Till We Have Faces*, however, the situation is very different. There is again a character, Psyche, who feels the longings Lewis felt in his youth and journeys onward until she finds their Object despite the various efforts of the rationally minded to impede or dissuade her—much like John in *The Pilgrim's Regress;* but one can almost sense Lewis in the background asserting, "Yes, but that's not me." He clearly feels closer to Orual, the character caught in a tension, attracted to the imaginative but held back from it by the rational, and thus unable to assent fully to the one or the other. That closeness to Orual is reflected in the fullness with which her character is developed. As Father Zogby points out, a key difference between *Till We Have Faces* and *The Pilgrim's Regress* is that "in the former there is the evolution of a fully conscious person, while in the latter we have not evolution but rather an accomplished and staged fact."[15] The point could be generalized to the rest of Lewis's fiction: Orual is the only character whom Lewis seems to know deeply and to develop fully. It is as if his unwillingness to pay attention to his own personality for so many years prevented him from being able to get into the personalities of his characters in a detailed and convincing way. The prolonged attention to his own consciousness in *Surprised by Joy* enabled him to portray the consciousness of at least one character fully. Not surprisingly, that character is very much like himself. Humphrey Carpenter goes so far as to call Orual a "self-portrait of Lewis";[16] I think he is right, and in that lies the key relationship between the two books. For Lewis, like Orual, was seeking wholeness. Orual in one sense spoke for Lewis when she said, "I saw that for years my life had been lived in two halves, never fitted together" (p. 151). She needed to fit the rationalism of the Fox together with the longing and vision of Psyche and the "mystery" surrounding Ungit, as

Lewis needed the imaginative, the rational, and the spiritual to find salvation. *Surprised by Joy* shows Lewis's reconciliation, not yet union, of the three; *Till We Have Faces* depicts their synthesis, through which Orual is able to find completeness and peace, and thus beauty of soul.

From this perspective one can see that *Till We Have Faces* is a deeply Christian work, but in a very different way from the works of the previous decade. It does not have the clear answers and tidy packaging of the apologetic books, or the expository or allegorical explicitness of the Ransom trilogy. In them the reason and the imagination were addressed separately—story for the imagination, explanation for the reason. In *Till We Have Faces* the distinction and the separation break down and Lewis writes to the whole person, emphasizing not answers and formulas but struggles and the ultimate goal. "What happens, then, in *Till We Have Faces*," Gunnar Urang points out, "is that C. S. Lewis moves toward coming to terms with his own dividedness. . . . Do we dare say that he moves toward becoming genuinely 'incarnate' in his fantasy-creation?"[17] The result is a presentation through myth of the essential Christian experience: one is given a "taste" of Reality through the story of Orual's achievement of wholeness of self and with God.

At the same time that it is profoundly and pointedly Christian, it is also fully universal. The use of the classical myth and the pre-Christian setting help universalize the story. And the sense of fragmentation and the search for wholeness involve a universal situation. Thus the story's struggles with separation, of self and from others, and the efforts of its characters to find unity of reason and imagination, of the physical and the psychological, can speak meaningfully to a reader who would reject the more explicitly Christian implications. It is the most universal of Lewis's works; at the same time it is the most closely personal of Lewis's works. Only as he accepted himself and found personal wholeness could he get fully beyond the personal and particular to the artistic and universal wholeness of his finest work.

XIV

Personal Writer of the Sixties: Reason and Imagination United

THE shift in Lewis's emphases and ideas in the late 1940s, which led to a reconciliation of reason and imagination, is evident in his works of the early 1960s, the last few years of Lewis's life. It is apparent first in Lewis's literary criticism, where his willingness to take the self and subjectivity into account leads to new approaches and attitudes in his later work. It is even more apparent in his writings on personal and Christian topics. Lewis wrote no fiction after *Till We Have Faces,* but he began to direct his creative abilities toward the development of forms which would unite imagination and reason in treating personal and Christian topics. The results, in *A Grief Observed* and *Letters to Malcolm,* are among the most creative and impressive of Lewis's career.

Although *An Experiment in Criticism,* Lewis's most important critical work of the sixties,[1] is primarily a response to evaluative criticism, the sort of criticism which regards it as important to separate "good" or "worthwhile" books from the others,[2] it is also a book about *reading:* the "experiment" is, instead of judging people's literary taste by evaluating the books they read, to try judging books by the way people read them: "If all went ideally well we should end by defining good literature as that which permits, invites, or even compels good reading; and bad, as that which does the same for bad reading" (p. 104). The contrast between the approach and attitude here and in "The Personal Heresy" shows the extent to which Lewis's thinking had shifted over the years.

The emphasis in "The Personal Heresy" was on the object, and on reading as a quasi-mechanical process of absorbing the objects presented by the author. The personalities of author and reader were to be disengaged, in good reading, so that private images or overtones would not distort the universality of the things or ideas the author was depicting. Lewis's intention was to remove as far as possible the subjective element in writing (the writer should imitate universals) and in reading (the reader should simply look through the author's eyes at the universals the author was imitating). In keeping with his heavy emphasis on objectivism philosophically, and his avoidance of attention to the self, he advocated an objective, depersonalized approach to literature.

Two decades later one finds a good deal of Lewis's critical energy being directed toward the act of reading. That is the starting point in a chapter of a proposed book, written sometime after 1957: it begins, "There are more ways than one of reading old books," and goes on to compare them and argue for the advantages of a historical approach.[3] His essay on "Metre" asks not "which analysis . . . is 'true' but which is the most useful" within the "different and defensible ways of reading poetry aloud."[4] And in "The Anthropological Approach" Lewis argues that to approach literature as a source for data on ancient rites and practices differs from reading for its impact as *literature*.[5] Lewis was ahead of the times when, in the 1950s, he was treating the act of reading as central to the experience of literature—in the late 1960s and throughout the 1970s, reading theory became the most influential and controversial area of literary study.

As he focused on reading in his fifties, Lewis was picking up and developing a remark he made in his diary in his twenties: "A poem unread is not a poem at all."[6] The words in a book are only ink markings on paper: they are real ink marks, but they become a real work of literature only as an intelligence takes in the words and combinations of words and finds them meaningful. In *An Experiment in Criticism* Lewis put it as follows: "Whatever the value of literature may be, it is actual only when and where good readers read.

Books on a shelf are only potential literature" (p. 104). In evaluating literature, then, Lewis suggests that attention should be directed toward readers and reading rather than toward an abstract text.

For such an approach, one's definition of reading becomes crucial—and this may be where Lewis's approach becomes limited because of residues from his approaches in "The Personal Heresy." Thus, early in *An Experiment in Criticism,* he says that in reading one must be "carried through and beyond words into something non-verbal and non-literary" (p. 27). This sounds much like the mechanical process of "The Personal Heresy," and to the extent that it is, Lewis's definition of reading will not be able to account adequately for the imaginative activity reading involves. For reading is not just a matter of getting self out of the way so one can absorb, directly, what the author saw. Of course readers can and should, as Lewis says, lay aside their own set of beliefs while reading and "enter into other men's beliefs (those, say, of Lucretius or Lawrence) even though we think them untrue" (p. 138). But attaining "objectivity" is not so simple as this, for this deals only with a sort of large-scale subjectivity, but neglects a more basic, smaller-scale subjectivity: the words, images, and experiences the author uses can be received and "grasped" only as they are interpreted, shaped, felt, and reacted to in terms of the reader's own experience with similar words, images, and experiences. Thus, in one sense, no reader sees the thing or idea the author saw: the reader sees only his or her private version of it. In that sense it is often said that no two readings of a poem or novel are the same, or that the poem or novel itself is not the same for different readers of it. Reading involves an imaginative, emotional, and intellectual interaction between the words an author writes and a reader's understanding of and response to them. Subjectivity on the large scale can be set aside—systems of belief can be ignored while one is reading a work whose ideas one disagrees with. But subjectivity on the smaller scale hardly can be, for one cannot set aside or ignore the entire range of minute particulars which enables one to receive and respond to words themselves.

Lewis does at times seem to acknowledge the inescapability of subjectivism in the smaller scale. In *An Experiment in Criticism* he appears to regard reading less mechanically and objectively than in "The Personal Heresy." Thus he writes, "Admittedly, we can never quite get out of our own skins. Whatever we do, something of our own and of our age's making will remain in our experience of all literature" (p. 101). And thus he calls for a critical approach centered on "literature in operation" (p. 105) and compares reading to "taking part in a choric dance invented by a good choreographer" (p. 134). In such statements, together with the emphasis on "the very objects [works of literature] are" (p. 82), Lewis appears to be attempting to integrate the objectivity he had long believed crucial to right thinking with the subjective element in reading. He remains a firm objectivist, but does so while granting that objectivism is not as simple and clear-cut in practice as it had seemed to him in the thirties and forties. He attempts to develop an approach which accents the activity of reading, while retaining an emphasis on the work as object: one's perceptions must be kept in check by a steady attention to the "real" work, the "thing made" by the author. It is sound advice and potentially valuable as a corrective to criticism today, although, because it does not take the lower-scale subjectivity fully into account, it does not adequately resolve the issue of how one can come to know "the real" so that one can attend to it properly.[7]

It is in the context of his desire to acknowledge subjectivity, but use "reality" as a check upon it, that Lewis's distinction between "receiving" and "using"—which seems initially to strengthen the earlier, narrowly objective sort of reading—should be understood. Lewis elaborates the two terms as follows: "A Work of (whatever) art can be either 'received' or 'used.' When we 'receive' it we exert our senses and imagination and various other powers according to a pattern invented by the artist. When we 'use' it we treat it as assistance for our own activities" (p. 88). Such "use" may be fantasizing and castle-building, or isolating an author's "themes" and thus turning from the work experienced imaginatively to a reflective abstraction of one's own making. In any case, it is wholly subjective, without the restraint or corrective of an external frame of reference: "We are so busy doing things with the work that we give it little chance to work on us. Thus increasingly we meet only ourselves" (p. 85). In contrast, "receiving" seems initially to be wholly objective, the reader simply taking in and processing the verbal signals emitted by the work. But if Lewis is, throughout the book, acknowledging and taking into consideration a subjective element in reading, then "receiving" cannot be quite the mechanical process its metaphor implies. Then Lewis's distinction is not between a nonsubjective activity (receiving) and a subjective one (using), but between an acceptable kind and degree of subjectivity (one kept in check by contact with external reality) and a kind less acceptable because it is unrestrained by reality. That this is Lewis's intent for the terms comes out in his application of them to art:

> We sit down before the picture in order to have something done to us, not that we may do things with it. The first demand any work of any art makes upon us is surrender. . . . I do not mean by this that the right spectator is passive. His also is an imaginative activity; but an obedient one. He seems passive at first because he is making sure of his orders. (p. 19)

There is, here, less tension than there was in the 1930s between the subjective and the objective in Lewis. His literary criticism of the late 1950s and early 1960s shows a movement toward reconciliation of the inner and the outer, an acceptance of and comfortableness with ambiguity, and an awareness of the importance of self and the subjective, which is evident also in his writings about Christianity at the same time.

Without that willingness to give attention to self and to use the subjective, Lewis would not have been able to write *A Grief Observed,* a beautiful, sensitive book based on his feelings after the death of his wife, Helen Joy Davidman.

The point is precisely that the book is about his feelings: it necessarily is subjective; instead of rejecting the subject because it is personal, Lewis here seeks a form and style which will allow him to take advantage of its personalness.

The text states that the book originated as "notes" jotted as a sort of diary in four empty manuscript books that happened to be in the house. According to Walter Hooper, Lewis seemed always to have a notebook on his desk in front of him in which he would scribble ideas as they occurred to him. Drafts of the opening paragraphs of essays and books, such as "Reply to Professor Haldane" and *That Hideous Strength,* are in such notebooks.[8] Perhaps *A Grief Observed* began so, too—the evidence suggests to me that it did not. The important thing, however, is that, even if Lewis did not write in four such books, they did give him the idea for a form in which he could express deep and private feelings in a way that could be helpful to others. It is crucial to separate the truth of the book from biographical accuracy. Lewis wrote what was—in its published form, at any rate—a fictional diary, and used in it a "persona," an imaginary "diarist" through whom he could express himself. He indicates the separation of the diarist from himself by using a pseudonym, N. W. Clerk—the book was published under Lewis's own name only after his death—and by including a reference to "J." (that is "Jack," his own nickname) as a third person, in addition to the diarist and H.[9] The "I" in the book, therefore, must not be completely identified with Lewis, and great caution should be used in treating the book as a source of information about Lewis's life or marriage. In its form it was an imaginative book, one for which matters of historical factuality are not relevant.

But the truth value of the book does not depend on its biographical accuracy, or on its being a transcript of notes Lewis wrote in manuscript books to vent his grief. The real test is its value as an account of the stages of grief: if this is successful, and I think it is, then Lewis's choice of form and approach was a wise one. The use of a fictional framework does not mean that Lewis did not experience the feelings he describes. Surely much of the book is a firsthand record of what grief feels like, particularly the unexpected emotions and reactions: "There is a sort of invisible blanket between the world and me. I find it hard to take in what anyone says. Or perhaps, hard to want to take it in" (p. 7). Similarly, grief "gives life a permanently provisional feeling. It doesn't seem worth starting anything. I can't settle down. I yawn, I fidget, I smoke too much. Up till this I always had too little time. Now there is nothing but time. Almost pure time, empty successiveness" (p. 29). And, "the agonies, the mad midnight moments, must, in the course of nature, die away. But what will follow? Just this apathy, this dead flatness?" (p. 30). If they are emotions and reactions he remembers he had rather than ones recorded immediately in a journal, that would not make them less real, or less valuable—valuable to those who go through the experiences he has just passed through, and to others who may misunderstand them. Thus the "diary" suggests its own purpose: "Why has no one told me these things? How easily I might have misjudged another man in the same situation" (p. 37). What Lewis should have been told but wasn't, he will seek to tell others.

Although Lewis intended that the book be instructive, he chose not to make it expository. To have organized what he experienced and learned into neat essays would have cost much of its immediacy and impact. So he turned instead to a form which would engage the imagination and emotions. To the extent that the book could be made to sound convincingly like a private diary, it would be both moving and instructive: a fruitful blending of reason and imagination. It was necessary, therefore, that the "diary" have sufficient detail to seem genuine. Thus precise details are given about the manuscript books: "This is the fourth—and the last— empty MS. book I can find in the house. . . . I resolve to let this limit my jottings. I *will not* start buying books for the purpose" (p. 47). And thus he lingers over the motives that led to the diary-keeping: "What am I to do? I must have some drug, and reading isn't a strong enough drug now. By writing it all down (all?—no: one thought in a hundred) I believe I get a little outside it" (p. 12). Such devices for cre-

169

ating verisimilitude—a semblance of truth—are old and conventional features of imaginative writing.

The writing must seem casual and informal in tone and manner, but also be sufficiently attractive and orderly to be pleasing and inviting to a reader. Lewis achieves this balance by unobtrusive, but effective, rhetorical techniques. There are the parallel phrasings—"No one ever told me that grief felt so like fear" (p. 7); "And no one ever told me about the laziness of grief'" (p. 8); "And grief still feels like fear" (p. 29)—and the repeated images, which unify the book and give it a sense of movement and progress:

> But go to Him when your need is desperate, when all other help is vain, and what do you find? A door slammed in the face, and a sound of bolting and double bolting on the inside. (p. 9)

> I have begged to be given even one hundredth part of the same assurance [of continued existence after death] about H. There is no answer. Only the locked door. (p. 11)

> Turned to God, my mind no longer meets that locked door. (p. 49)

> When I lay these questions before God I get no answer. But a rather special sort of "No answer." It is not the locked door. (p. 54)

The prose style is equally effective: "Slowly, quietly, like snow-flakes—like the small flakes that come when it is going to snow all night—little flakes of me, my impressions, my selections, are settling down on the image of her. The real shape will be quite hidden in the end" (p. 19). The beauty—in image, rhythm, and sound—of such a passage exceeds that of much of his other published work.

There is also a tidiness in the development of the four parts, a sense of completion at the end of each stage and of a terminus in style. This is true especially of the final section. The conclusion goes back to H.'s last words, "I am at peace with God" (p. 24), first quoted when the diarist was very much not at peace and very much wished her back with him. When the phrase returns, supplemented by a line from *The Divine Comedy,* it gives a sense of acceptance and assurance: "How wicked it would be, if we could, to call the dead back! She said not to me but to the chaplain, 'I am at peace with God.' She smiled, but not at me. *Poi si tornò all' eterna fontana"* (p. 60). The quoted line is from the *Paradiso,* XXXI, 93, as Beatrice, Dante's beloved and his spiritual guide, leaves him and returns to her heavenly throne high above him. In response to his words of praise and gratitude for what she meant to him, she, "it seemed, did smile," and "then to the eternal fountain turned her head."[10] The identification of H. with Beatrice, the suggestion that H. has led the writer to a deeper spiritual maturity, as Beatrice did for Dante, and the gentle affirmation that H. too has gone to a heavenly throne, creates a beautiful, touching, deeply satisfying—and carefully crafted—ending.

The central theme of the book is grief—a description not of the "state" but the "process" of sorrow (p. 47) offered in the hope that a description of one person's experience may be of help to others in their efforts to deal with bereavement. Beyond that theme is another, which could be explored only with the deliberate, willing acceptance of "self" shown in the book's form and style. Central to the book is a further, and more successful, effort to reconcile the "subjective" and the "real." The issue grows out of the writer's initial desire to remember H. as she "really was"; he fears that he will forget what she was really like, for he has no good photograph of her and cannot picture her accurately in his mind. He is nearly always thinking about her, but he realizes that his mind selects and groups the memories, and he fears he will replace the real person with an illusory one of his own devising: "Already . . . I can feel the slow, insidious beginning of a process that will make the H. I think of into a more and more imaginary woman" (p. 18). He must avoid the trap into which Dymer nearly fell, of attaching himself to an illusion, a projection of an ideal lover who "will do whatever you want, . . . smile or frown, be tender, gay, ribald, or argumentative just as your mood demands" (p. 20). That is not at all his desire: "It was H. I loved. As if I wanted to fall in love with my memory of her, an image in my own mind! It would be a sort of incest" (p. 19).[11] The subjective is unavoidable, but he must not allow his own perceptions to replace reality, as Lewis's father so often did in *Surprised by Joy*. Perceptions and images must be kept in check by comparison with the real. The difficulty comes in knowing where that reality is to be found and how it is to be held.

The answer now, unlike earlier in Lewis's life, is not a total rejection of subjectivity and an unrelenting pursuit of that which is solid, universal, and unchangingly "objective." The answer begins with acknowledgment of the subjective: "Five senses; an incurably abstract intellect; a haphazardly selective memory; a set of preconceptions and assumptions so numerous that I can never examine more than a minority of them—never become even conscious of them all. How much of total reality can such an apparatus let through?" (p. 51). The position Lewis now puts forward is a conscious interaction between the "self" and the "real." The images and impressions of the subjective self must, time after time, be brought into contact with external stimuli, must be confronted so that which is merely projection or illusion may be shattered. The diarist's experience in desiring an awareness of H.'s continuing existence illustrates this. He had formed his own impressions of how that awareness would come and how it would feel. But his impressions had to be shattered in order for the awareness to come, and it proved to be very different from what he expected. It was not a mental image or an emotional fullness, but a mental or intellectual intimacy: "Not at all like a rapturous re-union of lovers. Much more like getting a telephone call or a wire from her about some practical arrangement. Not that there was any 'message'—just intelligence and attention" (p. 57). Something like this was Lewis's experience; that of others may not be the same—Lewis's was what it was because Lewis was the sort of man he was. But others also must avoid being locked in by their preconceptions, and Lewis's recounting of his experience may form part of the external data which will help others shatter their "idols" and become open to reality.

As he does so often, Lewis uses the lower to illuminate the higher, a human relationship to illuminate relationship with the divine. Here too there must be an acceptance of, but a check upon, the subjective. As we form images of others which must be shattered by contact with and reception of their real personalities, so it must be with our approach to God: "My idea of God is not a divine idea. It has to be shattered time after time. He shatters it Himself. He is the great iconoclast. Could we not almost say that this shattering is one of the marks of His presence? The Incarnation is the supreme example; it leaves all previous ideas of the Messiah in ruins" (p. 52). As in "Myth Became Fact," Lewis here moves away from sight imagery, his earlier model for reception of the objective, as inadequate. Loving H., now that she is dead, has become, for the writer, somewhat like loving God: "In both cases I must stretch out the arms and hands of love—its eyes cannot here be used—to the reality, through—across—all the changeful phantasmagoria of my thoughts, passions, and imaginings" (pp. 52–53). "Reality" cannot be "grasped" or "taken in" by the sight, but must be "embraced" by the hands and arms—enclosed as an object of affection, not clutched as if a possession. Such an embrace involves subjectivity, but it keeps one turning outward, critically, toward external stimuli, to ensure that the subjective is processing external data rather than projecting one's own perceptions in front of, or in place of, the external (as in *An Experiment in Criticism,* the subjective must be kept in check by steady attention to the text). The outward reflex leads naturally into another familiar image: the writer's experience of H.'s presence "was quite incredibly unemotional. Just the impression of her *mind* momentarily facing my own" (p. 57). "Facing," intentionally or not, takes one back to *Till We Have Faces.* Until the writer was able to get past his selfish need of H. and his ideas about how he was to experience her presence, until his subjective projections could be broken by and reshaped by reality, he did not have a face, did not have a real and receptive means to meet and accept the face of her present being.

Near the end of his life, in a book published after his death, Lewis attempted a new fusion of reason and imagination. In *Letters to Malcolm: Chiefly on Prayer* Lewis carries on a fictional correspondence with an imaginary friend, doing it so realistically that many readers have found it hard to believe there was no actual Malcolm. It is in a sense an expository work, intended to clarify and illuminate ideas; but it is at the same time a creative work, engaging many of the same writing skills as a story or novel. The two sides, rational and imaginative, are fully integrated and reveal the wholeness and ease Lewis achieved in his final years.

To make the correspondence effective required first that Lewis develop for Malcolm a clear and fairly rounded character, much like that of a character in a story. Malcolm is a long-time friend, one with whom Lewis had corresponded on previous occasions. Lewis recalls their undergraduate years with their "interminable letters on the *Republic,* and classical metres, and what was then the 'new' psychology."[12] Malcolm is a layman, probably a teacher or a don (p. 51; Letter VI), apparently in the natural sciences, since Lewis yields to Malcolm's superior knowledge when he introduces a scientific issue (p. 57; VII). He is middle-aged, for he proposed marriage some twenty-five years ago (p. 58; VII), and married—his wife is named Betty; they have a son named George. He, like Lewis, is an Anglican, but he seems, from his dislike of written prayers, to be less "High Church" than Lewis. He is also less flexible and accepting of new or "different" ways than is Lewis: Malcolm wants simply to reject theologian A. R. Vidler's call for a "religionless Christianity" (p. 45; VI), while Lewis finds value in what Vidler says,[13] and Malcolm is bothered by Lewis's "frivolousness" in using the metaphors of "dance" and "game" for religion (p. 121; XVII).

Lewis also uses a story-like approach in building a larger context for his acquaintance with Malcolm. He gives it both a past history and a continuing present. Thus Lewis refers to a visit from Malcolm when "the great blow had fallen upon me" and Lewis had tried at first to act as if nothing were wrong (p. 36; IV). He mentions various times they were together: in a pub at Coton (p. 43; V); with Betty at Mullingar (p. 103; XV); on a walk in the Forest of Dean (p. 116; XVII); and in Edinburgh on a night they nearly came to

blows (p. 121; XVII). He reminds Malcolm of a "famous occasion" when a friend named Bill came to them and very
reluctantly, hesitantly, asked to borrow a hundred pounds
(pp. 53–54; VII). At present Malcolm is receiving and reply-
ing to Lewis's letters. Thus Lewis refers to Malcolm's letters
(e.g., p. 31; IV) and even quotes from them (as on p. 22 and
p. 126; II, XVIII). He sometimes disagrees with what Malcolm says in his letters (p. 53; VII), answers questions raised
by Malcolm (p. 138; XX), and follows Malcolm's example in
digressing to a related topic (p. 124; XVIII). One letter makes
arrangements for Malcolm and George to join Lewis for din-
ner in college (p. 143; XX), and the last letter concludes
with details about Lewis's approaching weekend visit to
Malcolm and Betty's home (p. 159; XXII). This is another
example, more sustained and elaborate, of the kind of verisimilitude Lewis employed in *A Grief Observed*. If he can
be so specific and can go into all that detail, surely it must
be true; and if readers are taken in by the apparent truth,
the writer has managed the technique very well. To notice
the skill with which the author employs his craft becomes
one of the pleasures of the book.

The fictional correspondence is also functional. At an
initial level it serves to remove Lewis from a position of
authority. He is not an "expert" qualified to deliver talks on
the BBC, or a scholar who has worked out a carefully reasoned defense of the possibility of miracle. These are just
"letters"—he does not even dignify them with the label "correspondence." Thus the form itself suggests a casual, unstud-
ied, personal approach, quite in contrast to what he would
need to do if he were "writing a book." With tongue in cheek,
he notes,

> However badly needed a good book on prayer is, I shall never
> try to write it. Two people on the foothills comparing notes in
> private are all very well. But in a book one would inevitably
> seem to be attempting, not discussion, but instruction. And
> for me to offer the world instruction about prayer would be
> impudence. (p. 87; XII)

The approach he adopted gives formal cognizance to the uncertainties he felt and allows him to proceed honestly and naturally, without recourse to the disclaimers and apologies which often seem awkward or artificial in an essay.

But the form is not merely functional: it is not just another imaginative vehicle serving the ends of reason, as in *The Screwtape Letters* or *The Great Divorce*. This Robert Merchant failed to appreciate when, about a decade ago, he called *Letters to Malcolm* "the worst (or should I say, Least attractive?) of Lewis's books." He criticizes it as being "self-consciously clever, almost pretentious" and as having "a great deal of somewhat useless filler." Obvious and valid as he believes these criticisms are, he concludes "they do not negate the essential contents of *Malcolm*."[14] Such charges betray a deep lack of sympathy with, or understanding of, what Lewis was attempting, shown particularly in the effort to separate the "contents" from the "useless filler" of the form Lewis adopted. For the "filler" is integral to the content and reflects Lewis's new ability to live with ambiguity, to accept greys instead of seeking a black and a white side to every issue. No longer does Lewis adopt a rigid attitude and insist on absolutes. He seems to have learned through experience that life does not break down into such formulas, and *Letters to Malcolm* reflects such experience in its ideas and its form.

For the book is meant, like a story or a poem, to be read straight through and to be received primarily through the imagination rather than the intellect. To endeavor to distill the "contents" of *Letters to Malcolm* into an outline and set of notes proves frustrating and futile; one ends up with mostly disconnected ideas and some very quotable snippets. Lewis, however, was not seeking to express a set of insights or lessons which could be listed and discussed quite apart from the form in which they appeared—as can be done quite readily and profitably with his expository works, or with *The Screwtape Letters*, for example. He was attempting to achieve a key effect of myth in a nonmythical work: to fuse the "knowing" of ideas crucial to Christian growth with the "taste" of experienced reality necessary to give that knowledge vitality. And to a great extent, I believe, he succeeded.

176

His approach is perhaps best illustrated by Letter VIII, particularly when it is contrasted with an essay written some ten years earlier and touching on many of the same points. In "Petitionary Prayer: A Problem without an Answer," Lewis treats many of the points covered in *Letters to Malcolm,* in the "simple essay" format Father Merchant would have preferred.[15] The problem Lewis explores is that the New Testament instructs one, on the one hand, to offer petitionary prayers conditionally, always with the qualifier, "Thy will be done," and on the other hand to pray with unwavering faith that the very things asked for will be received. He explores the biblical basis for both positions, discusses solutions others have offered for the problem, and ends by admitting that after much searching he has found no answer to the problem. It is an excellent essay: clear, orderly, well-supported, honest, and warm. But it remains a rather abstract, distanced discussion of a problem, one step removed from the experiences that make it vital and relevant.

In *Letters to Malcolm* Lewis attempts to eliminate that step. After a discussion in Letter VII of the relation between petitionary prayer and determinism, Lewis creates a dramatic situation in which George (Malcolm and Betty's son) is ill, perhaps seriously ill; the diagnosis awaits the results of medical tests. Letter VIII opens with a comment on the difference this situation makes: "The distance between the abstract, 'Does God hear petitionary prayers?' and the concrete, 'Will He—can He—grant our prayers for George?' is apparently infinite" (p. 60). The abstract issues discussed in Letter VII, and in "Petitionary Prayer," somehow seem hollow, for the moment, in the face of an immediate, personal situation and the anxiety it causes. Lewis examines at some length that sense of anxiety and anguish and abandonment. Anguish, in the face of such uncertainty, does not show a defective faith—indeed, Christ felt such anguish in the garden of Gethsemane. It is, rather, characteristic and representative, "the human situation writ large. These are among the things it means to be a man. Every rope breaks when you seize it. Every door is slammed shut as you reach it. To

177

be like the fox at the end of the run; the earths all staked"
(p. 64). Such a situation, such anxiety (the imagery of the
door echoes the passages of near-desperation in *A Grief Observed*), strips away the abstractions and forces one to take
matters seriously:

> Certainly we were talking too lightly and easily about these
> things a fortnight ago. We were playing with counters. One
> used to be told as a child: "Think what you're saying." Ap-
> parently we need also to be told: "Think what you're think-
> ing." The stakes have to be raised before we take the game
> quite seriously. I know this is the opposite of what is often
> said about the necessity of keeping all emotion out of our
> intellectual processes—"You can't think straight unless you
> are cool." But then neither can you think deep if you are. I
> suppose one must try every problem in both states. (p. 66)

Lewis uses the episode about George, and other similar
touches, to raise the stakes for the reader, to take the reader
beyond an abstract discussion to a deep and serious involvement in a situation.[16]

To all this may come the reply that it is not real: since
there was no Malcolm and the letters are a fiction, it is still
a game of counters. It is if one reads the book with the
intellect, searching for principles to draw out and testing
the historical accuracy of the details. But so too is every
myth a game of counters, unless one receives it imaginatively, as it was meant to be received. Lewis expects a reader
to enter with the imagination the world he creates in *Letters
to Malcolm,* to accept—for as long as one is reading the
book—the pretense that Malcolm and Betty and George,
and their problems and anxieties, are real. Lewis intended
to deceive no one about their actual reality: he was using
an old literary convention, an imaginary correspondence,
a convention he had used before; he expected readers to
recognize it and accept it for what it was, as he had expected
them to in *The Screwtape Letters* and the letter at the end
of *Out of the Silent Planet.* The convention demands that
readers share the anxiety when George is ill and the relief
when Lewis hears that the danger is past. Through such
imaginative involvement in the correspondence, one is taken

outside the self to share the experience of another; one gains knowledge, not through abstract intellectual means but embodied in the experiences and personalities of others.

There is much Lewis wanted to communicate in *Letters to Malcolm,* often points or ideas he had expressed elsewhere in essays. But unlike *The Screwtape Letters* and *The Great Divorce,* the imaginative structure is not there to serve reason, in getting a message across. The sense of separation, the tension between reason and imagination, is gone. In *Letters to Malcolm* reason and imagination do more than cooperate: they are unified. Neither has priority over the other; neither is held back by a sense of "limitation" upon it. Form and ideas are virtually inseparable: the ideas must be experienced through the form, through the letters and through the characters and lives the letters create, to do the ideas justice. In *Letters to Malcolm* Lewis achieved outside of myth what he had achieved, at last, through myth in *Till We Have Faces:* a full reconciliation and unification of the reason he admired with the imagination he loved.

Having examined Lewis's attitude toward reason and imagination across his career, we should perhaps return to "Reason," the poem discussed briefly in the Preface. Its endorsement of reason is strong and unequivocal:

> Set on the soul's acropolis the reason stands
> A virgin, arm'd, commercing with celestial light,
> And he who sins against her has defiled his own
> Virginity: no cleansing makes his garment white;
> So clear is reason.[17]

Lewis associates reason with Athena, Greek goddess of defensive warfare and practical reason, who resided in the Acropolis, the highest point of her city Athens, and became protectress of the ruling kings. He depicts reason in a protectress role, defending the soul not against the imagination but against unreason or error, which assaults and attempts to capture the soul, the citadel of the human personality. Lewis's high regard for the reason is best revealed by the sexual and religious imagery he uses. Reason is clear and pure and stable—there is nothing indulgent, or lax, or compromising about her; the life of reason is closely linked with sexual virginity, with its traditionally strong positive connotations. Those connotations lead into the equally close links with religion: reason is "celestial" and can be sinned against, not just in the sense that one human can wrong another but in the sense of a violation of divine expectations.

By contrast, the imagery given to imagination is dark and seductive—she is desirable, even sexually appealing, but thus has a slightly dangerous and questionable character:

> But how dark, imagining,
> Warm, dark, obscure and infinite, daughter of Night:
> Dark is her brow, the beauty of her eyes with sleep
> Is loaded, and her pains are long, and her delight.[18]

The "daughter of Night" is Demeter, Greek goddess of vegetative growth and harvest, by some accounts also a goddess of the underworld—a *chthonia,* or earth goddess. The earth-mother image stresses the creative and generative aspects of the imagination. The warmth, sleep, and delight, with their sensual and sexual overtones, are in sharp contrast with the virginity of Athena, for Demeter was linked traditionally with the Eleusinian mystery religions, which celebrate ritually the loss of virginity as a symbol of "death" giving birth to new life. Thus the endorsement of the imagination is definitely equivocal: for "dark" to be used three times in three lines gives it heavy emphasis and moves beyond suggestions of richness and mysteriousness to a sense of impenetrability and danger.

The imagery suggests a strong opposition between reason and imagination. Lewis sees positive elements in both—the clarity and strength of reason, the beauty and creativity of imagination—and he recognizes that both must be present in a balanced personality. Thus he urges the reader to "Tempt not Athene" and to "Wound not in her fertile pains / Demeter, nor rebel against her mother-right." The poet longs for something that will ease the tension in their relationship, that will "make imagination's dim exploring touch / Ever report the same as intellectual sight."[19] But such a total harmony of intellect and imagination would seem difficult when the two elements are so strongly opposed as they seem here, or when one is regarded as preferable to or more reliable than the other, as is surely the case here. That Lewis is more comfortable with reason, that it sets the standard to which imagination must reach, is shown by the imagery of "light," "height," and "sight": the "dim exploring touch" of the imagination falls far short of the firm, assured grasp of "intellectual sight."

It appears to me most likely, therefore, that the poem was written in the late 1920s, after or near Lewis's acceptance of Theism but before his conversion to Christianity. What he seems to be seeking is not a general harmony of reason and imagination but a concord between them in the area of Christian doctrines. In his letter to Greeves describing his late-night talk with Tolkien and Dyson, Lewis indicated that the barrier to his acceptance of Christianity was imaginative acceptance of the mythical elements, not— at that point, anyway—difficulty in accepting its doctrines intellectually. With Tolkien's guidance, Lewis reached a harmony of imagination and intellect which enabled him to become a Christian. But it was not the broad concord the poem mentions, in which the imagination and reason always arrive at ("Ever report") the same result. The spiritual wholeness he found as a Christian did not lead directly to a wholeness in the areas of reason and imagination.

That wholeness did come, but it was much later in his life, under different circumstances, long after he became able to believe in Christianity. Late in his life a shaking of his confidence in the rational and the cumulative effects of a steady growth of confidence in the imaginative and mythical made possible a full reconciliation of the "maid and mother" he had written of so much earlier. The result was a wholeness, not just in Lewis's writings but in his life generally. It is as if he had adopted much earlier the role of "the fully rational arguer" and attempted to live out that role as tutor, lecturer, apologist, and conversationalist, until, in the 1950s, he was able to let the role fall away, accept the limitations of a totally rational approach, and become a more relaxed and balanced person. He seems to move away from a certain rigidity and dogmaticness in his later years, and to grow in grace and wisdom beyond the growth that often comes with the mellowing of old age. The works of his last decade have a breadth of outlook, a depth of experience, and a unity of the imaginative with the intellectual greater than those of the earlier works. The tension between Athena and Demeter, between reason and the imagination, which ran throughout Lewis's life and exerted differing influences in much of it, was at last resolved and gave way to a personal wholeness, a concord of intellectual depth with imaginative height, and his finest works as a Christian writer and story-teller.

Notes

Preface

1. Lewis, "Reason," first published in Lewis's *Poems,* ed. Walter Hooper (London: Geoffrey Bles, 1964), p. 81. For a discussion of the poem, relating it to *The Pilgrim's Regress* and *Till We Have Faces,* see Kathryn Lindskoog, "Getting It Together: Lewis and the Two Hemispheres of Knowing," *Mythlore,* 6 (Winter 1979), 45–47.

2. Lewis nowhere defines imagination explicitly, and he uses the term in a number of ways: as the image-making power ("imagine two books lying on a table"), the creative or inventive power ("fired the imagination of the *hrossa*"), the power to make up things ("of course one can imagine things"), the power to create fiction ("solely an imaginative supposal"), the mysteriousness and adventurousness of romance ("almost everything the imagination craves—irony, heroism, vastness, unity in multiplicity, and a tragic close"), and " 'Imagination' in some high Coleridgean sense."

The essential concept, however, is that expressed by Tolkien in "On Fairy-Stories": "The human mind is capable of forming mental images of things not actually present. The faculty of conceiving the images is . . . called Imagination" (*Essays Presented to Charles Williams* [London: Oxford University Press, 1947], p. 66). That emphasizes imagination's involvement with the concrete in contrast with reason's concern with abstractions; with fiction rather than fact; with making up, "creating," rather than observing; with integration rather than analysis and identification. In a recent article Owen Barfield gives as imagination's concerns "resemblance" rather than a logical nexus, "metamorphosis" rather than sequence and aggregation, "interpenetration" rather than a fixed shape or pattern. The resemblance of these qualities to the "mishmash" of modern relativism and philosophical subjectivism, Barfield believes, accounts for some of Lewis's reluctance to commit himself to a theory of imagination. Barfield sees a bifurcation between Lewis the logician and Lewis the imaginative writer similar to what I describe, but explains Lewis's attitude toward imagination not as distrust but as a "desire to protect . . . and insulate imagination, so that it could continue to live its own pure and chaste life" ("Lewis, Truth and Imagination," *Kodon* [Wheaton College], Winter 1978, pp. 17–26).

3. Smith, *Patches of Godlight: The Pattern of Thought of C. S. Lewis* (Athens: University of Georgia Press, 1981), p. x.

SECTION ONE: THE WORK ITSELF

I—Introduction: The Background

1. The text and a reliable translation may be found in *The Golden Ass, being the Metamorphoses of Lucius Apuleius,* with an English translation by W. Adlington, Loeb Classical Library (London: Heinemann, 1915), pp. 184–99. I have drawn here upon the selective summary of Apuleius's story which Lewis appended to the American edition of *Till We Have Faces.*

2. Boccaccio, *The Book of Theseus,* trans. Bernadette M. McCoy (New York: Medieval Text Association, 1974), p. 201; William Warburton, *The Divine Legation of Moses Demonstrated* (1738; rpt. London: Thomas Tegg and Son, 1837), I, 324 (original in italics); Robert Graves, "Introduction," *The Golden Ass* (New York: Farrar, Straus, and Giroux, 1951), p. xix.

3. For Lewis's ideas on myth, see pages 122–26 and 137–39. Also Peter Macky, "Myth as the Way We Can Taste Reality: An Analysis of C. S. Lewis's Theory," *The Lamp-Post of the Southern California C. S. Lewis Society,* 6 (July 1982), 1–7; Dean Loganbill, "Myth, Reality, and *Till We Have Faces,*" *Man's 'Natural Powers': Essays for and about C. S. Lewis,* ed. Raymond P. Tripp, Jr. (n.p.: The Society for New Language Study, 1975), pp. 55–58. Also, Don D. Elgin, "True and False Myth in C. S. Lewis' *Till We Have Faces,*" *South Central Bulletin,* 41 (1981), 98–101.

4. Otto, *The Idea of the Holy: An Inquiry into the Non-rational Factor in the Idea of the Divine and its Relation to the Rational,* trans. John W. Harvey (1920; London: Oxford University Press, 1923). Lewis summarized Otto's points in the first chapter of *The Problem of Pain* (London: Geoffrey Bles—Centenary Press, 1940), and more briefly in his reply to H. H. Price's paper "Is Theism Important?", *Socratic Digest,* No. 5 (1952), 49–50 (reprinted in *God in the Dock: Essays on Theology and Ethics,* ed. Walter Hooper [Grand Rapids, Mich.: Eerdmans, 1970], pp. 174–75; in Britain, *Undeceptions: Essays on Theology and Ethics,* ed. Walter Hooper [London: Geoffrey Bles, 1971], pp. 140–41).

5. From Lewis's diary entry for 9 September 1923, included in volume VIII, page 150, of the unpublished *Memoirs of the Lewis Family, 1850–1930,* compiled and typed from original documents by Warren Lewis, now in the Wade Collection, Wheaton College, Wheaton, Illinois. Used by permission of C. S. Lewis PTE Limited and the Wade Collection.

6. *Memoirs of the Lewis Family,* VIII, 163–64.

7. Lewis, diary entry for 23 November 1922, in *Memoirs of the Lewis Family,* VII, 281.

8. Lewis, *Till We Have Faces: A Myth Retold* (London: Geoffrey Bles, 1956), p. [1].

II—Chapters 1-2: Methods, Motives, Materialism

1. The letter is dated 10 February 1957, and is found in *Letters of C. S. Lewis,* ed. W. H. Lewis (London: Geoffrey Bles, 1966), pp. 273–74. The imagined location of the setting is not very important. The Kingdom of Glome was, Chad Walsh suggests, "somewhere on the fringes of Asia Minor,

... possibly in what is now Turkey, or near the Black Sea" (*The Literary Legacy of C. S. Lewis* [New York: Harcourt Brace Jovanovich, 1979], p. 161). But, as Thomas Howard has written, myth requires a world that is remote from us and at the same time rooted in our world: "We don't want our myths taking place in 1929, or even 1066, nor do we want them to occur in East Lansing or Gary, Indiana" ("Myth: A Flight to Reality," in *The Christian Imagination: Essays on Literature and the Arts,* ed. Leland Ryken [Grand Rapids, Mich.: Baker Book House, 1981], p. 203). Lewis's use of an indeterminate time and place functions nicely to enhance his remythologizing of Apuleius.

2. Como, *"Till We Have Faces*: A Preface to Comprehension," *CSL: The Bulletin of the New York C. S. Lewis Society,* 7 (November 1975), 3. For a fuller analysis of Lewis's changes in Apuleius's tale, see Steve J. Van Der Weele, "From Mt. Olympus to Glome: C. S. Lewis's Dislocation of Apuleius's 'Cupid and Psyche' in *Till We Have Faces,"* in *The Longing for a Form: Essays on the Fiction of C. S. Lewis,* ed. Peter J. Schakel (Kent, Ohio: Kent State University Press, 1977), pp. 182–92. Also, Andrew Howard, *"Till We Have Faces* and its Mythological and Literary Precursors," *Mythlore,* 4 (March 1977), 30–32; and Gisbert Kranz, "Amor und Psyche: Metamorphose eines Mythos bei C. S. Lewis," *Arcadia: Zeitschrift für vergleichende Literaturwissenschaft,* 4 (1969), 285–99; see also his *C. S. Lewis: Studien zu Leben und Werk* (Bonn: Bouvier, 1974).

3. Diogenes Laertius, *Lives of Eminent Philosophers,* VII.88, trans. R. D. Hicks, Loeb Classical Library, 2 vols. (London: Heinemann, 1925), 2: 195, 197.

4. *Lives of Eminent Philosophers,* VII.138, 134–35, 148 (2: 243, 239, 241, 253).

5. *Lives of Eminent Philosophers,* VII.136, 149 (2: 241, 253).

6. See Epictetus, *Discourses,* IV.vii.14–15; and Josiah B. Gould, *The Philosophy of Chrysippus* (Albany: State University of New York Press, 1970), p. 165.

7. Lewis, *Surprised by Joy* (London: Geoffrey Bles, 1955), pp. 130, 132 (Ch. 9). The Fox's rationalism underlies Charles Moorman's suggestion that "the conflict of faith and scientific rationalism, apparent in all of Lewis's work, emerges as the dominant theme of *Till We Have Faces"* (*Arthurian Triptych: Mythic Materials in Charles Williams, C. S. Lewis, and T. S. Eliot* [Berkeley: University of California Press, 1960], p. 105).

8. See, for example, Clyde S. Kilby, *"Till We Have Faces*: An Interpretation," in *The Longing for a Form,* p. 179. The Fox's name, Lysias, is mentioned only once in the book (p. 186). According to Edward G. Zogby, S. J., "his name in Greek, ironically, means ransomer" ("Triadic Patterns in Lewis's Life and Thought," in *The Longing for a Form,* p. 34). In choosing the name, Lewis might also have had in mind that Lysias was the name of an Athenian orator (5th–4th century B.C.) who spent considerable time in exile.

9. Lewis's aggressiveness in argument is a recurring motif of the essays in *C. S. Lewis at the Breakfast Table and Other Reminiscences,* ed. James T. Como (New York: Macmillan, 1979). See Leo Baker, "Near the Beginning," p. 6; John Wain, "A Great Clerke," p. 69; Peter Bayley, "From

Master to Colleague," p. 81; and Walter Hooper, "Oxford's Bonny Fighter," p. 142.

10. Clyde S. Kilby, *The Christian World of C. S. Lewis* (Grand Rapids, Mich.: Eerdmans, 1964), pp. 57–58; and Margaret Patterson Hannay, *C. S. Lewis* (New York: Ungar, 1981), p. 124. Evan K. Gibson, *C. S. Lewis: Spinner of Tales* (Washington, D. C.: Christian University Press, 1980), pp. 232, 242–43, lists a number of illustrations, but concludes that Psyche is not a symbol of Christ but "the ideal pattern for the Christian soul" (p. 244). Martha C. Sammons takes the Christian interpretation much further, to a nearly allegorical reading (though she labels the approach "transposition" rather than allegory): "Christian Doctrines 'Transposed' in C. S. Lewis' *Till We Have Faces*," *Mythlore*, 7 (March 1980), 31–35.

11. *Letters of C. S. Lewis*, p. 274.

12. The poem by Simonides (556–467 B.C.) can be translated as follows: "There's a tale that Virtue dwelleth on a rock hard to climb and with a pure band of Goddesses to watch over it, nor may she ever be seen by eye of mortal, unless heart-devouring sweat come out of one and he reach unto the very top of manliness" (*Lyra Graeca*, trans. J. M. Edmonds, 3 vols., rev. ed. [London: Heinemann, 1964], 2: 321). The poem by Sappho (flourished about 590 B.C.) is,

> The Moon is gone
> And the Pleiads set,
> Midnight is nigh;
> Time passes on,
> And passes; yet
> Alone I lie.
>
> (trans. C. M. Bowra—*Lyra Graeca*, 1: 263).

13. The sources of the story are the *Homeric Hymn to Aphrodite*, 45–200, and Hyginus, *Fabula*, 94.

III—Chapters 3–5: Of Divine Mysteries and Sacrifice

1. But, as Thomas Howard reminds us, she is more like the Babylonian than the Greek Aphrodite, "a much darker, more bloody, more earthy deity than the lithe and statuesque figure we know from the Greeks and Romans" (*The Achievement of C. S. Lewis* [Wheaton, Ill.: Harold Shaw Publishers, 1980], p. 166). Jean Marie Chard, "Some Elements of Myth and Mysticism in C. S. Lewis's Novel *Till We Have Faces*," *Mythlore*, 5 (Autumn 1975), 15, points out that Lewis also drew upon the Babylonian myth of the love goddess Ishtar. W. D. Norwood, Jr., goes further in suggesting that "Ungit—Aphrodite, as she is identified by the Fox, or Venus—is one 'face' of the true God; i.e. she is God in his aspect of Love" ("C. S. Lewis' Portrait of Aphrodite," *The Southern Quarterly*, 8 [1970], 255). Cf. Setsuko Nakao, "A Reading of *Till We Have Faces*," *Sophia English Studies*, 2 (1977), 53–67.

2. Von Rad, *Old Testament Theology*, trans. D. M. G. Stalker, 2 vols. (1957; New York: Harper and Brothers, 1962), 1: 208.

3. Otto, *The Idea of the Holy: An Inquiry into the Non-rational Factor in the Idea of the Divine and its Relation to the Rational,* trans. John W. Harvey (1920; London: Oxford University Press, 1923), p. 18.

4. Lewis, *The Problem of Pain* (London: Geoffrey Bles—Centenary Press, 1940), pp. 27–29 (Ch. 3).

5. Lewis, "Religion without Dogma?", *Socratic Digest,* No. 4 (1948), 92. It was read to the Socratic Club in Oxford in May 1946 (reprinted in *God in the Dock: Essays on Theology and Ethics,* ed. Walter Hooper [Grand Rapids, Mich.: Eerdmans, 1970], pp. 142–43; in Britain, *Undeceptions: Essays on Theology and Ethics,* ed. Walter Hooper [London: Geoffrey Bles, 1971], p. 111).

6. Lewis, *The Lion, the Witch and the Wardrobe* (London: Geoffrey Bles, 1950), pp. 117–18 (Ch. 12). In depicting the divine nature as consubstantial parent and son, Lewis indicates his belief in the mysterious, "irrational" doctrines affirmed by Athanasius and the writers of the "Athanasian Creed." Lewis says of Athanasius, "He stood for the Trinitarian doctrine, 'whole and undefiled,' when it looked as if all the civilised world was slipping back from Christianity into the religion of Arius [who taught that Jesus was a supernatural being created by God, neither fully human nor wholly divine]—into one of those 'sensible' synthetic religions which are so strongly recommended to-day" (Introduction to *The Incarnation of the Word of God, Being the Treatise of St. Athanasius "De Incarnatione Verbi Dei,"* trans. Sister Penelope, C. S. M. V. [London: Geoffrey Bles—Centenary Press, 1944], p. 11; reprinted in *God in the Dock,* p. 206 [*Undeceptions,* p. 166]—retitled "On the Reading of Old Books").

7. Sophocles, *Oedipus the King,* trans. R. C. Jebb, *The Complete Greek Drama,* ed. Whitney J. Oates and Eugene O'Neill, Jr., 2 vols. (New York: Random House, 1938), 1: 380, 11. 412–13.

IV—Chapters 6-7: Love and Longing

1. Lewis, quoted by Walter Hooper in "An Evening with Walter Hooper," *CSL: The Bulletin of the New York C. S. Lewis Society,* 6 (July 1975), 4.

2. Lewis, *The Great Divorce* (London: Geoffrey Bles, 1946), p. 85. Pagination is the same in the Fontana paperback edition (London: Collins, 1972); the British edition is not divided into chapters. In the text the page number given first is in the Bles edition; the page number given second, in italics, is in the Macmillan paperback edition (New York, 1946)—here, p. 94.

Janice Witherspoon Neuleib, in "The Empty Face of Evil," *Christianity Today,* 28 March 1975, calls such descriptions of possessiveness and jealousy "Lewis's final statement on evil. Essentially, it is the wrong kind of love" (p. 16).

3. Lewis, *The Four Loves* (London: Geoffrey Bles, 1960), p. 50 (Ch. 3).

4. *The Four Loves,* p. 63 (Ch. 3).

5. Lewis, *Surprised by Joy* (London: Geoffrey Bles, 1955), pp. 23–24 (Ch. 1).

6. *Surprised by Joy,* p. 74 (Ch. 5) and p. 24 (Ch. 1).

7. Lewis, *The Problem of Pain* (London: Geoffrey Bles—Centenary Press, 1940), pp. 139–40 (Ch. 10).

8. *Surprised by Joy,* p. 22 (Ch. 1).

9. Lewis, "The Weight of Glory," *Theology,* 43 (1941), 266 (reprinted in *Transposition and Other Addresses* [London: Geoffrey Bles, 1949], p. 24; in the United States, *The Weight of Glory and Other Addresses* [New York: Macmillan, 1949], p. 5).

10. Lewis, *Christian Behaviour: A Further Series of Broadcast Talks* (London: Geoffrey Bles—Centenary Press, 1943), p. 53 (reprinted in *Mere Christianity* [London: Geoffrey Bles, 1952], Bk. III, Ch. 10).

11. Cf. Lewis's own expression of longing in a letter to Dom Bede Griffiths, 5 November 1959: "About death I go through different moods, but the times when I can *desire* it are never, I think, those when this world seems harshest. On the contrary, it is just when there seems to be most of Heaven already here that I come nearest to longing for a *patria*. It is the bright frontispiece which whets one to read the story itself" (*Letters of C. S. Lewis,* ed. W. H. Lewis [London: Geoffrey Bles, 1966], p. 289).

12. *Great Dialogues of Plato,* trans. W. H. D. Rouse, ed. Eric H. Warmington and Philip G. Rouse (New York: New American Library, 1956), pp. 101-2.

13. "Recently, what seemed to be the right form presented itself and themes suddenly interlocked: the straight tale of barbarism, the mind of an ugly woman, dark idolatry and pale enlightenment at war with each other and with vision, and the havoc which a vocation, or even a faith, works on human life"—Lewis, *Till We Have Faces: A Myth Retold* (London: Geoffrey Bles, 1956), p. [1]. The preceding sentences in this explanation are quoted on page 6. Carolyn Keefe uses the term "mystic experience" to clarify for herself the significance of such "vision": "Mystic Experience in *Till We Have Faces,*" *CSL: The Bulletin of the New York C. S. Lewis Society,* 7 (November 1975), 4–7.

V—Chapters 8-11: Believing and Perceiving

1. The main source of the story is Aeschylus's *Agamemnon.*

2. The source of the story is Sophocles' *Antigone.*

3. Earlier Psyche had observed, "If I am to go to the god, of course it must be through death" (p. 72).

4. See page 67. Some critics have argued that the name *Maia* invokes the Hindu word for illusion and thus is a way of exposing the deceptiveness of the modes of thought Orual relies on (see, for example, Martha C. Sammons, "The God within: Reason and its Riddle in C. S. Lewis's *Till We Have Faces,*" *Christian Scholar's Review,* 6 [1976], 133; and John H. Timmerman, "The Epistemology of C. S. Lewis: Reason and Belief in 'Till We Have Faces,' " *Religion in Life,* 46 [1977], 505). However, from the context in which the name is introduced, on pages 67–68, and the way it is generally used, it seems more appropriate to regard it as drawing on Roman mythology, where Maia was the mother of Hermes and her name means simply "mother" or "nurse." Thomas Howard adds that the name derives "from

the root *mag,* signifying growth or increase," and ties it to the pregnancy image in the story (*The Achievement of C. S. Lewis* [Wheaton, Ill.: Harold Shaw Publishers, 1980], pp. 172–73).

5. "Note" appended to the American edition of *Till We Have Faces,* p. 313.

6. Gerard Watson, *The Stoic Theory of Knowledge* (Belfast: The Queen's University, 1966), p. 9.

7. Charles H. S. Davis, *Greek and Roman Stoicism and Some of its Disciples* (Boston: Herbert B. Turner, 1903), p. 70.

8. Diogenes Laertius, *Lives of Eminent Philosophers,* VII.49, trans. R. D. Hicks, Loeb Classical Library, 2 vols. (London: Heinemann, 1925), 2: 159, quoting Diocles the Magnesian.

9. A. A. Long, *Hellenistic Philosophy: Stoics, Epicureans, Sceptics* (New York: Charles Scribner's Sons, 1974), p. 126.

10. Lewis in an unpublished letter to Clyde S. Kilby, 20 November 1962. All of the unpublished letters quoted from in this book are in the Wade Collection, Wheaton College, Wheaton, Illinois (copies in the Bodleian Library, Oxford). They are used with the permission of C. S. Lewis PTE Limited and the Wade Collection.

11. Lewis, *Perelandra* (London: John Lane—The Bodley Head, 1943), p. 232 (Ch. 16).

12. Lewis, *Out of the Silent Planet* (London: The Bodley Head, 1938), p. 46 (Ch. 7).

13. Barfield, *Saving the Appearances: A Study in Idolatry* (London: Faber and Faber, 1957), p. 20. Barfield's thought draws heavily upon the work of the eighteenth-century German philosopher Immanuel Kant. For a quite different, and I think questionable, interpretation of the influence of Barfield's ideas on *Till We Have Faces,* see Robert J. Reilly, *Romantic Religion: A Study of Barfield, Lewis, Williams and Tolkien* (Athens: University of Georgia Press, 1971), pp. 125–29.

14. From a letter dated 17 June 1918, in *They Stand Together: The Letters of C. S. Lewis to Arthur Greeves (1914–1963),* ed. Walter Hooper (London: Collins, 1979), p. 223.

15. From an unpublished letter, the longest in the Great War series, written, according to Lionel Adey, while Lewis was vacationing in Perranporth, Cornwall, September 1929 (*C. S. Lewis's "Great War" with Owen Barfield,* English Literary Studies Monograph Series, No. 14 [Victoria, British Columbia: University of Victoria, 1978], p. 43 and note).

16. *Saving the Appearances,* p. 21.

17. Lewis, *Prince Caspian* (London: Geoffrey Bles, 1951), p. 112 (Ch. 9). Subsequent quotations will be cited in the text.

18. Notice how, in the fourth series of radio talks, Lewis in handling essentially the same subject avoids making it so very subjective by placing the emphasis on God's revealing himself, rather than, as in *Prince Caspian,* on an individual's perceiving him: "When you come to knowing God, the initiative lies on His side. If He doesn't show Himself, nothing you can do will enable you to find Him. And, in fact, He shows much more of Himself to some people than to others—not because he has favourites, but because it is impossible for Him to show Himself to a man whose whole

mind and character are in the wrong condition"—*Beyond Personality*: *The Christian Idea of God* (London: Geoffrey Bles—Centenary Press, 1944), p. 18 (reprinted in *Mere Christianity* [London: Geoffrey Bles, 1952], Bk. IV, Ch. 2).

19. Lewis, *The Last Battle* (London: The Bodley Head, 1956), pp. 147, 150 (Ch. 13).

20. Lewis, *Surprised by Joy* (London: Geoffrey Bles, 1955), p. 15 (Ch. 1).

21. Lewis in a letter dated 12 October 1915, in *They Stand Together*, p. 85.

22. Lewis's diary entries for 4 July 1922 (VII, 171), 12 September 1923 (VIII, 151), 22 February 1924 (VIII, 184), and 3 June 1926 (IX, 101), respectively, in *Memoirs of the Lewis Family, 1850–1930*, compiled and typed from original documents by Warren Lewis, now in the Wade Collection, Wheaton College, Wheaton, Illinois. Used by permission of C. S. Lewis PTE Limited and the Wade Collection.

23. Lewis, *Dymer* (London: J. M. Dent, 1926); *Out of the Silent Planet*, pp. 20–21; *The Voyage of the "Dawn Treader"* (London: Geoffrey Bles, 1952), p. 167 (Ch. 12).

24. *The Last Battle*, pp. 170–71 (Ch. 15).

VI—Chapters 12-15: Seeing and Knowing

1. A character in *The Great Divorce* experiences a similar sense of shame when she appears beside heavenly beings: "How *can* I go out like this among a lot of people with real solid bodies? It's far worse than going out with nothing on would have been on earth" ([London: Geoffrey Bles, 1946], p. 56 [New York: Macmillan, 1946], p. 61).

VII—Chapters 16-20: Loving, Hating, Hiding

1. Lewis, *The Great Divorce* (London: Geoffrey Bles, 1946), p. 85 (New York: Macmillan, 1946), p. 94. Gunnar Urang notes that "the epigraph to [*Till We Have Faces*] reads: 'Love is too young to know what conscience is.' But the next line in that Shakespearean sonnet [number 151] is 'Yet who knows not conscience is born of love?' The story now follows this development of 'conscience' in Orual" (*Shadows of Heaven: Religion and Fantasy in the Writing of C. S. Lewis, Charles Williams, and J. R. R. Tolkien* [Philadelphia: Pilgrim Press, 1971], p. 44).

2. *The Great Divorce* (Bles), p. 84 (Macmillan), p. 92.

3. See W. B. Carnochan, "The Minister's Black Veil: Symbol, Meaning, and the Context of Hawthorne's Art," *Nineteenth-Century Fiction*, 24 (1969), 182-92. A valuable discussion of the veil symbolism appears in Margaret Hannay's "Orual: The Search for Justice," *Mythlore*, 2 (Winter 1971), 5–6.

VIII—Chapter 21: The Myth and the Retelling

1. Sir James G. Frazer, *The Golden Bough*: *A Study in Magic and Religion* (New York: Macmillan, 1922), p. 383.

2. Lewis, "Myth Became Fact," *World Dominion,* 22 (1944), 269 (reprinted in *God in the Dock: Essays on Theology and Ethics,* ed. Walter Hooper [Grand Rapids, Mich.: Eerdmans, 1970], p. 66; and in Britain, *Undeceptions: Essays on Theology and Ethics,* ed. Walter Hooper [London: Geoffrey Bles, 1971], p. 42).

3. Lewis, *Broadcast Talks* (London: Geoffrey Bles—Centenary Press, 1942), p. 50 (reprinted in *Mere Christianity* [London: Geoffrey Bles, 1952], Bk. II, Ch. 3). See also Stella Gibbons, "Imaginative Writing," in *Light on C. S. Lewis,* ed. Jocelyn Gibb (London: Geoffrey Bles, 1965), p. 94.

4. Lewis, "Religion without Dogma?", *Socratic Digest,* No. 4 (1948), 84 (reprinted in *God in the Dock,* p. 132; *Undeceptions,* p. 102).

5. Lewis, *Miracles* (London: Geoffrey Bles—Centenary Press, 1947), p. 161 n (Ch. 15).

6. Lewis, "The Grand Miracle," *The Guardian,* 27 April 1945, p. 161 (reprinted in *God in the Dock,* pp. 82–84; *Undeceptions,* pp. 58–60).

7. "Myth Became Fact," p. 269 (reprinted in *God in the Dock,* pp. 66–67; *Undeceptions,* p. 42).

8. Mink, "History and Fiction as Modes of Comprehension," *New Literary History,* 1 (1970), 557.

9. Louch, "History as Narrative," *History and Theory,* 8 (1969), 69. In defense of narrative, see Alasdair MacIntyre, *After Virtue: A Study in Moral Theory* (Notre Dame, Ind.: University of Notre Dame Press, 1981), Ch. 15; also Johannes B. Metz, *Faith in History and Society,* trans. David Smith (1977; New York: Seabury Press, 1980), pp. 205–18.

10. Antoine Roquentin in Sartre's *La Nausée* (Paris: Gallimard, 1938).

IX—Part II: "Real Life Is Meeting"

1. Joe R. Christopher, in "The Labors of Psyche: A Sorting of Events," *CSL: The Bulletin of the New York C. S. Lewis Society,* 7 (November 1975), 7–10, neatly outlines the differences between Lewis's four versions of the labors: in the Priest of Essur's tale, in Part II of the main story, in the pictures through which Orual and the Fox observe moments of Psyche's life after she left the valley, and in the note which follows the text in the American edition.

2. The sifting, sorting, and separating nicely image the subjective element in narrative—and in autobiography particularly—discussed in Chapter 8. There is an apparent artificiality in sorting things into "separate piles, each all of one kind," yet it is actually, Lewis would affirm, in the interest of a truth that is *there.*

3. For "the Way of Exchange," see pp. 82–83.

4. Clyde S. Kilby describes Redival as "the selfish, lustful worldling more concerned about 'getting and spending' and a good time than anything else" ("*Till We Have Faces:* An Interpretation," in *The Longing for a Form, Essays on the Fiction of C. S. Lewis,* ed. Peter J. Schakel [Kent, Ohio: Kent State University Press, 1977], p. 180). Evan Gibson looks deeper into her: "Redival is robbed of the companionship and love of her older sister by invasions of their happiness in which she can have no part. Born

without intellectual capacities, it is no wonder that she hates the lessons of the Fox and fills her lonely hours by plaguing him and encouraging others to do the same. And the arrival of Psyche, who robs her of what love Orual still has for her, is, no doubt, regarded as the final collapse of her world." It is only natural, therefore, that she should become spiteful and indulgent and turn to Tarin and then to Batta for the companionship she could not find elsewhere (*C. S. Lewis: Spinner of Tales* [Washington, D.C.: Christian University Press, 1980], p. 240).

5. Barfield, *Poetic Diction: A Study in Meaning* (London: Faber and Gwyer, 1928), p. 77 (Ch. 4). Albert F. Reddy, S. J., comments, "[Orual] writes her book for the Greek reader, the man of pure reason and cultivated sensibility like the Fox; and Lewis writes his book for the modern Greeks among us. These are the secularists of our day who regard the beliefs of primitive man as harmful superstitions and who desire to demythologize and rationalize all religion" ("*Till We Have Faces*: 'An Epistle to the Greeks,' " *Mosaic,* 13 [1980], 156).

6. Much of the "ugliness" of Ungit may, in fact, be a projection of Orual's feelings about herself upon Ungit. Here again the matter of perspective becomes important. Almost all that we know about Ungit comes through, and may be affected by, Orual.

7. The publishers turned down Lewis's choice of a title, *Bareface,* because, they felt, it made the book sound too much like an American "western" (see Roger Lancelyn Green and Walter Hooper, *C. S. Lewis: A Biography* [London: Collins, 1974], p. 261).

8. Corbin S. Carnell, in *Bright Shadow of Reality: C. S. Lewis and the Feeling Intellect* (Grand Rapids, Mich.: Eerdmans, 1974), pp. 114–16, points out Jungian features of the story suggested particularly by the descent into herself. See also Laura A. Ruskin, "Three Good Mothers: Galadriel, Psyche and Sybil Coningsby," *Mythcon I Proceedings,* ed. Glen GoodKnight (Los Angeles: The Mythopoeic Society, 1971), pp. 12–14; and Helen M. Luke, *The Way of Woman, Ancient and Modern* (Three Rivers, Mich.: Apple Farm, n.d.).

9. Lewis, *The Voyage of the "Dawn Treader"* (London: Geoffrey Bles, 1952), pp. 101–2 (Ch. 7).

10. Lewis, "Dogma and Science," *The Guardian,* 26 March 1943, p. 107 (reprinted as the second half of "Dogma and the Universe" in *God in the Dock: Essays on Theology and Ethics,* ed. Walter Hooper [Grand Rapids, Mich.: Eerdmans, 1970], p. 47; and in Britain, *Undeceptions: Essays on Theology and Ethics,* ed. Walter Hooper [London: Geoffrey Bles, 1971], p. 25).

11. Lewis, *Letters to Malcolm: Chiefly on Prayer* (London: Geoffrey Bles, 1964), pp. 32–33 (Letter IV). Similarly, in *Reflections on the Psalms,* he asks, "Shall we, perhaps, in Purgatory, see our own faces and hear our own voices as they really were?" ([London: Geoffrey Bles, 1958], p. 8).

12. *Letters to Malcolm,* pp. 33–34 (Letter IV).

13. See Lewis, *The Pilgrim's Regress* (London: J. M. Dent, 1933), p. 230 (Bk. X, Ch. 3).

14. Lewis, "Christian Apologetics," delivered as a lecture in 1945; first published in *God in the Dock,* p. 102 (*Undeceptions,* p. 76). Lewis was re-

pelled by the "obscenities and cruelties" ("Religion without Dogma?", *Socratic Digest,* No. 4 [1948], 93 [reprinted in *God in the Dock,* p. 143; *Undeceptions,* p. 112]) of paganism at its worst—its temple prostitution and human sacrifice, from which even worship of Ungit was not entirely free (pp. 7–8). "*Real* paganism at its best [however] is the next best thing to Christianity" (letter to Arthur Greeves, 6 December 1931, in *They Stand Together: The Letters of C. S. Lewis to Arthur Greeves [1914–1963],* ed. Walter Hooper [London: Collins, 1979], p. 433), for in its numinousness and acknowledgment of the importance of sacrifice it contains the more vibrant and compelling of the two halves of "the real religion"—that is, a religion which combines the "thick" with the "clear," the numinous with ethical teaching ("Christian Apologetics," in *God in the Dock,* p. 103; *Undeceptions,* p. 76).

15. "Religion without Dogma?", pp. 93–94 (reprinted in *God in the Dock,* p. 144; *Undeceptions,* pp. 112–13).

16. Lewis, *The Problem of Pain* (London: Geoffrey Bles—Centenary Press, 1940), p. 139 (Ch. 10).

17. *Letters to Malcolm,* p. 146 (Letter XXI).

18. Lewis, *Arthurian Torso: Containing the Posthumous Fragment of "The Figure of Arthur" by Charles Williams and a Commentary on the Arthurian Poems of Charles Williams by C. S. Lewis* (London: Oxford University Press, 1948), p. 123. For discussions of Exchange by Williams, see especially the sixth chapter of *Descent into Hell* (1937) and section five of *The Image of the City and Other Essays,* ed. Anne Ridler (London: Oxford University Press, 1958). Its thematic and biographical implications are examined in detail by J. R. Christopher, "Archetypal Patterns in *Till We Have Faces,*" in *The Longing for a Form,* pp. 206–10. See also Nathan Comfort Starr, *C. S. Lewis's* Till We Have Faces: *An Introduction and Commentary,* Religious Dimensions in Literature, ed. Lee A. Belford (New York: Seabury Press, 1968), pp. 16–17; Dorothy Hobson Fitzgerald, "Themes of Joy and Substitution in the Works of C. S. Lewis and Charles Williams," *CSL: The Bulletin of the New York C. S. Lewis Society,* 12 (January 1981), 1–9; and Dabney A. Hart, *Through the Open Door: A New Look at C. S. Lewis* (forthcoming—University, Ala.: University of Alabama Press, 1984).

19. I differ with Clyde S. Kilby, however, in that I take Psyche's husband to be the Cupid of Greek myth; he is the Christ-figure of the story, but is known by the people of Glome only as the Shadowbrute. Kilby reads it as follows: "Cupid we know as the god of love, and Psyche means, in Greek, soul, that is, the immaterial essence or spiritual principle resident in a human body. Psyche is lovingly rescued from captivity by West-wind, another character in Greek mythology, and here a symbol of Christ, whom the pagan people of Glome can see and fear only as the Shadowbrute. He becomes 'husband' to one who from childhood had experienced a great longing (*Sehnsucht*) for him. Contrary to her sister Orual, who demands always to see, Psyche is willing to live by faith with her unseen Lord" (*Images of Salvation in the Fiction of C. S. Lewis* [Wheaton, Ill.: Harold Shaw Publishers, 1978], p. 139).

20. Bardia's words, "I wonder do the gods know what it feels like to be a man" (p. 66), also anticipate the Incarnation.

21. *Letters of C. S. Lewis,* ed. W. H. Lewis (London: Geoffrey Bles, 1966), p. 274. The reference is to Tertullian, *Apology,* XVII, 197.

22. Lewis, *That Hideous Strength* (London: John Lane—The Bodley Head, 1945), pp. 394–95 (Ch. 14, Sect. vi). As Orual was "being unmade," so too was Jane, when she first met with Ransom: "Her world was unmade; she knew that. Anything might happen now" (p. 173 [Ch. 7, Sect. i]). Similarly, in *Surprised by Joy* (London: Geoffrey Bles, 1955), Lewis says, "If I could only leave off, let go, unmake myself, it [the Object of his desirings] would be there" (p. 170; Ch. 11).

SECTION TWO: THE WORK IN CONTEXT

X—Poet of the Teens and Twenties

1. Barfield, "Introduction," *Light on C. S. Lewis,* ed. Jocelyn Gibb (London: Geoffrey Bles, 1965), p. ix.

2. Barfield, "Introduction," p. xvi.

3. From a letter dated 30 January 1930, in *They Stand Together: The Letters of C. S. Lewis to Arthur Greeves (1914–1963),* ed. Walter Hooper (London: Collins, 1979), p. 339.

4. Lewis, *Surprised by Joy* (London: Geoffrey Bles, 1955), p. 130 (Ch. 9). Subsequent quotations will be cited in the text.

5. Humphrey Carpenter, *The Inklings: C. S. Lewis, J. R. R. Tolkien, Charles Williams, and Their Friends* (London: George Allen and Unwin, 1978), pp. 35–36.

6. Lewis in a letter dated 12 October 1916, in *They Stand Together,* pp. 134–35.

7. Ibid.

8. Lewis in a letter dated 12 September 1918, in *They Stand Together,* p. 230.

9. Clive Hamilton (pseud.), *Spirits in Bondage: A Cycle of Lyrics* (London: Heinemann, 1919), p. 16. Further quotations from this volume will be cited in the text. The work will soon be reprinted for the first time (*Spirits in Bondage,* ed. Walter Hooper [New York: Harcourt Brace Jovanovich, 1984]).

10. Clive Hamilton (pseud.), *Dymer* (London: J. M. Dent, 1926), Canto I, Stanza 24 (reprinted in *Narrative Poems,* ed. Walter Hooper [London: Geoffrey Bles, 1969]). Quotations hereafter will be cited in the text by canto and stanza numbers.

11. See the Preface added to a later edition of *Dymer* (London: J. M. Dent, 1950), pp. xi–xii (reprinted in *Narrative Poems,* pp. 4–5).

12. Lewis in a letter dated 12 September 1918, in *They Stand Together,* p. 230.

13. Lewis in a letter dated 2 December 1918, in *They Stand Together,* p. 239.

14. The epigraph is not included in *Narrative Poems.* For a recent version of the *Hàvamàl,* see *The Elder Edda: A Selection,* trans. Paul B.

Taylor and W. H. Auden (London: Faber and Faber, 1969); the stanzas Lewis drew upon are on pp. 56–57.

15. For Sartre on choice as the projection of the self which gives one existence, and his affirmation that "in choosing for himself he chooses for all men," see *Existence and Humanism,* trans. Philip Mairet (London: Methuen, 1948), pp. 28–29—a translation of *L'Existentialisme est un humanisme* (Paris: Nagel, 1946).

16. Barfield, from an unpublished lecture delivered at Wheaton College, Wheaton, Illinois, 16 October 1964. Used with Mr. Barfield's permission.

17. Thus I do not expect, as George Sayer does, that "the time may come when [*Dymer*] will be ranked higher than much of Lewis's prose work"—"C. S. Lewis's *Dymer*," *VII: An Anglo-American Literary Review,* 1 (1980), 113. Sayer provides a detailed and valuable reading of the poem, with emphasis on the theme of guilt in it. Richard Hodgens, "Notes on *Narrative Poems,*" *CSL: The Bulletin of the New York C. S. Lewis Society,* 7 (April 1976), 4–8, points out an Oedipal motif in *Dymer.* See also J. R. Christopher, "A Study of C. S. Lewis's *Dymer,*" *Orcrist,* No. 6 (Winter 1971–72), 17–19.

18. Milne, "*Dymer*: Myth or Poem?", *The Month,* n.s. 8 (1952), 171, 173.

XI—Critic and Story-Writer of the Thirties

1. Lewis, *Surprised by Joy* (London: Geoffrey Bles, 1955), pp. 221–22 (Ch. 15).

2. From a letter dated 1 October 1931, in *They Stand Together: The Letters of C. S. Lewis to Arthur Greeves (1914–1963)* ed. Walter Hooper (London: Collins, 1979), p. 425.

3. Lewis in a letter dated 18 October 1931, in *They Stand Together,* pp. 426–27, 427–28.

4. Coghill, "The Approach to English," *Light on C. S. Lewis,* ed. Jocelyn Gibb (London: Geoffrey Bles, 1965), pp. 51–52.

5. Lewis, "The Personal Heresy in Criticism," *Essays and Studies,* 19 (1933), 8 and 7; page numbers for following references to this essay will be included in the text. The essay was reprinted, with two further pieces by Lewis and three replies by E. M. W. Tillyard, in *The Personal Heresy: A Controversy* (London: Oxford University Press, 1939).

6. Lewis, "A Sacred Poem," *Theology,* 38 (1939), 272.

7. Lewis, *Broadcast Talks* (London: Geoffrey Bles—Centenary Press, 1942), p. 60.

8. Lewis, *Mere Christianity* (London: Geoffrey Bles, 1952), p. 51 (Bk. II, Ch. 5).

9. Lewis, "Rejoinder to Dr. Pittenger," *The Christian Century,* 75 (1958), 1359 (reprinted in *God in the Dock: Essays on Theology and Ethics,* ed. Walter Hooper [Grand Rapids, Mich.: Eerdmans, 1970], p. 177; in Britain, *Undeceptions: Essays on Theology and Ethics,* ed. Walter Hooper [London: Geoffrey Bles, 1971], p. 143).

10. "The 'Personal Heresy': Style and the Man in Poetry—A Critical Controversy," *Times Literary Supplement,* 29 April 1939, p. 248.

11. In "Christianity and Literature," read to a religious society in Oxford in the late 1930s, Lewis develops an imitative theory of literature which corresponds closely to the critical approach in "The Personal Heresy": " 'Originality' in the New Testament is quite plainly the prerogative of God alone. . . . The duty and happiness of every other being is placed in being derivative, in reflecting like a mirror. . . . Our whole destiny seems to lie in . . . being as little as possible ourselves, in acquiring a fragrance that is not our own but borrowed, in becoming clean mirrors filled with the image of a face that is not ours" (*Rehabilitations and Other Essays* [London: Oxford University Press, 1939], p. 191; reprinted in *Christian Reflections,* ed. Walter Hooper [London: Geoffrey Bles, 1967], pp. 6–7).

12. Lewis, "Donne and Love Poetry in the Seventeenth Century," *Seventeenth Century Studies Presented to Sir Herbert Grierson* (Oxford: Clarendon Press, 1938), pp. 64–84 (reprinted in *Selected Literary Essays,* ed. Walter Hooper [Cambridge: Cambridge University Press, 1969], pp. 106–25).

13. Lewis, *Hamlet: The Prince or the Poem?,* Annual Shakespeare Lecture of the British Academy, 1942, *The Proceedings of the British Academy,* 28 (London: Oxford University Press, 1942), p. 10 (reprinted in *Selected Literary Essays,* p. 96).

14. Ibid., pp. 12–15 (reprinted in *Selected Literary Essays,* pp. 98–101).

15. Lewis, *The Allegory of Love: A Study in Medieval Tradition* (Oxford: Clarendon Press, 1936).

16. See Lewis, "What Chaucer Really Did to *Il Filostrato,*" *Essays and Studies,* 17 (1931), 56–75 (reprinted in *Selected Literary Essays,* pp. 27–44); "A Metrical Suggestion," *Lysistrata,* 2 (1935), 13–24 (reprinted in *Selected Literary Essays,* pp. 15–26); "The Fifteenth-Century Heroic Line," *Essays and Studies,* 24 (1938), 28–41 (reprinted in *Selected Literary Essays,* pp. 45–57); and *A Preface to Paradise Lost* (London: Oxford University Press, 1942).

17. Lewis, *The Pilgrim's Regress* (London: J. M. Dent, 1933). Quotations are from this edition, cited in the text by book and chapter number. The epigraph, from Proverbs 25:25, is on the title page.

18. Compare with these lines from "To Sleep" (*Spirits in Bondage: A Cycle of Lyrics* [London: Heinemann, 1919], p. 30):

> And when he meets me at the dusk of day
> To call me home for ever, this I ask—
> That he may lead me friendly on that way
> And wear no frightful mask.

19. Lewis, *The Pilgrim's Regress,* rev. ed. (London: Geoffrey Bles, 1943), p. 10.

20. Ibid., p. 176.

21. Ibid., p. 13.

22. Lindskoog, "Getting It Together; Lewis and the Two Hemispheres of Knowing," *Mythlore,* 6 (Winter 1979), 45.

23. Lewis, "Myth Became Fact," *World Dominion,* 22 (1944), 269 (reprinted in *God in the Dock,* p. 66; *Undeceptions,* p. 42).

24. Lewis, *Surprised by Joy,* p. 64 (Ch. 4).

25. Lewis, *Miracles* (London: Geoffrey Bles—Centenary Press, 1947), p. 161n (Ch. 15). For the dates of the writing of *Miracles,* see Roger Lancelyn Green and Walter Hooper, *C. S. Lewis: A Biography* (London: Collins, 1974), p. 225. Parts of the footnote are expanded in "Religion without Dogma?", *Socratic Digest,* No. 4 (1948), 83–84 (reprinted in *God in the Dock,* pp. 131–32; *Undeceptions,* pp. 101–2).

26. A discussion of myth in "Is Theology Poetry?" is similar to the other early discussions of it: *Socratic Digest,* No. 3 (1945), 29–31 (reprinted in *They Asked for a Paper: Papers and Addresses* [London: Geoffrey Bles, 1962], pp. 157–59). However, one should note Lewis's claim, in "Bluspels and Flalansferes" in the 1930s, that "it must not be supposed that I am in any sense putting forward the imagination as the organ of truth" (*Rehabilitations and Other Essays,* p. 157; reprinted in *Selected Literary Essays,* p. 265). There is no inconsistency: though myth contains truth (in a nonabstract sense of the term), it is not the vehicle of truth (as abstraction). Lewis goes on to say, in the same paragraph, "I am a rationalist. For me, reason is the natural organ of truth; but imagination is the organ of meaning." The "but" in that sentence renders it ambiguous: one could read the sentence as elevating imagination and meaning above reason and truth. The context, however, would not support that interpretation. "Bluspels and Flalansferes" is Lewis's contribution to a contemporary dispute over the relation of meaning and metaphor. His particular issue was the extent to which "dead" metaphors condition meaning. Lewis was not setting forth a general theory of metaphor or a theory of imagination. The sentences quoted here are from the final paragraph of the essay, which places the discussion of meaning and metaphor in the context of Lewis's metaphysics for clarity and honesty. He is asserting the value, the indispensability, of metaphor and imagination even for a rationalist, but the final paragraph is added to avoid appearing to claim more for imagination than he actually is. In the hierarchical terms Lewis uses repeatedly in *Rehabilitations,* "truth" clearly ranks higher than meaning. But imagination and metaphor are in many cases the prior condition of apprehending truth, and thus are obviously of the highest importance to Lewis.

27. Compare "How can they meet us face to face till we have faces" with Exodus 33:11—"Thus the Lord used to speak to Moses face to face, as a man speaks to his friend." The phrase "face to face" is used frequently throughout the Bible for a direct, personal relationship. Equally frequent is the image of hiding one's face, out of fear or shame: for example, "And Moses hid his face, for he was afraid to look at God" (Exodus 3:6).

28. Lewis, "On Science Fiction," first published in *Of Other Worlds: Essays and Stories,* ed. Walter Hooper (London: Geoffrey Bles, 1966), p. 68. Given as a talk to the Cambridge University English Club, 24 November 1955.

29. Lewis, *Out of the Silent Planet* (London: The Bodley Head, 1938), pp. 136–37 (Ch. 18).

30. *Out of the Silent Planet,* pp. 152–56 (Ch. 20).

31. Lewis in a letter to Sister Penelope, 9 July 1939, *Letters of C. S. Lewis,* ed. W. H. Lewis (London: Geoffrey Bles, 1966), p. 167.

32. Tolkien, "On Fairy-Stories," in *Essays Presented to Charles Williams* (London: Oxford University Press, 1947), p. 67.

33. Ibid., p. 83.

XII—Apologist of the Forties

1. Lewis, unpublished letter, 5 October 1938. (See p. 189, n. 10).

2. Lewis, *The Problem of Pain* (London: Geoffrey Bles—Centenary Press, 1940), p. 4. Subsequent quotations will be cited in the text.

3. Roger Lancelyn Green and Walter Hooper, *C. S. Lewis: A Biography* (London: Collins, 1974), p. 187.

4. The series, entitled "Right and Wrong: A Clue to the Meaning of the Universe," is the first half of the book *Broadcast Talks* (London: Geoffrey Bles—Centenary Press, 1942). The book's American title, *The Case for Christianity* (New York: Macmillan, 1943) emphasizes even more the logical, argumentative nature of the work. I will cite passages in the text by page number in the first British edition and by book and chapter of its later reprinting in *Mere Christianity* (London: Geoffrey Bles, 1952).

5. Lewis, quoted by Green and Hooper in *C. S. Lewis: A Biography*, p. 202.

6. Lewis, "Difficulties in Presenting the Christian Faith to Modern Unbelievers," *Lumen Vitae*, 3 (1948); I am quoting from the reprinting, retitled "God in the Dock," in *God in the Dock: Essays on Theology and Ethics*, ed. Walter Hooper (Grand Rapids, Mich.: Eerdmans, 1970), pp. 243–44 (in Britain, *Undeceptions: Essays on Theology and Ethics*, ed. Walter Hooper [London: Geoffrey Bles, 1971], p. 200).

7. Lewis, quoted by Green and Hooper in *C. S. Lewis: A Biography*, p. 202.

8. Lewis, *Miracles* (London: Geoffrey Bles—Centenary Press, 1947), p. 15 (Ch. 2). The third chapter was later revised, expanded, and given the new title "The Cardinal Difficulty in Naturalism" (London: Fontana Books, 1960). Because my interest here is the place of *Miracles* in the development of Lewis's thought, not the final form his argument took, I will continue to quote from the first edition.

9. For example, "authority, reason, experience; on these three, mixed in varying proportions all our knowledge depends" ("Religion: Reality or Substitute?", *Christian Reflections*, ed. Walter Hooper [London: Geoffrey Bles, 1967], p. 41). The line was added to the essay after it was published in *World Dominion*, 19 (1941), 277–81, but summarizes ideas that were there originally.

10. Lewis, "Myth Became Fact," *World Dominion*, 22 (1944), 268 (reprinted in *God in the Dock*, pp. 64–65; *Undeceptions*, pp. 40–41). Also on myth, see Lewis's Preface to *George MacDonald: An Anthology* (London: Geoffrey Bles—Centenary Press, 1946), pp. 14–17; and, for a later elaboration of its ideas, the fifth chapter of *An Experiment in Criticism* (Cambridge: Cambridge University Press, 1961).

11. Alexander, *Space Time and Deity: The Gifford Lectures at Glasgow, 1916–1918*, 2 vols. (London: Macmillan and Company, 1920), 1: 11–13.

12. For example, "The Personal Heresy in Criticism," *Essays and Studies,* 19 (1933), 15.

13. "Myth Became Fact," p. 269.

14. "The Personal Heresy," p. 10.

15. "Myth Became Fact," p. 270.

16. "The Personal Heresy," p. 15.

17. About the same time, in an article in *The Coventry Evening Telegraph,* 17 July 1945, Lewis put Alexander's theory into popular terms; here too he stresses the need to unify: "One must look both *along* and *at* everything" ("Meditation in a Toolshed," *God in the Dock,* p. 215; *Undeceptions,* p. 174).

18. "Myth Became Fact," p. 270.

19. Green and Hooper, *C. S. Lewis: A Biography,* p. 171.

20. Lewis, *Perelandra* (London: John Lane—The Bodley Head, 1943), pp. 45–46 (Ch. 3).

21. Lewis, "On Stories," in *Essays Presented to Charles Williams,* ed. C. S. Lewis (London: Oxford University Press, 1947), p. 101 (reprinted in *Of Other Worlds: Essays and Stories,* ed. Walter Hooper [London: Geoffrey Bles, 1966], p. 15.

22. *Perelandra,* p. 52 (Ch. 4).

23. "Vivisection" was first published as a pamphlet by the New England Anti-Vivisection Society in 1947 (reprinted in *God in the Dock,* pp. 224–28; *Undeceptions,* pp. 182–86). "The Humanitarian Theory of Punishment" appeared first in *Twentieth Century: An Australian Quarterly Review* in 1949 (reprinted in *God in the Dock,* pp. 287–94; *Undeceptions,* pp. 238–45).

24. Lewis, *That Hideous Strength* (London: John Lane—The Bodley Head, 1945), p. 83 (Ch. 3, Sect. iv).

25. Lewis, *The Allegory of Love: A Study in Medieval Tradition* (Oxford: Clarendon Press, 1936), p. 45 (Ch. 2, Sect. i); also, "Transposition," preached as a sermon in 1944, published in *Transposition and Other Addresses* (London: Geoffrey Bles, 1949), pp. 9–20; in the United States, *The Weight of Glory and Other Addresses* (New York: Macmillan, 1949), pp. 16–29.

26. Lewis, *The Great Divorce* (London: Geoffrey Bles, 1946), p. 57 (New York: Macmillan, 1946), p. 62. In the text the page number given first is in the Bles edition; the page number given second, in italics, is in the Macmillan edition.

27. Green and Hooper, *C. S. Lewis: A Biography,* p. 222.

28. Remarks by Owen Barfield summarized by Lewis in a journal-letter to Arthur Greeves, 5 November 1929, in *They Stand Together: The Letters of C. S. Lewis to Arthur Greeves (1914–1963),* ed. Walter Hooper (London: Collins, 1979), p. 316. (Cf. *Till We Have Faces,* p. 76.)

29. Walsh, *C. S. Lewis: Apostle to the Skeptics* (New York: Macmillan, 1949), p. 158.

XIII—Autobiographer of the Fifties

1. Miss Anscombe's paper was published in the *Socratic Digest,* No. 4 (1948), 7–15, and recently reprinted in *Metaphysics and the Philosophy of*

Mind, volume II of *The Collected Philosophical Papers of G. E. M. Anscombe* (Oxford: Basil Blackwell, 1981), pp. 224–31.

2. Miss Anscombe's objections have been analyzed and rebutted by E. L. Mascall, *Christian Theology and Natural Science: Some Questions in their Relations* (1956; rpt. Hamden, Conn.: Archon Books, 1965), pp. 214–16; and Richard Webster, "The Emperor Clothed and in his Right Mind?", *VII: An Anglo-American Literary Review,* 2 (1981), 21–23. See also Walter Hooper's essay on the Socratic Club: "Oxford's Bonny Fighter," in *C. S. Lewis at the Breakfast Table and Other Reminiscences,* ed. James T. Como (New York: Macmillan, 1979), pp. 161–65.

3. Brewer, "The Tutor: A Portrait," in *C. S. Lewis at the Breakfast Table,* p. 59. See also Roger Lancelyn Green and Walter Hooper, *C. S. Lewis: A Biography* (London: Collins, 1974), pp. 227–28. But cf. Miss Anscombe in the Introduction to *Metaphysics and the Philosophy of Mind:* "The meeting of the Socratic Club at which I read my paper has been described by several of his friends as a horrible and shocking experience which upset him very much. Neither Dr Havard . . . nor Professor Jack Bennett remembered any such feelings on Lewis' part. . . . I am inclined to construe the odd accounts of the matter by some of his friends . . . as an interesting example of the phenomenon called 'projection' " (p. x).

4. Carpenter, *The Inklings: C. S. Lewis, J. R. R. Tolkien, Charles Williams, and Their Friends* (London: George Allen and Unwin, 1978), p. 216.

5. Lewis, "Christian Apologetics," *God in the Dock: Essays on Theology and Ethics,* ed. Walter Hooper (Grand Rapids, Mich.: Eerdmans, 1970), p. 103; in Britain, *Undeceptions: Essays on Theology and Ethics,* ed. Walter Hooper (London: Geoffrey Bles, 1971), p. 76. See also "The Apologist's Evening Prayer," in *Poems,* ed. Walter Hooper (London: Geoffrey Bles, 1964), p. 129.

6. Having examined Lewis's use of myth in the Narnian Chronicles at length in *Reading with the Heart: The Way into Narnia* (Grand Rapids, Mich.: Eerdmans, 1979), I will not comment on it further here.

7. Lewis, "As the Ruin Falls," lines 9–12. The poem is undated and was published first in *Poems,* p. 110. See Carpenter, *The Inklings,* pp. 248–49; Chad Walsh, Afterword to *A Grief Observed* (New York: Bantam, 1976), pp. 143–46, and *The Literary Legacy of C. S. Lewis* (New York: Harcourt Brace Jovanovich, 1979), p. 232; and Lyle W. Dorsett, *And God Came In* (New York: Macmillan, 1983), pp. 116–17 and 146–47.

8. Lewis, *Surprised by Joy* (London: Geoffrey Bles, 1955), p. 7 (Preface). Subsequent quotations will be cited in the text.

9. W. H. Lewis, "Introduction," *Letters of C. S. Lewis,* ed. W. H. Lewis (London: Geoffrey Bles, 1966), p. 5.

10. Lewis, *The Pilgrim's Regress,* rev. ed. (London: Geoffrey Bles, 1943), p. 7.

11. Lewis, "On Three Ways of Writing for Children," *Proceedings, Papers and Summaries of Discussions at the Bournemouth Conference 29th April to 2nd May 1952* (London: The Library Association, 1952), p. 27 (reprinted in *Of Other Worlds: Essays and Stories,* ed. Walter Hooper [London: Geoffrey Bles, 1966], p. 32).

12. Lewis, "Sometimes Fairy Stories May Say Best What's to be Said,"

The New York Times Book Review, Children's Book Section, 18 November 1956, p. 3 (reprinted in *Of Other Worlds,* p. 36).

13. Lewis, "It All Began with a Picture . . . ," *Junior Radio Times,* No. 47, p. [2], supplement to *Radio Times,* 15 July 1960 (reprinted in *Of Other Worlds,* p. 42).

14. Lewis, in 1954, prior to the Society's December 28th meeting, in *Letters of C. S. Lewis,* p. 260.

15. Zogby, "Triadic Patterns in Lewis's Life and Thought," in *The Longing for a Form: Essays on the Fiction of C. S. Lewis,* ed. Peter J. Schakel (Kent, Ohio: Kent State University Press, 1977), p. 35.

16. Carpenter, *The Inklings,* p. 245. Similarly, Leanne Payne, *Real Presence: The Holy Spirit in the Works of C. S. Lewis* (Westchester, Ill.: Cornerstone Books, 1979), p. 57—"Orual is really Lewis, and her tale is not only his but it is the story of all men." Also, Donald Glover, *C. S. Lewis: The Art of Enchantment* (Athens, Ohio: Ohio University Press, 1981), p. 191; and Carol Ann Brown, "Who is Ungit?", *CSL: Bulletin of the New York C. S. Lewis Society,* 13 (April 1982), 2; and Margaret Hannay, *C. S. Lewis* (New York: Ungar, 1981), p. 125.

17. Urang, *Shadows of Heaven: Religion and Fantasy in the Writing of C. S. Lewis, Charles Williams, and J. R. R. Tolkien* (Philadelphia: Pilgrim Press, 1971), p. 49. Urang's book traces a shift in Lewis from "satirical particularizing" in the earlier works, to a more open and experiential attitude and freer use of myth in the later ones like *Till We Have Faces, A Grief Observed,* and *Letters to Malcolm.*

XIV—Personal Writer of the Sixties

1. Quotations from *An Experiment in Criticism* (Cambridge: Cambridge University Press, 1961), will be cited in the text. It might well be argued that *The Discarded Image: An Introduction to Medieval and Renaissance Literature* (Cambridge: Cambridge University Press, 1964) is a more important book than *An Experiment in Criticism.* I would not dispute the claim, but I am hesitant to treat *The Discarded Image* as a work of the sixties. It puts into published form lectures Lewis began delivering in the twenties and thirties. If there is research or new interpretation in the sixties, it is likely to appear in the Epilogue, which in its emphases and expressions seems very much to reflect the openness to Barfieldian approaches late in Lewis's life.

2. Margaret Hannay, in a lengthy chapter on Lewis's literary criticism, explains *An Experiment in Criticism* as a response to the evaluative criticism of F. R. Leavis (*C. S. Lewis* [New York: Ungar, 1981], pp. 151–55).

3. Lewis, " 'De Audiendis Poetis,' " published for the first time in *Studies in Medieval and Renaissance Literature,* ed. Walter Hooper (Cambridge: Cambridge University Press, 1966), p. 1.

4. Lewis, "Metre," *A Review of English Literature,* 1 (January 1960), 46, 45 (reprinted in *Selected Literary Essays,* ed. Walter Hooper [Cambridge: Cambridge University Press, 1969], pp. 281, 280.

5. Lewis, "The Anthropological Approach," in *English and Medieval Studies Presented to J. R. R. Tolkien on the Occasion of His Seventieth*

Birthday, ed. Norman Davis and C. L. Wrenn (London: George Allen and Unwin, 1962), pp. 219–30 (reprinted in *Selected Literary Essays,* pp. 301–11).

6. From an entry in Lewis's diary, 6 March 1926, sent to Arthur Greeves with a letter dated 18 August 1930, in *They Stand Together: The Letters of C. S. Lewis to Arthur Greeves (1914–1963),* ed. Walter Hooper (London: Collins, 1979), p. 382.

7. Scott Oury, in an article on the objective, also fails to resolve the issue of how one could come to know "the real": " 'The Thing Itself': C. S. Lewis and the Value of Something Other," in *The Longing for a Form: Essays on the Fiction of C. S. Lewis,* ed. Peter J. Schakel (Kent, Ohio: Kent State University Press, 1977), pp. 1–19. On Lewis's objectivism, see also Robert H. Smith, *Patches of Godlight: The Pattern of Thought of C. S. Lewis* (Athens: University of Georgia Press, 1981), pp. 1–27. Paul L. Holmer explores Lewis's reconciliation of the objective and subjective in *C. S. Lewis: The Shape of His Faith and Thought* (New York: Harper and Row, 1976), pp. 86, 104. Cf. also the comments on the Narnian Chronicles and *Till We Have Faces* in Brian Murphy, *C. S. Lewis* (Mercer Island, Wash.: Starmont, 1983),pp. 71–81.

8. Father Hooper said further, in a conversation about *A Grief Observed,* that Lewis took good care of notebooks because they contained lecture notes and other things he intended to keep. Because no notebooks containing a draft of *A Grief Observed* have survived, Father Hooper suspects the book was not written in notebooks.

9. The last notebook was not quite empty, "for there are some pages of very ancient arithmetic at the end by J."—N. W. Clerk (pseud.), *A Grief Observed* (London: Faber and Faber, 1961), p. 47. Subsequent quotations will be cited in the text.

10. *The Comedy of Dante Alighieri . . . Cantica III: Paradise,* trans. Dorothy L. Sayers and Barbara Reynolds (Harmondsworth, Middlesex: Penguin Books, 1962), p. 329.

11. There is an interesting parallel here to Wentworth's false Adela in Charles Williams' novel *Descent into Hell* (London: Faber and Faber, 1937), especially chaps. 5 and 8.

12. Lewis, *Letters to Malcolm: Chiefly on Prayer* (London: Geoffrey Bles, 1964), p. 11, Letter I. Subsequent quotations will be cited in the text.

13. Vidler, "Religion and the National Church," *Soundings: Essays Concerning Christian Understanding,* ed. A. R. Vidler (Cambridge: Cambridge University Press, 1962), pp. 239–63.

14. Merchant, "An Appraisal of *Malcolm,*" *CSL: Bulletin of the New York C. S. Lewis Society,* 4 (February 1972), 2.

15. "Petitionary Prayer" was read to the Oxford Clerical Society, 8 December 1953; published in *Christian Reflections,* ed. Walter Hooper (London: Geoffrey Bles, 1967), pp. 142–51.

16. See also Hannay, *C. S. Lewis,* pp. 264–65.

17. Lewis, "Reason," in *Poems,* ed. Walter Hooper (London: Geoffrey Bles, 1964), p. 81.

18. Ibid.

19. Ibid.

Table for Converting Page References in *Till We Have Faces* to Chapter Numbers

To locate quotations in other editions of *Till We Have Faces*, use the page numbers below (from the Harcourt Brace Jovanovich paperback edition cited in this book) to identify the chapter and the approximate location in the chapter of passages cited by page number in the text.

Index

Index

Greeves, Arthur, Lewis's letters to, 123, 124, 181, 199 n. 28, 202 n. 6; on dreams, 44; on *Dymer*, 101; on Lewis's conversion, 109–111; on paganism, 193 n. 14; on perception, 41; on pride, 89; romanticism and rationalism in, 92–93

Grief Observed, A, 163, 167–71, 175, 178, 202 nn. 8, 9; the subjective in, 167, 171–73

Imagination in Lewis, x, 88, 96, 98, 138, 155, 165, 180–82, 183 n. 2, 197 n. 26; and conversion, 109–11; in *A Grief Observed*, 168–70; in *Letters to Malcolm*, 173–79; limitations on, 121–27, 128, 139–42, 145; in *Out of the Silent Planet*, 126; in *Perelandra*, 140, 158; and reason, 147, 169, 173–74, 182; in *That Hideous Strength*, 140–41; in *Till We Have Faces*, x, 14, 30–34, 61, 74, 83. **See also** Knowledge: through imagination

Joy. **See** Longing

Knowledge: through imagination, 138, 178–79; through reason or the senses, 90, 93, 110–11, 135, 136, 150, 176

Last Battle, The, 43, 45

Law of nature (moral law), 89, 111, 131, 132, 133, 146

Letters to Malcolm, 79, 82, 174–79

Lewis, C. S.: conversion to Christianity, 108–11, 122, 128, 160, 181; and fictional characters, his closeness to, 160–62; literary criticism by, 111–16, 163–67; and metaphors, 106, 197 n. 26; pride of, 89, 136; reading theory of, 115, 163–66; romantic inclinations of, 91–101, 106–7, 116–17, 120–22, 156, 159; tension, personal, and reason and imagination, ix, x, 99–101,

106–7, 108, 111, 116, 119, 126–27, 128, 139–40, 141, 145, 157, 159–62, 167, 179, 180; wholeness, personal, and reason and imagination, 161–62, 174, 179, 181–82. **See also** Imagination in Lewis; **and titles of individual works**

Longing, 188 n. 11; in *Dymer*, 100; in *The Great Divorce*, 142–43; in *The Pilgrim's Regress*, 116–17, 119–22, 156; in *Spirits in Bondage*, 98; in *Surprised by Joy*, 156, 159–61; in *Till We Have Faces*, 30–32

Love: in *The Four Loves*, 27–29; in *The Great Divorce*, 28–29, 54, 55, 143–44; in *Till We Have Faces*, 20, 29–30, 53–56, 71–72, 82–83

MacDonald, George, 78, 159–60

Masks motif: in *Dymer*, 103; in *The Pilgrim's Regress*, 118; in *Spirits in Bondage*, 96, 196 n. 18; in *Till We Have Faces*, 103, 118

Mere Christianity, 114

Metaphors in Lewis, 106, 197 n. 26

Miracles, 129, 134–36, 148, 149

Moral law. **See** Law of nature

Myth, 5, 61, 83, 184 n. 3, 197 n. 26; allegorical explanation of, 72–73, 92–93; attitude of Lewis toward, 6, 108, 121–27, 128, 137–39, 149–50, 158–60, 181, 198 n. 10; and conversion of Lewis, 110–11; and *The Great Divorce*, 147; in *Letters to Malcolm*, 176–79; in *Perelandra*, 140; in *The Pilgrim's Regress*, 120–26; in *Till We Have Faces*, 61, 63, 64–65, 162. **See also** "Myth Became Fact"

"Myth Became Fact": and dying god myth, 63, 65; and myth as "tast-

Index